THE STRUCTURE OF SOCIAL INCONSISTENCIES

THE STRUCTURE OF
SOCIAL INCONSISTENCIES

A contribution to a unified theory of play, game,
and social action

by

RICHARD H. GRATHOFF

MARTINUS NIJHOFF / THE HAGUE / 1970

ISBN 90 247 5006 7

PRINTED IN THE NETHERLANDS

PREFACE

Few phenomena have found such divergent descriptions in sociological literature as have social inconsistencies. They were studied by George Herbert Mead as eruptive "natural" events constituting a social temporality. Alfred Schütz described them as "explosions" of the individual actor's anticipatory action patterns. Talcott Parsons attempted to grasp social inconsistencies into his frame of "pattern variables," while Erving Goffman dealt with them as disruptions of "fostered impressions of reality" maintained by one or the other dominant team.

The present study traces these divergent approaches back to various unchecked assumptions concerning the structure and the constitution of social types. Thus, to further clarify the relationship between social types and the relevance structure of interactional situations has been my first objective. This initially rather limited intention widened when the rôle of social inconsistencies for analysing the differences between play, game, and social action proper in the immediate context of social interaction became apparent. The structure of social inconsistencies seems to hold a key to unifying the theories of play and social action.

The conceptual frame for this endeavor is developed from a main hypothesis, namely, that perceptual experience of social objects has a structure different from that of visual perception. Edmund Husserl's theory of intentionality and Charles S. Peirce' theory of abduction are the points of departure for explicating this hypothesis in a "moderate" phenomenological approach. In recent years, phenomenology and pragmatism have shown a considerable rapprochement in the social sciences: With this study I am following an already established trend. Methodological questions, however, which have been the main impetus for that trend, have been bracketed where they do not immediately contribute to my objective.

On the other hand, short-cutting the methodological discussion probably will disappoint some readers who, in my opinion, correctly expect some intrinsic relationship to prevail between social and logical inconsistencies. But their disappointment most likely is based on a too confident extrapolation of Peirce' work, while Husserl's problematic theory of intersubjectivity, the major stumbling block for any study of that relationship, is left aside. Such difficulties have been recognized most clearly and elaborated upon with an admirable intellectual honesty by Alfred Schütz in his analyses of the reality of everyday life. The changes concerning his theory of social types and relevance, which the problem at hand and the main hypothesis of this study have suggested to me, do nowhere, I hope, obscure my general indebtedness to his work.

The first two chapters of this book are introductory. They describe the precise locus of the problem at hand and set the methodological frame for its solution. They are followed by a step by step presentation of the most important theories of relevance, which are basic for the general concept formation in chapter four. There, the main thesis is developed: Social inconsistencies arise within and modify typificatory schemes that pattern social interaction. The temporal structure of this process, as analysed in chapter five, opens a way to discriminate the interactional modes of play, of game, and of social action proper from one another (chaps. 6–7). The import of social inconsistencies for the formation of teams and audiences is the main theme of chapter eight, followed by a review and some concluding remarks on open ends of this study and their relationship to sociological theory in general.

Much of what is presented in the following treaties will bear the imprint of men whom I was fortunate enough to meet as a student, or as a colleague, without my being able to acknowledge their influence by explicite quotation in more than a few important instances. My interpretation of Emile Durkheim, especially of his notion of anomie, is largely dependent on the teaching of the late Albert Salomon. Aron Gurwitsch (Graduate Faculty, New School for Social Research) influenced most profoundly my critique of Schütz by his somewhat different approach to the problem of relevance. From the first draft of this manuscript Thomas Luckmann (University of Frankfurt) supported my project with relentless criticism and matiring interest. I am equally indebted to Peter L. Berger (New School for Social Research) and Joseph Kockelmans (Pennsylvania State University). For stylistic corrections and the typing of this manuscript I would like to thank my wife Ruth.

Schwalbach, September 1969 Richard Grathoff, Ph. D.

TABLE OF CONTENTS

Preface   V

Table of contents   VII

CHAPTER I. INTRODUCTION: SOCIAL ACTION AND PLAY   1

  1.1 Sociological Interest in Game and Play   2
  1.2 Contextual Inconsistencies and the Marginality of Games and Play   4
  1.3 Some Studies of Contextual Inconsistencies   7
  1.4 The Topic and its Methodological Frame   12

CHAPTER 2. CONSISTENCY IN SOCIAL INTERACTION   14

CHAPTER 3. SOME PHENOMENOLOGICAL AND PRAGMATISTIC THEORIES OF
      RELEVANCE   19

  3.1 Schütz' Theory of Relevance   22
  3.11 Thematic Relevance   24
  3.12 Motivational Relevance   25
  3.13 Interpretational Relevance   27
  3.2 Gurwitsch' Theory of Relevance   28
  3.3 James' Theory of Fringes and Peirce' Abductive Reasoning   34
  3.31 The First Stage of Inquiry: Abduction, which is Related to the Emergence of
      Incipient Events   40
  3.32 The Second Stage: Deduction, which is Related to Typification   43
  3.33 The Third Stage: Induction, which is Related to the Formation of Types 43
  3.34 Summary   44

CHAPTER 4. SOCIAL INCONSISTENCIES AND SOCIAL TYPES   45

  4.1 The Structure of Social Relevance   46
  4.2 The Rôle of Play in Processes of Typification   51
  4.3 The Notion of Typificatory Scheme   53
  4.4 Gaps and Social Inconsistencies   56
  4.41 Permanent Gaps   56
  4.42 Definition of Social Inconsistencies   58
  4.5 The Arisal of Social Types   61
  4.51 The First Stage: Arisal of an Incipient Event   62
  4.52 The Second Stage: Typification by the Incipient Event   66
  4.53 The Third Stage: Type and Social Object   70
  4.6 Conclusion   74

CHAPTER 5. TEMPORAL TYPIFICATION AND SOCIAL TEMPORALITY   76

5.1   Typificatory Schemes and Social Temporality   77
5.11 Temporal Typification and Inner Time   78
5.12 A Necessary Condition for Social Temporality   79
5.13 Schütz' Notion of "Vivid Present" and Social Temporality   79
5.14 Parsons' "Pattern Variables" and Social Temporality   80
5.2   Social Temporality and Incipient Events   85
5.21 Social Inconsistencies in Parsons' Frame of Pattern Variables 85
5.22 Incipient Events in Schütz' Notion of We-Relation   87
5.23 A More Stringent Condition for Social Temporality   96
5.3   G. H. Mead's Notion of the Present and Social Temporality   98
5.4   A Comparison with Some Notions of Sartre   101
5.5   Summary   108

CHAPTER 6. SOCIAL INCONSISTENCIES AND SYMBOLIC TYPES IN PLAY   111

6.1   Reduction of Types in Play and Social Action   112
6.11 A First Characteristic of Play: Reduction of Types in Play 113
6.12 Reduction of Types as "Entlastung" in Social Action   114
6.2   Social Limits and Symbolic Types in Play   117
6.21 Anomie, Social Relevance, and Symbolic Types   119
6.22 The Symbolic Type of the Fool   122
6.23 Social Limits: Anomie and Alienation   125
6.24 Play and Symbolic Types (Second Characteristic of Play)   127
6.25 Summary: The Nomic Rôle of Play   130
6.3   The Rôle of the Body in Play   131
6.31 The Body as Incipient Event   131
6.32 The Body in Play (Third Characteristic of Play)   133

CHAPTER 7. TOWARD A UNIFIED THEORY OF GAME, PLAY, AND SOCIAL
          ACTION   139

7.1   Common Symbolic Types in Play and Game   142
7.2   Inconsistencies and Relevance in Play, in Game, and in Social Action 144
7.3   The Closure of a Game's Typificatory Scheme   148
7.4   Conclusion: Game and Social Action   151

CHAPTER 8. TEAM AND AUDIENCE   155

8.1   Team and Audience: Theory   155
8.2   Practice: The Relation between Career Patterns and the Structure of Games 161

CHAPTER 9. CONCLUSION: THE CONSTRUCTION AND SOLUTION OF SOCIAL
          INCONSISTENCIES   174

Bibliography   180

Index   185

CHAPTER I

INTRODUCTION: SOCIAL ACTION AND PLAY

THEME:
The dualism of play and social action is supported by common sense and by a peculiar ethic of work. It is enforced by certain social factors in modern industrialized societies and acknowledged by the methodology of the social sciences. The marginality of games and play is a social fact. But is it also an irreducible fact?

This introductory chapter points out some intrinsic relationship between the common-sense notions of play and game and the social relevances and symbolic types of a social group. This relationship can be reduced to constitutive problems in the theory of social types, providing some methodological difficulties in the study of social inconsistencies are recognized. These difficulties can be solved within the framework of a moderate phenomenological approach.

The totem of modern man is his game. Soccer and baseball, the Olympic games, and the World Series have all the trappings of totemic designs. They decorate not only the walls of modern man's dwelling and the bumpers of his car, they classify not only his reading and his TV-time into "Sports" and "Other News," but he wears them also on his sweat shirt and pins them on the lapel of his business suit. His game is surely respected by those he works with in the office or in the shop, conjoined by those he meets in his club or in his church, and played by those he lives with at home.

There is no safer way "out" among one's colleagues and no better move to spoil a party than to question the games those people play. A joke about their religious beliefs, contempt about their political preferences or derision about their sexual mores seldom evokes considerable dissonance. But to relate among American football fans, for instance, the "trading" of football players to transactional principles of a slave economy proves only one's "ignorance" or marginal status as a "resident alien." The sentiments related to the common-sense notions of play and game are founded in the social relevances and symbolic types of a social group.

1.1 Sociological Interest in Game and Play

Systematic scholarly interest has turned toward phenomena of game and play only late in the history of sociology. Its great theoreticians Emile Durkheim, Max Weber, and Vilfredo Pareto referred to games and play mainly only for illustrative purposes. But in spite (or because?) of its marginality a plurality of systematic approaches and a diversity of "Standpunkte," so typical for sociology at large, arose here, too. If one were asked to name a decade in which the major positions of today's sociology of games were formulated, one would probably think of the years immediately preceding the second world war.

In *1928*, a young Hungarian-born mathematician published a paper on the theory of strategic social games which was to lead to a reorientation of several mathematical fields of study.[1] But John von Neumann's paper had even a greater impact on some realms outside his own discipline. While previously, methods derived from the limit theorems of calculus allowed the formulation of only maximum and minimum conditions in models of social behavior, it now became possible to calculate optimal behavior patterns between multiple actors in strategic interactional situations.[2] Cybernetics, "computer sciences," mathematical theories of learning, and especially the various studies of strategic behavior in economics, ecology, and more recently also in anthropology, relate at one or the other central point to John von Neumann's investigations.

Buytendijk's book on the game and play of man and animal appeared in *1932*.[3] It was the first systematic effort to overcome the evolutionistic and utilistic notions of play and game (Stanley Hall, Herbert Spencer, Karl Groos)[4] from within their own realm of argumentation, by keeping the distinction between human and animal characteristics open and attempting to find separating criteria in the phenomenal structure of play and game. Buytendijk and also Plessner, who elaborated especially on the subsequent implications for a sociology of knowledge and a "philosophic anthropolo-

---

[1] John von Neumann, *Zur Theorie der Gesellschaftsspiele*, Mathematische Annalen, 100, 1928, pp. 295–320.

[2] The conjecture that such calculation ought to be possible had been stated by Leibniz in 1710. He described also clearly the difference between games of chance and games of strategy. *See* for a summary of the early history of games Oskar Morgenstern, *Spieltheorie*, Handwörterbuch der Sozialwissenschaften (Göttingen, Vandenhoek, 1956).

[3] F. J. J. Buytendijk, *Het spel van mensch en dier als openbaring van levensdriften* (Amsterdam, 1932). German translation: *Wesen und Sinn des Spiels* (Berlin, Wolff, 1934).

[4] See, for instance, Helmuth Plessner, *Spiel und Sport*, in his collected essays *Diesseits der Utopie* (Düsseldorf-Köln, Diederichs, 1966), pp. 160–162.

gy," saw play and game as arising in the fundamental condition of an "ambivalence" between creative independence and an urge to tie oneself to the dependency of the situation and its objects. Play and game arise in ambivalent human interaction and play back at that mode of interaction.[5]

In *1934,* George Herbert Mead's "Mind, Self and Society" was published posthumously (from his own and his students' lecture notes) presenting a first comprehensive statement of his theory of the social genesis of the human self.[6] For Mead, play and game are descriptive for specific phases of individual human genesis, and in this sense he is again more closely related to earlier evolutionary and behavioristic thinking than Buytendijk or Plessner. But especially with his notion of "generalized other" he was able to make the constitutive processes of that genesis so transparent that the modes of interaction he called play, respectively game, opened themselves to empirical analyses.

Finally, Johan Huizinga's most influential book "Homo Ludens" appeared in *1938,* exactly ten years after John von Neumann published his paper on the theory of games.[7] On first sight, the eloquent essay of the historian of culture and the ingenious theorems of the mathematician seem to have nothing in common except empty headings like "Games" or "Play." For Huizinga, play is a *total* phenomenon: culture and all its important social manifestations, from the realm of arts to the institutions of law, have their origin in play and game. Language and mythos, art and handicraft, ritual and "gallant" warfare are interspersed with elements of play. This notion of art and culture having its origin in play goes directly back to Schiller's theory of play.[8] Only in play, a balance between elementary drives of human nature may unfold; only in play is man free to choose or to reject, so-to-speak, some "optimum," some "median path" for his existence as a man of culture. The implicit *rationality* in Schiller's notion of *merely subjective choice in the realm of play* is also the main presupposition imputed to all actors within a strategic theory of games.[9]

---

[5] Helmuth Plessner, *Lachen und Weinen* (Bern–München, Francke, 3d. ed., 1961), pp. 100–106.

[6] George Herbert Mead, *Mind, Self, and Society* (Chicago, Univ. of Chicago Press, 1934).

[7] Johan Huizinga, *Homo Ludens* (Leiden, 1938). English translation under the same title published by Beacon Press, Boston, 1955.

[8] This dependency holds in spite of the fact that Huizinga refers only once to Schiller's theory, and in that case not even correctly. (p. 162) For Schiller also *rejected* the notion criticized by Huizinga that some "play impulse" may be inherent in human nature. Rather, it is constituted as a free and redundant human activity; it is hence close to Huizinga's notion. See also *sect.* 6.2.

[9] The convergence of mathematical game theory and cybernetics with the aesthetic

If this were a study in the sociology of games and play, the multiple interrelations of those four important theories, their roots, for instance, in the philosophical systems of Locke, Kant, and Hegel, in the aesthetic theories of Schiller and Spencer, to name only a few, would have to be worked out, before the present state of the discipline could be studied. A less ambitious project is to be pursued here, one which is mainly concerned with a dual phenomenon. All theories of game and play seem to deal with their objects of study as marginal phenomena: they can be realized only in the limit case of totally formalized rational behavior (von Neumann); they fall into the vague span between creative freedom and situational dependency (Buytendijk); they separate the still incomplete constituting phases of social genesis from the fully constituted adult self (Mead); they are altogether redundant, impractical elements of "mere fun" in all human endeavor involving a refined art and culture (Huizinga). – None of these theories, on the other hand, has been developed as a *sociological* theory, if this term implies a close orientation or at least a critical reflection of the major body of sociological thought.[10] Two circumstances, marginality of the phenomena and isolation of their study, only reinforced the already prevalent notion among sociologists that "serious" social action and "mere" play have nothing in common, that sociology is *the* science of social action, and that game and play ought to be left to psychologists, educationalists, et al.

1.2 Contextual Inconsistencies and the Marginality of Games and Play.

Every formation of divisive classes in the social field is most problematic, and I am going to refer later to several scholars and their investigations of play and game which do not fit that contrasting picture drawn above. But again, I am not interested in pursuing a study in the sociology af play and

---

theories of play in a total unity of art and culture has found, for instance, an institutional form quite recently at the University of Frankfurt (Germany). The "Institut für experimentelle Kunst und Aesthetik" intends to use computer-simulated experiments to develop a "cybernetical aesthetics".

[10] If Huizinga's attempt to deal with play and game as total phenomena could stand up also under close scrutiny, i.e., if consequently sociology as the study of those cultural phenomena also had its theoretical basis in game and play, then this latter request to control a theory of play and game by otherwise-developed sociological notions would be empty. Precisely this, however, is the theoretical position of Roger Caillois, who pleads for a sociology taking its start from a theory of game and play. (Roger Gaillois, *Les jeux et les hommes,* Paris, Gallimard, 1958). His position, which is in certain respects more radical and definitely more consistent than Huizinga's, will be dealt with later in detail.

games, and hence I may be allowed to use this provisional frame to illustrate the present project of study.

The isolation of the study of games and play from the major course of sociological theory and the marginality of its objects of study finds further support. Common sense, for instance, assumes generally the marginality of play and game and has developed "protective" devices (customs, proverbs, etc.) to shelter the child and to shield the card player from the "reality" of man's everyday struggle to sustain his existence. The universal literacy of modern industrialized societies and the "magic" of their automated processes and machines has only built still higher walls to protect the so-called "play-world" of the child.

But these social phenonema would hardly have led to the common-sense assumption of a dualism between "play" and "serious action," if they were not supported by a similarly divisive social philosophy. Max Weber's study of the Protestant ethic of work has exposed the basis of a "mundane asceticism" *(innerweltliche Askese)* which led man to perceive his daily chores as a fulfillment of eternally assigned worldly tasks and obligations.[11] Friedrich Oetinger has shown convincingly, though with the passion of an occasionally too strongly concerned educational reformer, how Kant's Categorical Imperative with its similarly ascetic implications has penetrated, and partly dominated, German civic education in its schools and may be held partly responsible for the seemingly unbridgeable gap between "play" and "serious work."[12] A closer look at Kant's conception of play supports Oetinger's opinion: Play originates for Kant in "aesthetic common-sense" and delineates the boundaries of representative social action in the modus of "as-if," of "serious" and "responsible" action guided by the norms, regularities, and "laws of nature" circumscribed in the Categorical Imperative.

The epistemological principles of sociology as a science of social action have been strongly influenced by Kant's conceptions. Alfred Schütz, for instance, remarked on this fundamental assumption that social action in the modus of "as-if" is *the* object of study of modern social sciences:

---

[11] "Es kommt also in dem Begriff 'Beruf' jenes Zentraldogma aller protestantischen Denominationen zum Ausdruck, welches . . . als das einzige Mittel, Gott gefällig zu leben . . . ausschließlich die Erfüllung der innerweltlichen Pflichten kennt, wie sie sich aus der Lebenseinstellung des einzelnen ergeben, die dadurch eben sein 'Beruf' wird." Max Weber, *Die protestantische Ethik und der Geist des Kapitalismus,* in: *Gesammelte Aufsätze zur Religionssoziologie* (Tübingen, Mohr, 1934), vol. 1, p. 69.

[12] Friedrich Oetinger, *Partnerschaft* (Stuttgart, Metzler, 1953).

It is a methodological postulate of modern social sciences that the conduct of man has to be explained *as if* occurring in the form of choosing among problematic possibilities.[13]

Only *strategic* games, which may (at least in principle) be studied in the conceptual frame of mathematical game analysis, are characterized by such a notion of probabilistic choice. Other forms of play, as well as the ambivalent forms of infant conduct, are on one side or the other not covered by that "methodological postulate of modern social science." They are marginal forms of human conduct.

The marginality of play and game, i.e., the dualism of play and social action is supported by common-sense and by a peculiar ethic of work. It is enforced by certain social factors in modern industrialized societies and acknowledged by the methodology of the social sciences. The marginality of games and play is a social fact. But is it also an irreducible fact? Or is it possible to describe structural determinants in the immediate context of social interaction, which are related to or perhaps even constitutive for this divisive social phenomenon?

I am aware that these questions pose serious methodological difficulties. Again, Alfred Schütz has described them most clearly. If the "methodological postulate of modern social sciences" is to be upheld, then the social scientist, in his attempt to construct adequate models of interactional patterns in typical social situations, has to observe that these constructs "are subject to the postulate of logical consistency and to the postulate of adequacy."[14] *Logical* consistency within an *adequate* construct of some behavior pattern presupposes, however, *contextual* consistency in social interaction.

On the other hand, the marginality of play and game seems to rest precisely in what one could call tentatively "contextual inconsistencies." John von Neumann was able to balance seemingly discrepant strategic goals by means of his "minimax theorem"; Buytendijk and Plessner circumscribed in their notion of "ambivalence" inconsistent configurations in human "nature"; G. H. Mead acknowledged the discrepancies in the child's play explicitly in his dictum: "You cannot count on the child; you cannot assume that all the things he does are going to determine what he will do at any moment. He is not organized in a whole."[15] And Huizinga assumed play to be the consistency-producing vehicle of all meaningful social life, to be the "cement" in all human art and culture.

---

[13] Alfred Schütz, *Collected Papers* (The Hague, Nijhoff, 1962), vol. 1, p. 83.
[14] *Coll. Pap.*, vol. 1, p. 64.
[15] Mead, *Mind*, p. 159.

The direction of the problem to be pursued in this study has been indicated above. How are "contextual inconsistencies" in immediate social interaction to be described? What modes of social interaction may "solve" and "overcome" these "inconsistencies"? And finally what is the part of play and game in the construction and solution of these "inconsistencies"?

1.3 Some Studies of Contextual Inconsistencies.

Three approaches to the problem of "contextual inconsistencies" and their relationship to modes of play and game can be presented to the extent that the necessary methodological frame for studying my problem at hand can be clarified. It will suffice to look briefly at some basic assumptions of the works of Leon Festinger, Eric Berne, and Erving Goffman. All three theories will be discussed later in more detail, whenever specific material problems relate to their studies.

Leon Festinger's "Theory of Cognitive Dissonance" is perhaps best known among empirical social scientists because of its considerable capacity to yield both hypotheses concerning specific observational data and inherently related measures to judge these data.[16] This power of Festinger's model rests on its close affinity to the related notions of propositional logic.[17] Festinger assumes that all knowledge, all expectations and motivations, all opinions and experiences of a person can be understood as a distinct set of "cognitive elements," which either have "nothing to do with each other" (irrelevance) or are in some "relevant" relationship. If two relevant cognitive elements, say p and q, are in such a relation that p "follows from" q or vice versa, then they are consonant. If not-p "follows from" q and if not-q "follows from" p, then p and q are dissonant cognitive elements. These dissonant elements are understood as a motivational constellation stimulating some purposive activity of the individual:

Cognitive dissonance can be seen as an antecedent condition which leads to activity oriented toward dissonance reduction.[18]

---

[16] Festinger presented his theory in his book *A Theory of Cognitive Dissonance* (Stanford, Stanford Univ. Press, 1957). My present purpose allows me to restrict myself to this original publication. For later refinements of the theory, for references to its critics, and for an eloquent application of the theory see: Schönbach, *Dissonanz und Interaktionssequenzen*, Kölner Zeitschrift für Soziologie und Sozialpsychologie, 18, 1966, pp. 253–270.

[17] This close affinity exists in spite of an understandable insistence (one tries to counter the attempt to *equate* Festinger's model with one in propositional logic) that the notion of implication (p "follows from" q) as a psychological intention can still not be defined exactly. See: Schönbach, *op. cit.*, p. 253.

[18] Festinger, *Dissonance*, p. 3.

Contextual inconsistency is reduced by Festinger to cognitive dissonance. This allows him, for instance, to study phenomena which I am going to describe later as "permanent gaps".[19] But Festinger's reduction can only be maintained, if the relations of relevance between cognitive elements *represent* intersubjective relevance structures constitutive for contextual inconsistencies. For cognitive dissonance is a hypothetical model for motivational constellations leading to overt social behavior, but having its ultimate roots in intersubjective contexts. Theoretical interest in the constitution of contextual inconsistencies can hardly be satisfied by Festinger's assumption that "these elements of cognition are responsive to reality" and "mirror, or map reality".[20] His pragmatic hint that the "unanswered question," how cognitive elements may form a set, "does not present a problem in connection with measurement" is not much more reassuring. If contextual inconsistencies and their relationship to marginal modes of social interaction are investigated further, I contend, then Festinger's attempt to formulate "clear" and "distinct" (set-theoretical) conditions for cognitive dissonance will prove to be contradictory to the essential ambivalence and diffuseness of their corresponding contextual inconsistencies.

Eric Berne's "transactional analysis" of dissonant social interaction disagrees with Festinger's theory at a crucial point. While for Festinger overt activity in dissonant situations has to aim at reduction of dissonance, Berne advocates the opposite thesis. People play certain "games" to create contextual inconsistencies which let them experience certain idiosyncratic feats endured and supported by their fellow-men.[21] Though Berne saw clearly the social constitution of cognitive dissonance, his descriptive model of contextual inconsistencies hardly animates a sociological study of these problems, though it may suffice the therapeutic purposes of a psychoanalyst. Berne reduces the interactional context to the multiple tendings between two or more actors, each of whom may address himself to any other from either

---

[19] See *sect.* 4.41.

[20] See, also for the following quote, *Dissonance*, p. 10. – The epistemological problems of such "representation" are studied in detail by Prof. Gurwitsch under the title of "constancy hypothesis": Aron Gurwitsch, *The Field of Consciousness* (Pittsburgh, Dusquesne Univ. Press, 1964).

[21] Eric Berne, *Games People Play* (New York, Grove, 1964). – To answer the critic who may object that Berne's "transactions" are not related to what Festinger called "dissonant cognitive elements" here is one random example from Berne (*Games*, p. 33). A salesman offers some product to a housewife. Berne assumes the salesman insists: "This one is better, but you can't afford it." And the housewife reacts: "That's the one I'll take." The dissonant cognitive elements in the housewife's mind are "I cannot afford it" and "I am going to buy it." Festinger discusses the same example: "If a person were already in debt and also purchased a new car, the corresponding cognitive elements would be dissonant with one another." *Dissonance*, p. 13.

of his three levels (ego states) of Child, Adult, or Parent. Interaction from and to any of these levels may be classified into procedures, rituals, pastimes, and games. It is interaction in a frame of repression (Parent), of objectivity (Adult) and of submissiveness (Child), which may take on multiple shades depending on the various combinations among the respective levels of mutual tending. But in any case, interaction in these stereotyped modes is not "autonomous"; it is programmed and not under the sovereign, creative control of the individual; it is overt, "social behavior": "Pastimes and games are substitutes for the real living of real intimacy."[22] Berne is correct in describing all social interaction as occuring in typified form. But it is highly questionable and rests not on empirical evidence, but on (non-quoted) philosophical opinion, that below this "ostensible, or social, level"[23] is hidden a nontypified, "psychological" level of "reality," which man may live in if he attains or recovers "autonomy." "Awareness, spontaneity, and intimacy" are for Berne the three essential human capacities to live an autonomous existence:

Awareness means the capacity to see a coffeepot and hear the birds sing in one's own way, and not the way one was taught.
Spontaneity means . . . liberation from the compulsion to play games and have only the feelings one was taught to have.
Intimacy means the spontaneous, game-free candidness of an aware person, the liberation of the eidetically perceptive, uncorrupted Child in all its naiveté living in the here and now.[24]

The "uncorrupted" innocence in this, in the last analysis, a-social state of "autonomy" is closely related to Heidegger's theory of man's "inauthentic" mode of social existence, which will be referred to again later. The most poignant question as to the possibility of man's existing and living with his fellowmen in such an "autonomous" mode has been studied by Camus:

Our purpose is to find out whether innocence, the moment it becomes involved in action, can avoid committing murder.[25]

For man's existence is a constant and immediate involvement in social interaction, constituted by social types and enacted within typical motivational frames of reference which he cannot take off like an old shoe. It is not sociology and social psychology, as Berne wants us to believe,[26] which take

---

[22] Berne, *Games,* p. 18.
[23] *op. cit.,* pp. 33 and 51–53.
[24] *op. cit.,* pp. 178–180.
[25] Albert Camus, *The Rebel* (New York, Vintage Books, 1961), p. 4.
[26] *Games,* p. 51.

a detached and less committed attitude toward human individuals, but it is Berne's own view of "social psychiatry".[27]

Erving Goffman has carried, most consequentially, the methodological "postulate of modern social sciences" (i.e., social action has to be described in the representative mode of "as-if") into studies of informal social gatherings. Similarly to Berne (a view, by the way, which is also shared by his critic Szasz), Goffman knows that contextual inconsistencies can be grasped within the vocabulary of play and games. But, in difference to Berne's hypothesis of an ulterior "psychological reality," and also in difference to Festinger, who assumed cognitive dissonances to be "mappings" of the reality of contextual inconsistencies, Goffman describes *all* social interaction in terms of *presentations of typified "fronts"* and of *typical orientation at presented "fronts":*

It will be convenient to label as "front" that part of the individual's performance which regularly functions in a general and fixed fashion to define the situation for those who observe the performance.[28]

The individual actor *presents* in all interaction typical aspects of his typified projects and motives; he does not *represent* some "front" which has to be questioned further for its "real" or "true" significance. Social reality presents itself only in types valid for a specific social group. In Goffman's terms: "Impressions of reality" are "fostered" among teams and audiences. What common-sense likes to call "impostures," or "lies," or "false representations" can be grasped in terms of inconsistent impressions of reality:

The crucial sociological consideration, for this report at least, is merely that impressions fostered in everyday performances are subject to disruption. We will want to know what kind of impression of reality can shatter the fostered impression of reality, and what reality is can be left to other students.[29]

Contextual inconsistencies, or "disruptions of fostered impressions of re-

---

[27] It is outside of my competence to enter into the methodological dispute among psychoanalysts. But one opposing position to Berne's view ought to be cited. Thomas S. Szasz presents his "contractual psychoanalysis" as an *integral* part of social science. The analyst's task cannot be to penetrate the "ostensible" cover of social behavior to reveal some "real" basis, in order to attempt to alter the patient's "overt" conduct. "The analyst's task is to listen: but to what? To inconsistencies between what the patient says and how he acts." And these inconsistencies may be bridged and overcome, if at all possible, only by alterations of the immediate social context he lives in. See: Thomas S. Szasz, *The Ethics of Psychoanalysis* (New York, Basic Books, 1965). The quote is on p. 58.

[28] Erving Goffman, *The Presentation of Self in Everyday Life* (New York, Doubleday, 1959), p. 22.

[29] *Presentation,* p. 66.

ality" in Goffman's language, arise where a presented impression is in variance with the prevalent impression of a social group. In other words: *Contextual inconsistency is an inconsistency between social types*. This thesis of Goffman will be established later from a somewhat different approach.

Goffman describes the interactional attempts to overcome contextual inconsistencies as an "impression management" by individual performers or by teams, which try to impress their definition of social reality on the situation. Impression management occurs in the frame of typified performances, i.e. along pre-established patterns of typical interaction:

The team and the team-performance may well be the best units to take as the fundamental point of reference.

Goffman's footnote: "The use of the team (as opposed to the performer) as the fundamental unit I take from Von Neumann, op. cit., especially p. 53, where bridge is analysed as a game between two players, each of whom in some respects has two separate individuals to do the playing." [30]

John von Neumann and Oskar Morgenstern do not talk about "teams" but about "coalitions". And coalitions are in principle not different from individual performers or even "opposed" to them. To the contrary, coalitions are "represented" by individual players in the strict sense of mathematical representation: interaction between two coalitions may be dealt with as if it were a two-person-game. "Team-performances," as Goffman calls them, are in mathematical game theory reduced to individual performances. This, however, is precisely what Goffman wants to avoid. He proposes to "assimilate" also "two-person interaction into the framework (of team and audience) by describing these situations as two-team interaction in which each team contains only one member." This intention makes Goffman's reference to Von Neumann not only terminologically, but also materially empty.

Already a fugitive acquaintance with both Goffman's and Von Neumann – Morgenstern's writings shows that they have little in common.[31] But why does Goffman refer to the mathematical theory at all? Why does he take refuge in some "impression management" of his own? I contend that Goffman's references are of methodological significance. Strategic games can be studied in the conceptual frame of mathematical game analysis and are in line with the "methodological postulate of modern social sciences" in the

---

[30] *Presentation*, p. 80. For the "quote" see: John von Neumann and Oskar Morgenstern, *Theory of Games and Economic Behavior* (New York, Wiley, 1964), p. 53.

[31] This holds also for Goffman's other references to Von Neumann: *Presentation*, p. 16. See also his essay "Fun in Games" in: *Encounters* (Indianapolis, Bobbs-Merrill, 1961), p. 35.

rigorous formulation of Schütz stated above. Hence, Goffman adheres to a strategic notion of game and his reference to Von Neumann is a declaration of intent. And indeed, Goffman assumes that *pre-established* patterns for typical interactional performances prevail in society and may be assumed by a team, according to its strategic purpose, to maintain its definition of the situation.[32] Goffman does not study the constitution of these pre-established typical patterns. This leaves him wide open to critics, who are out to prove that Goffman's teams find their scripts for impression management in some "Book of Etiquette." But such critique would be against the sociological intention of Goffman's work, which ought to be seen against a background of sociological analyses dealing with the constitution of social types.

1.4 The Topic and its Methodological Frame.

This study deals with problems that fall into the margin between what is generally called the "theory of social action" and the "sociology of game and play." Contextual inconsistencies, disruptions of typified patterns of social interaction, dissonance in an actor's orientation toward the goals he intends to realize are phenomena occurring in the realm of social action. The subsequent "ambivalence," the indeterminedness of "what-to-do-next," the disequilibrium of competitive strategic goals or "natural drives" are constitutive notions in the various theories of play and game. In short: contextual inconsistencies arise as problematic phenomena in social action; their phenomenal structure and the interactional modes to "solve" contextual inconsistencies refer to games and play.

Consequently, I could not pursue a study of contextual inconsistencies, without prejudging its results, if I were to accept from the start a dualism between the realms of social action and play as an unquestioned social fact. This holds in spite of the marginality of games and play acknowledged both in common-sense and in relevant social theory. Rather, if such a dualism

---

[32] This argument only seems to be circular. For two very different arguments have to be seen: 1. Goffman does not accept the notions of "play" and of "team" from Von Neumann-Morgenstern. He develops his own concepts, which allow him to describe the solution of contextual inconsistencies in his theory of "impression management". – 2. The patterns of interaction in "impression management" have a strategic character, which *could* be formalized in set-theoretical terms of mathematical theory. Only Goffman would neither recognize his theory any more nor could he accept the subsequent, highly subjectivistic notions of rational interaction. The methodological postulate, however, requires merely that *in principle* such a formalization is possible regardless of how its mathematical form may compare with the original.

has to be maintained in one form or the other, then it ought to reveal itself also from the structure of contextual inconsistencies themselves.

This implies considerable methodological difficulties. It is generally accepted that social action has to be described as typified interaction within typified patterns of conduct. Inconsistencies are thus to be located as arising between configurations of social types. To reveal the structure of those inconsistencies is to ask for the constitutive modes of the arisal of types. If a "methodological principle of social science" insists that all social phenomena are to be grasped as typical phenomena (for instance by a method of construction by ideal types), then the *arisal* of social types would also be described by types. Hence, one would have to typify a type-producing process and the constitutive context of social types would probably fall altogether through the grid of those analytic methods. This problem, which will be dealt with later as "reification of social types," has to be carefully noted.

The problem is not without precedent solutions. Charles S. Peirce had to deal with it in his theory of types and symbols. George H. Mead encountered it in his study of significant gestures and their constitutive part in the genesis of a social self. Alfred Schütz, in elaboration of the ideas of Edmund Husserl, showed that the social types constitutive for social interaction refer back to intersubjective relevance structures, which also offer a descriptive frame to deal with contextual inconsistencies.

It is therefore a methodological necessity, and not a convenient choice, to study the construction and solution of social inconsistencies within a "phenomenological frame of reference." It is the only frame in which the constitution of social types as structures of consciousness may be studied. As long as a "phenomenological approach" is understood in such a broad sense, then Peirce, Mead and Schütz have pursued their studies within a common frame. However, a restriction to methods of "phenomenology proper," i.e., to certain procedures introduced into the study of social phenomena first of all by Alfred Schütz, will be necessary later. This will be evident in the actual presentation of my problem and of its solution, which I would like to submit for further discussion.

CHAPTER 2

CONSISTENCY IN SOCIAL INTERACTION

THEME:

How are interacting individuals to be assured that social objects constituted in their interacting are the "same" social objects for each participant? This question may be approached by studying carefully the implications of the main hypothesis: The intentionality of perceiving social objects has a structure different from the perceiving of visual objects. This hypothesis implies subsequent changes in those earlier theories of social types and relevance which have been developed in close analogy to phenomena of immediate sensory perception.

The main stream of contemporary sociology does not dispute that at least sectors, if not the whole of social reality, are socially constructed. Social objects are constituted in a context of social interaction. Though careful analysis even of common-sense perception, say of perceiving a tree, reveals this perceiving also as a highly complicated process of construction,[1] it still rests on a rather "solid" basis: The common-sense perception of a tree can rely upon *immediate* perceptual affirmations. My seeing or touching a tree immediately reaffirms the tree as "being-out-there"; it does not imply the mediary of social interaction in which the constitution of the tree as an object comes about.

My perceiving a social object, say a /"host" or a "family," cannot rely upon immediate perceptual affirmations. Neither by touch or sight, nor by hearing or smelling, can I immediately affirm somebody as a "host" or some group as a "family." "Host" and "family" are objects primarily dependent on an interactional context of meaning. Explication of such context, which is necessary in order to "understand" social objects, often contradicts that which is immediately perceivable.[2] The social construction of social objects may result in a multiplicity of contours. Their polar degener-

---

[1] See for example Schütz, *Coll. Pap.,* vol. 1, pp. 3ff.

[2] The notion of "social object" cannot be clarified by a simple definitory step at this point. For it is inseparably tied in with processes of social typification. These processes

ations are anomie (the dissolution of socially significant structural contours) and reification (the hardening of the contours of "host" or "family" into the thinghood, say, of "boss" or "clan").

Perceiving is an activity of consciousness. If there is a fundamental difference between perceiving a tree and perceiving a social object, it has to be established in structural differences in the attentional grasp of these objects of consciousness. Strangely enough, this problem has been studied nearly exclusively for the case of one of the most complex social objects: for my perceiving of and interacting with another human being *as a social object.* This problem is most difficult, since a human being is first of all a corporeal perceptual object comparable to a puppet or an ape, and secondly he may be constituted as a social object ("thief" or "lover") in an interactional context, in the constitution of which he has an eminent part himself.[3]

The topic of my present study allows dealing with social objects on a much simpler level. But in order to clarify further the constitutive realm of social inconsistencies I want to refer briefly to one problem in the theory of "intersubjectivity" and a solution proposed by Alfred Schütz. For, if social objects are constituted in a context of social interaction, then social interaction between human beings must be consistent. *Consistency in social interaction* shall mean simply that "somehow" one has to assure and all interacting individuals have to be assured that social objects constituted in their interacting are the "same" social objects for every one of them, i.e., that they are at least tolerably similar from the point of view of each participant. In simpler words: If I want to realize a certain social project in which others are also engaged, I must be sure that the others are "adequatly equipped" to cooperate. There must be some kind of intersubjective consent, some kind of "resonance" among the participants, if social interaction is to be consistent.

This problem has been a foremost topic of Alfred Schütz' work.[4] Any

have to be studied first in their intrinsic dependence on the phenomenon of social relevance, before any "definition" can be given. (See *sect.* 4.53) However, as an example for the frequent contradiction between the immediately perceivable and the social object one may take a sign like "No Entrance": By immediate perceptual affirmation I can assure myself that there *is* an entrance; however, as a social object defined in an interactional context there is *none.*

[3] This problem of "intersubjectivity" has found various, but divergent solutions. The most important theories are presented and criticized by Schütz in *Coll. Pap.*, vol. 1, part II.

[4] Important earlier notions to assure consistency in social interaction relied on "inference by analogy" or "empathy." For Schütz' critique of both notions in the context of a critique of Max Scheler on this and related matters see *Coll. Pap.*, vol. 1, pp. 159–179.

social activity, especially social action proper, in which a preconceived project is to be realized, occurs within a highly typified interactional context of meaning. Hence, consistency in social interaction can be described in terms of consistency between typical constructs of meaning constituted by the interacting partners. Aron Gurwitsch has given a very concise summary of this aspect of Schütz' theory:

Obviously, my project cannot have the same meaning to my prospective partner that it has to me, since even in the absence of a conflict of interests his "biographical situation" differs from mine. To conceive of the meaning my project might have for my partner, I have to impute to him typical goals, interests, motives, attitudes, and so on. I have to construct the image of a certain type of person who holds a certain type of position and pursues typical interests – those that the position of the type in question requires him to pursue, or at least those that are congruent with his position. To this construct I have to refer my project, in order to see it in the light and from the perspective of my partner's goals, motives, interests, as typified by me. And I have to impute to my partner some knowledge of the meaning the project has to me, a knowledge that I suppose him to attain in substantially the same way I form my knowledge of my project's meaning to him. A reciprocity of this sort prevails in all social interaction.[5]

The "reciprocity of this sort" is triadic. My conceiving a project implies two further constituents: 1. the typical aspect of the project as it appears to my partner, and 2. the typical aspect of myself as I appear to him. According to Schütz, my *imputing* "typical goals, interests, motives, attitudes, and so on" to my partner and my *imputing* to him "some knowledge of the meaning the project has to me" should take care of these constituents.

This is a weak point in Schütz' theory. Successful realization of my project and even a mere performance of my project in some form of social interaction[6] is supposed to rest mainly on *imputations*. Consistency in social interaction is supposed to be assured by reciprocal imputations of typical constructs of meaning between interacting partners. Consistency depends, therefore, on a subjective likelihood based on previously successful or frustrated experiences. It depends on the chance that my imputation and the intention of my partner correspond to one another. On the other hand, however, "resonance" between interacting partners in everyday life is much more frequent than could be expected on a basis of mere chance. Schütz gave three distinct answers to solve this problem. They relate respectively to the three main roots of Schütz' thinking: to Edmund Husserl, Max Weber, and William James.

---

[5] Introduction to Schütz, *Coll. Pap.*, vol. 3, p. xxvi.
[6] *Coll. Pap.*, vol. 1, pp. 67f.

1. The resonance between my imputation and the intention of my partner is built upon appresentations and processes of sense-transfer originating in the *intersubjective context of the life-world*.[7] Resonance between interacting partners is to be established by appresentational references based on the immediate experience of the "We-relation." – Yet despite Schütz' excellent grasp and critical elaboration of the theories of intersubjectivity of Husserl, Scheler, Heidegger, Sartre et al, his own conception of intersubjectivity, based on the paramount experience of the We-relation, is not beyond criticism.[8]

2. Resonance is assured through processes of typification and construction of *ideal types*.[9] Lacking a workable theory of intersubjectivity, which would allow him, for example, to analyse the rudimentary social interaction between children, Schütz has to restrict himself to the limiting case of purposive social action between fully awake, grown-up adults. Because of this difficulty, I contend, Schütz did not study phenomena of play.

3. Resonance between my imputations, when they are typical for my group, and the intentions of my partner, when they are typical for his group, is explained by Schütz in later writings by references to Cooley's theory of the *looking-glass self*.[10] Cooley introduced the concept in respect to relations between individuals:

The thing that moves us to pride or shame is not the mere mechanical reflection of ourselves, but an imputed sentiment, the imagined effect of this reflection upon another's mind.

Schütz, in referring to Cooley's concept, seems to acknowledge that through the process of social constitution of self the triadic structure of the looking-glass-effect becomes a characteristic of the relevance systems of competing groups.

I intend to show that these later references of Schütz to Cooley suggesting some relation between the structure of social relevance and the structure of what Cooley called the "Looking-Glass Self" may be worked out systematically. Schütz' assumption of a process of "imputations" among inter-

---

[7] See "Symbol, Reality and Society" in *Coll. Pap.*, vol. 1, esp. pp. 294–305.

[8] For Schütz' critique of these theories and a presentation of his own notions see *Coll. Pap.*, vol. 1, part II, and vol. 3, pp. 51–91. Schütz' notion of We-relation will be studied in detail in *sect. 5.22*.

[9] See "Constructs of Thought Objects in Common-Sense Thinking," *Coll. Pap.*, vol. 1, pp. 7–27.

[10] For Schütz' references see *Coll. Pap.*, vol. 2, pp. 98, 247, 260. – Charles H. Cooley presented this notion first in his book *Human Nature and the Social Order* (New York, Scribner, 1902), p. 184.

acting individuals leads, as shown, into the still unsolved problems of the theory of intersubjectivity. They can be bypassed, if reciprocal imputations can be either avoided or shown to be an intrinsic characteristic of social types themselves.

The latter path will be taken. It suggests itself not only by the frequent references to Cooley in Schütz' later writings, but also by an explicit conjecture by him.[11] In defending his theory of intersubjectivity against Fink's critique Schütz referred to the looking-glass-effect at a very crucial point of the argument. Fink had taken up Schütz' notion that "the experience of the Other involves a reciprocal relationship" and had insisted that "this reciprocal relationship allows, potentially, infinite reiterations." Schütz replied:

It may be of interest, in this connection, to mention that this comparison called the "looking glass effect" plays a great role in the theories of experience of the Other, advanced by some American philosophers (William James, Cooley, G. H. Mead). These writers even found the experience of my Self upon my experience (or anticipation) of the impression or image which the Other has of me. *But perhaps the inner reciprocal relation is not infinitely reiterable* because, retaining Fink's metaphor, the mirrors cannot of necessity, be placed parallel to each other. (My italics)

Fink's objection that "infinite reiterations" were to occur in the reciprocal We-relationship would have been correct if consistency in social interaction could be established *merely* on a process of imputations. The prevalent relationship would have a symmetrical structure insofar as reciprocal imputations of typified frames of references, of "mirrors" in Fink's metaphor, had to be assumed.

However, I take Schütz' reference to Cooley in this context as a conjecture that the triadic reciprocity in social interaction, leading on the one hand to the problem of imputations, may on the other hand be related more immediately to the process in which social types are constituted. The arisal of social inconsistencies, as I have shown in chapter 1, also ought to be studied within this process. Extrapolating Schütz' conjecture into a study of social inconsistencies will require, however, a critical reappraisal of his approach to the problem of social relevance and the introduction of a somewhat different solution to this problem.

---

[11] I am referring to comments by Eugen Fink on Alfred Schütz' paper "The Problem of Transcendental Intersubjectivity in Husserl," presented 1957 in Royaumont, and to Schütz' subsequent replies. This discussion has been published in Schütz, *Coll. Pap.*, vol. 3, pp. 84–91. The following quotes are on pp. 85 resp. 88.

CHAPTER 3

SOME PHENOMENOLOGICAL AND PRAGMATISTIC
THEORIES OF RELEVANCE

THEME:

The most explicit theories of relevance have been developed by Alfred Schütz and Aron Gurwitsch. They depend partially on certain notions of William James, which are traced back to Charles Peirce. His theory of abduction allows translating the main hypothesis into some constitutive principles for social types.

A theory of social types, which takes its constitutive context of social interaction for granted, can hardly answer the question how social types arise. For every social action is already a highly typified process implying typical actors, who try to reach typified goals by typical means in an already typified situation. Schütz has, to a considerable extent, clarified the typifications prevalent in such processes of social interaction.[1] To avoid the circularity indicated above, Schütz approached the problem of the constitution of social types from an analysis of the meaning structure of social action. Reciprocal processes of typification constitute the intersubjective context of meaning in social action. However, to explain this reciprocity by relying upon *imputing* certain typifications from one partner to the other leads, as indicated above, into a host of new and even more difficult problems.

Is perhaps a different approach possible? The exposition of the main topic in the previous chapters has suggested some intricate relations between social types, social inconsistencies, and the relevance structure of the social situation. In some detail, Schütz had already shown[2] that typifications are determined by, and take place in, the context of particular relevance systems. Hence, the hypothesis suggests itself: the problem may be solved by shifting the argument from the complex of meaning, which an individual actor attaches to his projecting and acting, to the structure of rele-

---

[1] See especially his paper *Common-Sense and Scientific Interpretation of Human Action,* reprinted in *Coll. Pap.,* vol. 1, pp. 3–47.

[2] *Coll. Pap.,* vol. 3, p. 125. See also a summary of this conception by Gurwitsch in his introduction to that volume, p. xx.

vance. Since relevance is co-constitutive for the meaning of social action, this shifting does, of course, not imply a rejection of Schütz' subsequent analyses.

Such a shift presupposes, on the other hand, that the "structure of relevance" can be clarified to some degree. In other words, certain hypotheses concerning this structure, which are suggested by Husserl's notion of intentionality, by Cooley's so-called "Looking-Glass-Self," and especially by Gurwitsch' theory of relevance will be checked for their consequences within a constitutive theory of social types. I intend to show that the particular relevance of social interaction has a "triadic structure." In other words, if I were able to show that "social relevance" means nothing but a specific intersubjective constellation of perspectives, then this structure of relevance, by becoming an implicit characteristic of the ensuing typifications, should be responsible for the particular reciprocity prevailing in social interaction. Hence, the problem of imputations in Schütz' conception of social interaction may be considerably reduced. The problem arose, since your conceiving of a project implies the typical aspect of the project as it appears to your partner and the typical aspect of yourself as you appear to him. This "implication," I suppose, does not primarily come about by your imputing, by your referring and constructing. It rests in, and is assured by, the structure of relevance. Available types and ongoing processes of typification in social interaction have an inherent "triadic structure": the "typical goal" of my project already indicates in its typicality the tending of a typical Other toward this typical goal and toward a typified Me.

In a certain sense, such a notion concerning the structure of social relevance had already occured to Schütz. In his earliest remark (1940) on the problem of relevance he introduced a very fortunate term:

> One can always reactivate the process which has built up the sediments of meaning, and one can explain the *intentionalities of the perspectives of relevance and the horizons of interest*.[3]

But what is the structure of these specific "intentionalities of the perspectives of relevance" in social interaction? In the technical language of phenomenological analysis this denotes merely that the attentional grasp of certain objects of consciousness is guided by perspectives of relevance.

Though Schütz does not refer explicitly to Husserl in this context, he seems to have had in mind here what Husserl has called "double intentionality of founded acts" (doppelte Intentionalität der fundierten Akte). Husserl distinguished between acts of tending toward "mere things" (bloße

---

[3] *Coll. Pap.*, vol. 1, p. 136. (My italics).

Sachen) and acts of tending toward values (wertende Akte). In acts of the latter kind, he proposed to distinguish two aspects of the intentional object:

In Akten der Art, wie es die wertenden sind, haben wir also ein intentionales Objekt in doppeltem Sinne: wir müssen zwischen der bloßen "Sache" und dem vollen intentionalen Objekt unterscheiden, und entsprechend eine doppelte intentio, und eventuell ein zwiefaches Zugewendetsein; in der Einheit eines cogito ist intentional verflochten ein doppeltes cogito. Sind wir in einem Akte des Wertens auf eine Sache gerichtet, so ist die Richtung auf die Sache selbst ein gegenständliches Achten auf sie, ein sie Erfassen; aber "gerichtet" sind wir – nur nicht in erfassender Weise – auch auf den Wert.[4]

This distinction between "mere things" and "values" is in respect to social objects – to say the least – problematic. But I can put that question aside for the present. The interesting point is the following: Intentionality of consciousness can have a manifold composition rather than the simple, immediate "from-here-to-there" directness of, for example, visual perception. Husserl's concept of "double intentionality" already shows a twofold composition. He did not occupy himself explicitly with studies of social relations.[5] Hence the problem of a manifold intentionality in acts involving social objects did not – to my knowledge – occur to him.

The hypothesis concerning the structure of social relevance can now be stated more precisely. The intentionalities of the perspectives of relevance have a manifold structure. My tending toward a social object has to imply the tending of the Other toward it and toward me.[6] Using Husserl's term, my tending toward a social object has to imply a "double intentio" of the Other.

This hypothesis has to be studied first in the context of the theories of relevance of Schütz and Gurwitsch. Both theories will require certain extensions and further assumptions, before a notion of social inconsistencies in relation to processes of type-constitution can be developed.

---

[4] Edmund Husserl, *Ideen zu einer reinen Phänomenologie und phänomenologischen Philosophie* (Den Haag, Martinus Nijhoff, 1950), vol. 1, § 37, p. 83.

[5] I am disregarding here Husserl's contested theory of intersubjectivity, published first in French in 1931, *Cartesianische Meditationen* (Den Haag, Nijhoff, 1950). For a critique and an exposition of Husserl's theory see, for instance, Schütz' essay: *The Problem of Transcendental Intersubjectivity in Husserl, Coll. Pap.*, vol. 3, pp. 51–91.

[6] This structure between Other, social object, and I is *not* symmetrical: I am tending toward the social object, and *not* toward the Other, while he is tending toward both. Consequently, the relation between I and Other is *not* infinitely reiterable. Fink's earlier objection against Schütz can be met at this point.

3.1 Schütz' Theory of Relevance

Schütz' later preoccupation with the problems of relevance and related processes of typification seems to have been stimulated by his study of Husserl's "Erfahrung und Urteil." [7] In a very short section of this important work Husserl touched upon the notion of "interest". He distinguished two kinds of interest:

1. Interest, in a narrow sense, is awakened with every tending toward an object and belongs essentially to all perceiving. However, interest is not a specific act of volition. It is not, for example, initiative for some purposive action. Beyond tending toward the object, interest implies a "positive feeling" toward it. This feeling may be an attraction toward an appreciated value; or it may be adverse, because of some detestable character involved. In any case, the texture of meaning of the object becomes filled and enriched by my *perceptual interest* in it (as I would like to call it here).

2. A wider notion it that of *thematic interest*. In "making the intentional object thematic" I am tending toward the intentional object in a double sense: first, I am tending toward it qua object; secondly, I am tending toward it qua theme. However, intentional object and theme do not have to coincide: the writing of this thesis is my present theme; the intentional object is the problem at hand. If I am suddenly distracted by noisy children, they become momentarily my intentional object. Nevertheless, the theme "writing-this-thesis" remains unaltered, their play does not become thematic, unless it stimulates me to make some notes about their play or to stop their rough-housing.

This second notion of "theme" and "thematic interest" has become germinal for the theories of relevance both of Schütz and of Gurwitsch. However, as fugitive as the remarks of Husserl on this topic have been, Schütz did not elaborate on the following link Husserl indicated between both kinds of interest: The "positive feeling" toward the object implied in perceptual interest leads to an enrichment of the texture of meaning of the intentional object. Husserl continues:

Daran knüpft sich ein eigenes Gefühl der Befriedigung an dieser Bereicherung, und mit Beziehung auf diesen Horizont sich erweiternder und steigernder Bereicherung ein Streben, dem Gegenstand "immer näher zu kommen," sich sein Selbst immer vollkommener zuzueignen. Auf höherer Stufe kann dieses Streben

---

[7] Schütz gave the most concise statement of these specific problems in one of his last publications (1959), *Type and Eidos in Husserl's Late Philosophy, Coll. Pap.,* vol. 3, esp. p. 98. He refers to Husserl's *Erfahrung und Urteil* (Hamburg, Claassen, 3d ed., 1964), pp. 91ff. Here and on the following page, I am referring to both texts.

dann auch die Form eines eigentlichen Willens annehmen, des *Willens zur Er-kenntnis*, mit absichtlichen Zielsetzungen usw . . . Dieses Streben, in den Gegen-stand einzugehen, und die Befriedigung an der Bereicherung seines Selbst stellt sich nicht ein, wenn ich dem Gegenstand bloß überhaupt zugewendet bin, son-dern nur dann, wenn ich ihm zugewendet bin im spezifischen Sinne des Themas.

Husserl described the link between both kinds of interest as "an effort to come closer and closer to the object." This effort originates in a "posi-tive feeling" toward the object; it is realized only by making the object the-matic. Here, Husserl ties the thematic interest in an object to the genesis of processes of inquiry. This idea, as will be shown later in detail, was advan-ced by Charles S. Peirce in a somewhat different manner. Unfortunately, Schütz was not acquainted with the writings of Peirce. Instead, the pragma-tism of William James only re-enforced Schütz' basic contention (derived from Bergson) that my thematic interest in the intentional object is guided by my "attention à la vie."[8] Thus, Schütz disregarded that link between the two kinds of interest, which will be shown to have a significant part in the constitution of theme and of the social object itself. By founding instead the constitution of theme and relevance on the broad and rather ambiguous conception of "attention à la vie," his theory of relevance becomes, on the one hand, consistent with his general theory, but, on the other hand, it gains a strongly subjective accent. This has to be established now in more detail. It may be done by presenting at the same time a short systematic survey of Schütz' theory of social relevances.[9]

Schütz distinguished three major types of social relevance: thematic, mo-tivational, and interpretational relevance. Roughly, these three types can be headed respectively by Schütz' questions:

How does it happen that a problem arises at all, that is to say, how does it hap-pen that that which has become questionable for us appears as worth being questioned? What is relevant for the solution of a problem? When does it ap-

---

[8] For Schütz' acceptance of this notion of Bergson see, for instance, *Coll. Pap.*, vol. 1, pp. 212ff.

[9] Since Schütz started to study the constitution of social types within an analysis of the meaning structure of social action, the notion of social relevance becomes problem-atic only relatively late in his work. I have already said that the notion is discussed first in 1940, *Coll. Pap.*, vol. 1, p. 136. In chronological order, further references occur (all in the *Coll. Pap.*) in 1943 (vol. 2, p. 84), in 1945 (vol. 1, p. 227), 1953 (vol. 1, p. 5), 1954 (vol. 1, p. 60), and in 1957 (vol. 2, p. 226). A first concise and comprehensive statement of this theory has been published only posthumously in a translation by Aron Gurwitsch: *Some Structures of the Life World, Coll. Pap.*, vol. 3, pp. 116—132. A further manuscript of Schütz dealing systematically with the problem of social relevance has just been edited by Richard Zaner: *Reflections on the Problem of Relevance* (New Haven, Yale University Press, 1970).

pear to us as sufficiently solved, as far as our purposes are concerned, so that we discontinue further investigations? [10]

3.11 Thematic Relevance

The concept of "thematic relevance" connects immediately with Husserl's notions of theme and "making an object thematic." If I am tending toward an object in that double sense, i.e. if theme and object coincide, then explication or elaboration can go on. However, the theme can either be forced upon me, or I may have chosen it because of an old theme, or I may have taken it up merely hypothetically. Accordingly, Schütz distinguishes three types of thematic relevance:

1. Forced thematic relevance. Schütz' central contention that our experiencing social reality is structured into distinct "finite provinces of meaning," each characterized by a specific cognitive style and some "attention à la vie," [11] leads him to distinguish four ways in which a theme can be forced upon me: a) Something "new" within a given frame of acquaintance catches my attention. I am not even sure if I am dreaming, or phantasying, or imagining, or indeed looking at something "new". In Schütz' terms: I am not even sure which is to be the dominant realm of meaning in which the "new" experience can be grasped. For example, playing a hand of bridge in Frankfurt (Germany) I suddenly see something moving in my partner's lap which I would "normally" call a cobra. b) If a finite province of meaning is unquestionably pre-given, a change of my "attention à la vie" within the same realm can impose a new theme. In a game of bridge, for example, I may suddenly get an urge and propose playing poker. This change would result from my own disposition, while c) it may, of course, be imposed by my social environment, say, by my partners in that game. d) The only remaining case is now a "leap" from one finite province to another, say from the world of play into that of "serious interaction," which brings about a wholesale transformation and recomposition of themes. This may happen, for instance, if my partner suddenly draws his pistol on me.

2. Motivated thematic relevance. Phenomenological analysis distinguishes the outer and inner horizon of any lived experience. Roughly, one could say that a theme delineates the outer from the inner horizon. Accordingly, a theme can change in two different ways: a) Via its outer horizon the present intentional object is related to previous experiences. Thus, elaborating on the present theme, I may be motivated to take up a theme related to some previous experience. For example, in listening to a dispute of the op-

[10] *Coll. Pap.*, vol. 3, p. 117.
[11] *Coll. Pap.*, vol. 1, pp. 230–232.

ponents in a game of bridge, I may be reminded of my mother-in-law.
b) Otherwise, motivation to change the present theme may come from an
attempt to explicate some implication of the inner horizon. For example,
playing a hand in "three no-trump" in bridge I may be suddenly interested
in knowing if I passed up the chance of a slam in a minor suit.

3. *Hypothetical thematic relevance.* I may cling to a certain theme explicitly for the purpose of testing the validity of some of its ingredients in
specific situations. For example, and again I am choosing it from the context of playing bridge, an observer or a total beginner notes that one of the
foursome puts all his cards face-up on the table, his partner immediately
does the same gesticulating in some undecipherable manner, and the others
follow suit. The observing beginner will probably carry this theme into the
next round of the game, validating the first step and invalidating the following steps as being part of the game.

Remembering Schütz' leading question concerning thematic relevance,
"how does it happen that that which has become questionable for us appears as worth being questioned," the notion of hypothetical thematic relevance goes somehow beyond the range of this question. It already implies
initial steps of a process of typification which will be shown in more detail
later. A similar critique can be raised against the other two remaining major
types of relevance.

3.12 Motivational Relevance

"What is relevant for the solution of a problem?" This leading question
gets a typically subjective twist in Schütz' solution and should have been
stated like this: "What do I, the acting participant in a social situation consider to be relevant for the solution of a problem, still better, for the definition of this situation?" Schütz analyses the structure of motives for an answer to this question. His fundamental distinction between "because-mo-
tives" and "in-order-to-motives" derives from the temporal structure of the
stream of consciousness, from its "past" in memory and retentions, from its
"future" in anticipations and protentions. This temporal dimension is fundamental for phenomenological analysis. Consequently, Schütz considers
the motivationally relevant context to be fundamental for the constitution
of theme and thus for thematic relevance in general.[12] The difference from
Husserl's notion of constitution of theme becomes apparent here: Husserl
talked vaguely about "a positive feeling," about "an effort to come closer
and closer to the object," thus indicating a link between thematic interest

[12] *Coll. Pap.,* vol. 3, p. 124.

and the genesis of inquiry. In contrast, Schütz refers the constitution of theme back into the structure of motives.

In a similar context Schütz suggested earlier "that the various solutions offered for the explanation of the origin of the interests might the grouped into two types: one which is concerned with the because motives, the other with the in-order-to motives constituting the so-called interests," [13] Quite in line with this earlier distinction, Schütz separates the motivational context of relevance into two realms.

1. The because-of context of motivational relevance. Each arising theme in a given context of social interaction depends also on how the individual actor defines his situation. This definition is bounded by what Schütz calls "the biographic determination of perspective": the elements relevant for the individual's present definition of the situation are part of his current interests, which are part of the prevailing particular plan, which in turn have their place in a hierarchy of plans forming, *in toto,* the life-plan of the individual. Every project of action, for instance, has its "objective" motivational basis in this context. In other words, if one is interested in finding out the "motivational relevance" of some accomplished act (for instance in some legal case), he has to ask for the biographic definition of that situation, which "led" to the *formation of* the preceding *project,* i.e., which "objectively" determined that project. Schütz stresses that the widening circle of biographic determinants shall *not* be considered as a series of types or as processes of typification. It lays out merely a future perspective which is a syndrom of expectations, hypothetical relevances, projects of action, capacities, elements of habitual knowledge, states of moods, etc. This perspective initiates *typical* in-order-to motivational series in *typical* situations.

2. The in-order-to context of motivational relevance. In-order-to motivational series are, for example, constitutive for social action. They extend from the project of action, from the state of phantasying typical acts under typical circumstances, into the future. These in-order-to motivations span, for instance, the "voluntative fiat," i.e. they determine the motivational context which leads to the "decision" to *perform some project* of action. Specifically, this "decision" orients itself at typifications of probabilities of certain typical events. These typified events are, so-to-speak, guideposts of conduct spanning the in-order-to context in which action will be performed.

Both the because-of-context (formation of project) and the in-order-to context (enactment of project) form the texture of relevance in which social

[13] *Coll. Pap.,* vol. 1, p. 77n.

action arises and takes place. My acting circumscribes the sum total of elements which are relevant for the solution of my problem at hand.[14]

3.13 Interpretational Relevance

Schütz connects the constitution of theme and his fundamental concept of "stock of knowledge" by means of his notion of "interpretational relevance." Certain aspects of the perceived object and certain elements of the stock of knowledge offer themselves for interpretation. A theme, once constituted in consciousness, is brought to "resonance" (Deckung) with certain relevant elements of knowledge. "Interpretational relevance" is thus a title for a complex process in which specific elements of the stock of knowledge suitable for "resonance" occur in the attentional foreground: the stock of knowledge "contains" compatible typifications; mutually "awakening" aspects of theme and typified elements of knowledge are brought to resonance; the process is broken off if the problem at hand seems to be sufficiently solved.

Apparently Schütz introduced this concept of interpretational relevance to be able to relate social relevance to processes of typification. In Schütz' words:

All typification is relative to some problem: there is no type at large but only types which carry an "index" pointing to a problem. If, by synthesis of cognition, an actually relevant theme is brought to coincidence as typically known, typically familiar, typically alike, with a type which pertains as habitual to the horizonally given stock of experience and displays the same degree of familiarity, then this foreknown type becomes interpretationally relevant with respect to the actual theme.[15]

An "index," pertaining to each type and pointing to the related problem indicates that types are intentional types having some directional structure. The question as to the composition of this structure is still open. Schütz merely gave the broad answer above, that "types . . . carry an index pointing to a problem." An example might serve to explain some of its open aspects.

Assume an informal gathering of, say, a social party at Mr. L.'s residence. The relevant theme is "being-at-a-party." Being invited to the party I attend it along habitual lines of highly typified conduct. To be more specific: the typification of Mr. L. as "host" is supposed to become "interpretationally relevant" with respect to the theme "being-at-a-party" if type and

---

[14] Though the motivational structure of social action is most important for Schütz, it cannot be described here in great detail. Schütz has presented that study in *Choosing among Projects of Action, Coll. Pap.,* vol. 1, pp. 67–96.

[15] *Coll. Pap.,* vol. 3, p. 128.

theme are "brought to coincidence." Coincidence – or resonance, as I prefer to call it – between theme and type is problematic, and reference to this problem of resonance is what Schütz circumscribes by the term "index." The type "host" carries an index pointing to the problematic resonance with the theme "being-at-a-party." The situational context of the party is the major source of possible problems which Schütz referred into the context of motivational relevance.

But the situational context, which is not identical with the theme, is also responsible for the constitution of the typified social objects "Mr. L. being the host of this party" and the correlative formation of "I being a guest at the party of Mr. L." Without this situational context, or independently of it, these two correlative typified social objects do not exist at all. They are socially constituted in an interactional context. Thus, they do not exist merely because of *my* imputing to the other some typical conduct, because of *my* assuming some learned typical behavior, because of *my* perceiving and regarding the situation in a specific cognitive style and "attention à la vie." There are semantic types like "host" and "guest," there are semantic themes like "being-at-a-party," but "host" and "guest" have *one common* situational reference, *one* "index": this situational link between type and theme has been analysed by Gurwitsch under the heading of "thematic field." [16] His studies lead a step further to reveal the structure of what Schütz called an "index." Later I shall go beyond Gurwitsch' theory and show that this *structure* of the index and that of relevance are essentially the same.

3.2 Gurwitsch' Theory of Relevance

Gurwitsch' theory of relevance is more closely related to Husserl's notion of interest. According to Husserl, "perceptual interest" – as I have called it – and thematic interest coincide when my tending toward the intentional object grasps it qua object and qua theme. Husserl pointed out that it is the mediary state between both kinds of interests, the indeterminateness and vagueness of a still only fugitive theme, which is germinal for processes of inquiry initiated by "an effort to come closer and closer to the object." Further elaboration of this problem therefore requires some notion of, and some method of approach to, the context in which object, inquirer, and inquiry are situated.

Schütz referred at this point to the because-of-context and the in-order-to context of motivational relevances, a distinction which, in the last analysis,

---

[16] Aron Gurwitsch, *The Field of Consciousness* (Pittsburgh, Dusquesne Univ. Press, 1964), pp. 307ff.

results from the temporal dimensions of inner time. Thus Schütz describes the phenomenon of context in terms of the motivational horizon which is constitutive for all projecting and acting in a given situation.

At this point Schütz differs basically from Gurwitsch. The latter insists that the phenomenon of context cannot be described in terms of phenomenal time:

> The phenomenon of context concerns *that which is experienced* rather than the *fact of its actually being experienced*. Therefore, it cannot be accounted for in terms of phenomenal time.[17]

Surely, the topics dealt with by Schütz and by Gurwitsch are different: Schütz had been concerned with the problem of relevance in social situations of mutual interaction, Gurwitsch addressed himself mainly to the question of scientific inquiry. But this has no import for the fundamental differences in their conception of context and consequently in their notions of relevance. As Gurwitsch puts it himself:

> Schütz does not search for the basic principle of context and unity of context by virtue of which the items of the thematic field are intrinsically related to one another due to their common intrinsic relationship to the theme. By relevancy Schütz means rather the comparative importance of objects and contexts of objects for the experiencing subject, the greater or lesser interest which the subject takes in objects and their contexts. . . . According to Schütz, relevancy denotes a relationship in which objects and items stand to the Ego with regard to the Ego's plans and designs, not, as with us, the relationship of mutual pointing reference of these items. . . . Schütz, though occasionally using the term in question in a sense close to ours, refers all relevancies and systems of relevancies to the Ego, or, as he prefers to say, to the self.[18]

Gurwitsch agrees here in part with Schütz' notion of "thematic relevance."[19] But the differences between both theories will guide my analysis. For interaction in a social context is a temporal process. If context and its social objects are constituted in this process, if furthermore the context is not supposed to be describable in terms of phenomenal time, then the temporality of social interaction has to occur in some other relationship to the social context.

---

[17] Gurwitsch, Field, p. 329. — This translation veils one important point: the context *as it presents* itself is to be distinguished from certain acts occurring within this context, which relate to different temporal modes of experiences: "Le phénomène de contexte concerne *ce qui se présente,* et non le fait que *certain actes sont, furent, ou seront vécus." Théorie du champs de la conscience* (Paris, Desclée De Brouwer, 1957), p. 260.

[18] Gurwitsch, *Field,* p. 342.

[19] Schütz compared his notion of relevance with Gurwitsch' theory in *Coll. Pap.,* vol. 3, p. 126.

Gurwitsch' theory of relevance is closely related to Husserl's distinction between intentional object and theme. He defines *theme* as that upon which the inquiring subject concentrates his mental activity, thus allowing, like Husserl, for a possible cleavage between his momentary object of attention (a noise, for example) and his theme of mental deliberation (measuring, for example, a certain distance in a right triangle). The theme, in Gurwitsch' words, "engrosses his mind and he concentrates his mental activity upon it." [20]

Gurwitsch proceeds to study the tie between theme and attentional object which Husserl already had indicated to be germinal for processes of inquiry. Referring to William James' "theory of the fringes" [21] Gurwitsch shows that the surrounding halo of fringes of each theme ties the theme to a *context* constituting a "sense of affinity":

Conveying awareness of the theme's pertinence to a broader context constitutes the principal function of the fringe defined as a "sense of affinity." [22]

But a theme is not tied to a unique specific context. Neither does some given context give rise to only one specific theme. (The properties of a right triangle, for example, may 1. be proved to be correct within a specific geometry, may 2. be used in some measurement of polygons, may 3. be postulated as a characteristic of an Euclidean space.) The multiplicity and variability of themes and contexts can be grasped and studied only if some invariant structure, some at least relative "fix point" can be revealed.

The *thematic field* [23] is introduced as "the totality of items to which a theme points and refers" in the following manner: 1. the items are constituents of the context as it presents itself; 2. every theme necessarily refers to some thematic field: *this reference is an invariant of consciousness;* 3. the *"appearance of a theme must* be described as *emergence from* a (thematic) *field* in which the theme is located occupying the center so that the field forms a background with respect to the theme." In the previous example, the thematic field "Pythagorean theorem" is the necessary referent of the various themes; deliberation of the inquirer has to reveal it as the source of the emergent themes. [24]

---

[20] *Field*, p. 319.

[21] William James, *The Principles of Psychology* (Dover Publications, 1950), vol. 1, pp. 258ff.

[22] *Field*, p. 319.

[23] For the following quotes see: Gurwitsch, *Field*, pp. 319–320.

[24] C. Wright Mills advanced (from a quite different theoretical perspective) a similar notion in his essay "On Intellectual Craftsmanship." He proposes to distinguish a "topic" from a "theme." While a "theme is an idea, usually of some signal trend, some master

Clarification of the tie between theme and attentional object can now be formulated more precisely as the problem to clarify a vague and undetermined thematic field. What are the guiding principles which lead the inquirer at the often diffuse start of his deliberations? What can be said about the situation in which neither typical interpretations nor typical projects are available to grasp a heretofore not even articulated problem?

In answer to these questions, Gurwitsch introduces first the term *relevance* as a correlate to the notion of context:

Besides being copresent with the theme, the data . . . appear, moreover, as *being of a certain concern* to the theme. They have something to do with it; they are relevant to it.[25]

The unity of the context is a unity by way of its relevance, by way of its "relationship of mutual pointing reference of these items."

Most important, the thematic field is never totally diffuse: "However diffuse, vague, obscure, and devoid of inner differentiation and discrimination the thematic field (may be), it is nevertheless tinged in a specific manner. . . .The experience of reference may assume the form of a mere awareness of direction. Still, it is a specific direction, namely, the consciousness of a 'whence' in contra-distinction to that of a 'whither.'"[26] Inquiry in such undetermined situations is guided by a "sentiment of direction." A "perspective" or "orientation" is impressed upon the theme by the thematic field thus determining a "positional index" locating the theme within the thematic field.[27] While relevance designates the reciprocal relation of reference between that which is given in a situation (such as it presents itself!), the positional index of the theme designates the correlative "sentiment of direction" pertaining even to a diffuse and undeterminate thematic field.

conception, or a key distinction" which frequently "will be found in the clotted and confused, the more badly written, sections of your manuscript," a topic is a short subject which "can readily be put into one chapter." C. Wright Mills, *The Sociological Imagination* (New York, Grove Press, 1961), p. 216. Though Mills' notion of "topic" is comparable with Gurwitsch' "theme," and Mills' "theme" reminds one of Gurwitsch' "thematic field," the differences are obvious: Mills never tried to develop these notions which remain for him recipes for an "Intellectual Craftsman."

[25] Gurwitsch, *Field*, p. 340. – Gurwitsch prefers the term "relevancy" to Schütz' concept of "relevance." I have adopted the latter term, though my notion of "relevance" is much closer to Gurwitsch' than to Schütz'. – The French term "données," i.e., "something given," has been rendered as "data" or "items" in the English version. The translation, of course, is not to give the impression that these "data" are in any way already typified. "Data," "items," or "données" are that which is given in a context as it presents itself.

[26] Gurwitsch, *Field*, p. 337. – Gurwitsch refers here to W. James' notion of the "consciousness of the whence and whither." See: James, *Principles,* vol. 1, p. 242.

[27] Gurwitsch, *Field*, pp. 358–365.

The previously mentioned example of an informal social party may be useful to show the extent to which Gurwitsch' theory can clarify the structure of *social* relevance and which aspects, in my opinion, are still to be studied. The situation may be this: I have received a written invitation from Mr. L., whom I never visited before, to come to his house at a given time. I know that he is a senior professor of philosophy at Z-College where I am working as a graduate assistent. Ringing the bell at the assigned time and location the door is opened by a young woman in a breathtakingly bold dress. She addresses me apparently in French, which I barely manage to speak, and gestures invitingly to enter and then to proceed toward a bar close by. Nobody else is present. The whole house seems to deserted. She asks me to mix her a drink and to start a game on the nearby cardtable. We are alone for quite a while before . . . etc.

The *thematic field* "being-at-a-party"[28] is diffuse and undetermined; any of the situational elements (her bold dress; her French language; my mixing a drink; etc.) may become a *theme* should I turn my attention toward it in an effort to "come to terms with the situation." The essential "données" of the *context* are, other than myself, the young female and, as a horizonal character, Mr. L.. But does Mr. L. belong to the context also? Gurwitsch insists that context as well as thematic field are to be taken strictly as they present themselves and not in relation to previous, present, or future acts. Thus, the context does not include Mr. L. and is restricted to the immediately present and perceivable situational setting encompassing the girl and myself. But the context as it presents itself is in this case (and Gurwitsch does not explicitly discuss this case!) a *social context:* it presents itself 1. to me; it presents itself 2. to the young woman; and it presents itself 3. to me by way of her presenting herself to me. Gurwitsch' definition of *relevance* (the relationship of mutual pointing reference among that which is given in a situation) should be extended to take care of this "triadic" contextual structure if applied to a social situation.

To avoid a possible misunderstanding: Gurwitsch' critique concerning Schütz' notion of relevance is not being watered down by my proposed extension: no reference to any motivational context is being made; neither is a

---

[28] One may notice that "being-at-a-party" has previously been called a "theme" in Schütz' theory. Gurwitsch distinguishes between "theme" and "thematic field" in order to keep the topic of my momentary thematic interest (theme) apart from the "invariant" structure of the thematic field. – I contend that this "invariance" as well as the "relative independence of the theme with regard to the thematic field" (*Field,* p. 354) can be assured in case of *social* relevance by giving the thematic field an intersubjective status.

"reciprocity of perspectives"[29] assumed at this elementary level. However, I do suggest that this triadic contextual structure of social relevance has its origin in a manifold structure of the intentionality of perceiving social objects.

This suggestion may become more apparant by a further interpretation of the previous example: the *thematic field* "being-at-a-party" guides my interest throughout that situation. Relevance in a social context, a relation of reciprocal indicative references, has, I contend, a specific "triadic" structure of references. All situational characters (the whole bearing of the young woman, her dress, her alien language, the setting of the bar room, my mixing a drink, the cards on the cardtable, etc. etc.) acquire a unity by way of this structure of relevance. Though the thematic field is diffuse and undetermined (I believe I have been invited; I think I have gone to the right address on the correct date; I remember vaguely his fancy for the French classics), any of these elements may become a dominant *theme* inducing a certain *sentiment of direction* and thus unifying all relevant contextual characters. For example, the theme may be "Mr. L. recently also lecturer of French literature at Vassar College": the thematic field "being-at-a-party" would confer upon this theme a *positional index* which had been originated, of course, by the French language of the young woman. All *subsequent* typifications will be oriented by this positional index unless apparent inconsistencies drive another theme or even another thematic field into the foreground. These processes of typification take place in the context of social relevance, in which the structure of relevance plays a constitutive part in the formation of social types. I suggest, in reference to some notions of G. H. Mead to be explicated later on, that these processes involve specific forms of play.

Since both Schütz and Gurwitsch developed their theories of relevance by elaborating upon some very central conceptions of William James (theory of fringes, knowledge of acquaintance and knowledge about, etc.), a synthesis and perhaps a further development might be possible by taking account of Charles S. Peirce' writings. He had the most profound influence in the formation of James' thought as well as having decisively determined the theoretical positions of Dewey and G. H. Mead.[30]

---

[29] See for ex. Schütz, *Coll. Pap.*, vol. 1, pp. 11ff: "Reciprocity of Perspectives" is for Schütz a set of idealizations leading to an interchangeability of standpoints of the I and the Other. Thus Schütz accounts for the *symmetry* of my Here to his or her There, which is *not implied* in the "triadic" constellation of the context, as proposed in this paper.

[30] Dewey was a student of Peirce' at Johns Hopkins University.

3.3 James' Theory of Fringes and Peirce' Abductive Reasoning.

The theories of relevance of Schütz and of Gurwitsch connect with and elaborate upon, Husserl's notion of thematic interest. This has been outlined in the previous sections. According to Husserl, a "positive feeling" toward the intentional object, a tendency and an effort "to come closer and closer" to it are fundamental for the constitution of a theme and for the genesis of processes of inquiry. A similar contention has been advanced by W. James:

Now what I contend for, and accumulate examples to show, is that "tendencies" are not only descriptions from without, but that they are among the *objects* of the stream (of thought), which is thus aware of them from within, and must be described as in very large measure constituted of *feelings* of *tendencies,* often so vague that we are unable to name them at all. It is, in short, the reinstatement of the vague to its proper place in our mental life which I am so anxious to press on the attention.[31]

This last phrase, the "reinstatement of the vague to its proper place in our mental life" could be taken as the leitmotif of pragmatism. It appeared first in 1877/78 in Ch. S. Peirce' critique of the logical theories of Descartes and Leibniz.[32] Both had insisted that an idea or a conception has to be "clear and distinct" in order to be acceptable for logical reasoning, while "the distinction between an idea *seeming* clear and really being so" never occured to them. Peirce points out that the intermediary state of diffuse and vague premisses, which is the only source of any possible advancement of our knowledge, has never been studied in the theory of logic. The structure of the vague[33] ought to be the foremost field of interest for the logician. "The very first lesson that we have a right to demand that logic shall teach us is how to make our ideas clear." It is *abductive reasoning* which serves that purpose. And Peirce went so far as to state later (1903) in his Lowell

---

[31] W. James, *Principles,* vol. 1, p. 254.

[32] Charles Sanders Peirce, *Collected Papers,* (Cambridge, Harvard Univ. Press, 2d and 3d printing, 1965–66), vol. 5, esp. §§ 391–393. – I use in the following the standardized abbreviation: *Coll. Pap.* 5.391–393.

[33] There seems to be a paradox implied in the term "structure of the vague" since "structure" often is understood as a set of clear and distinct (relational) elements on the background of some possibly diffuse horizon. (Such as for example, the notions of residues and residual elements by Pareto and Parsons.) A fundamental misconception (i.e., an unjustified reification of sets) underlies those notions of structure. There are "structures," like "the relationship of mutual pointing reference" in a context, which cannot be grasped in set-theoretical terms, and I am using the term "structure" precisely in this broad sense.

Lectures at Harvard: "If you carefully consider the question of pragmatism you will see that it is nothing else than the question of the logic of abduction." [34]

W. James tried to achieve the "reinstatement of the vague to its proper place in our mental life" by means of his theory of fringes. This broad intent is the reason for his quite heterogeneous usage of the term. [35]

The *stream of thought* is described by James as largely constituted of "feelings of tendencies." [36] That is, it implies a "permanent consciousness of whither our thought is going." There is a "sense of the whither" as well as a "sense of the whence" of consciousness founded upon cerebral processes due to some neurological cause. These "faint brain-processes" influence our thought, thus making the stream of thought "aware of relations and objects but dimly perceived." In short, this influence brings about a directional, temporal unity, i.e. the continuity of the stream of thought. It is a unity by "psychic overtones" or by "fringes."

James pointed out early [37] that his fringes were misunderstood as "some sort of psychic material," while he intends them to be "part of the object cognized, – substantive qualities and things appearing to the mind in a fringe of relations." Both his references to the neurological structure of the brain and his often flamboyant and loose language may account for the frequent misinterpretations by his critics. To separate the Jamesian chaff from its pragmatic wheat, a disciplined and theoretically refined scheme of interpretations, like that of phenomenological analysis applied by Schütz and by Gurwitsch, seems to be necessary. Similarly suitable are the highly consistent pragmatic theories of Ch. S. Peirce which offer in addition some hitherto undiscussed suggestions for a theory of social relevance and types. [38]

---

[34] *Coll. Pap.*, 5.196.

[35] See, for more detail, Gurwitsch, *Field*, pp. 309–318 and Schütz, *Coll. Pap.*, vol. 3, pp. 8–13. Both authors have analysed the various problems embraced by James' theory of fringes. They did not discuss James' dependence upon Peirce, which is my first interest here.

[36] *Principles*, vol. 1, pp. 255–258.

[37] *op. cit.*, p. 258n. James refers to a critique raised in 1885.

[38] The first sociologist who took a systematic interest in Peirce' social thought was C. Wright Mills. His dissertation *A Sociological Account of Pragmatism* (University of Wisconsin, 1942) has been published posthumously: C. Wright Mills, *Sociology and Pragmatism* (New York, Oxford Univ. Press, 1966). Mills' interpretation of Peirce has, however, several shortcomings. (Cf. my review in *Social Research,* 34, 1967, pp. 387–391.) – Among the most recent Peirce-interpretations one should mention Jürgen Habermas, *Erkenntnis und Interesse* (Frankfurt, Suhrkamp, 1968), esp. chapter 5: "Ch. S. Peirce's Logik der Forschung: Die Aporie eines sprachlogisch erneuerten Universalienrealismus." Habermas' excellent presentation of Peirce' "abductive reasoning" (in chapter 6) shows its implications for explanatory and for innovatory processes in

James described the "cognitive function of different states of mind" by means of fringes:

The difference between those (states) that are mere "acquaintance," and those that are "knowledges-about". . . is reducible almost entirely to the absence or presence of psychic fringes.[39]

Earlier he distinguished two essential states of mind, the "resting-places" of thought and the "places of flight":

Let us call the resting-places the "substantive parts," and the places of flight the "transitive parts," of the stream of thought. It then appears that the main end of our thinking is at all times the attainment of some other substantive part than the one from which we have just been dislodged. And we may say that the main use of the transitive parts is to lead us from one substantive conclusion to another.[40]

The same notion had been advanced before by *Peirce* under the headings of doubt (places of flight) and belief (resting-places). Peirce contends [41] "that there are such states of mind as doubt and belief, that a passage from one to the other is possible, the object of mind remaining the same, and that this transition is subject to some rules which all minds are alike bound by." And more specifically: "Doubt is an uneasy and dissatisfied state from which we struggle to free ourselves and pass into the state of belief." But what is in Peirce' terminology that which James called "the cognitive function of different states of mind?" Peirce says:

The irritation of doubt causes a struggle to attain a state of belief. I shall call this struggle inquiry . . . The irritation of doubt is the only immediate motive for the struggle to attain belief . . . The sole object of inquiry is the settlement of opinion.

A "cognitive function" according to Peirce has to be assigned solely to the state of doubt, to the "transitive parts" as James called them. Thus, Peirce does not primarily study the "substantive" state of belief, but the "transitive" state concerning the "fixation of belief."

On the other hand, James' introspective analysis of the transitive parts lead to "baleful" results as he admits.[42] Could it be simply a case of an incorrect or inadequate methodological approach? Very likely, his friend

scientific reasoning. This level of methodological discussion is, at present, not relevant to my presentation.

[39] *Principles*, vol. 1, p. 259.
[40] *op. cit.*, p. 243.
[41] *Coll. Pap.*, 5.369–375.
[42] *Principles*, vol. 1, p. 243f.

Peirce would have argued this point: He had rejected in an earlier paper (1868) any inquiry based on introspection.[43] In any case, James tried to overcome his unsuccessful analysis of the "transitive parts" of thought by postulating:

If there be such things as feelings at all, then so surely as relations between objects exist in rerum natura, so surely, and more surely, do feelings exist to which these relations are known.[44]

Consequently James uses the terms "transitive states" and "feelings of relation" synonymously[45] stating finally that "relation . . . to our topic or interest is constantly felt in the fringe."[46]

James' utilitarian conception of pragmatism[47] has one source in this short-circuited analysis of "transitive parts of thought." For James assigned them a major rôle, if one remembers that "the main use of the transitive parts is to lead us from one substantive conclusion to another"[48] and that "the important thing about a train of thought is its conclusion."[49] Important questions of the genesis of logical forms and of methods of inquiry in general are cut out or are merely touched upon because of James' disinterest in a further analysis of the constitution of fringes.[50] James can merely state in very vague and vulnerable form:

Any thought, the quality of whose fringe lets us feel ourselves "all right," is an acceptable member of our thinking, whatever kind of thought it may otherwise be. Provided we only feel it to have a place in the scheme of relations in which

---

[43] *Coll. Pap.,* 5.244–249. – Peirce, by the way, was quite frank in his criticism of James. A rich source is the – unfortunately only partly published – correspondence between Peirce and James. See *Coll. Pap.,* vol. 8.

[44] *Principles,* vol. 1, p. 245.

[45] *Principles,* vol. 1, p. 247.

[46] *op. cit.,* p. 259. – The "topic of thought" (James) is, roughly speaking, the same as what Gurwitsch called a "theme". For the difference see Gurwitsch, *Field,* pp. 318f.

[47] Especially established by his essay "The Will to Believe" (1897), republished as Dover Edition, 1956. Peirce comments on this conception of pragmatism in 1908: "In 1897 Professor James remodelled the matter, and transmogrified it into a doctrine of philosophy, some parts of which I highly approved, while other and more prominent parts I regarded and still regard, as opposed to sound logic." *Coll. Pap.,* 6.482.

[48] *Principles,* vol. 1, p. 243.

[49] *op. cit.,* p. 260.

[50] James occasionally touches upon the topic of logical relations: "We ought to say a feeling of *and,* a feeling of *if,* a feeling of *but,* and a feeling of *by* . . .". (*Principles,* vol. 1, p. 245). – Gurwitsch (*Field,* p. 309n) refers to the paper of E. B. McGilvary "The 'fringe' of William James' psychology, the basis of logic," Phil. Rev., 20, 1911, pp. 138ff, which is an interesting attempt to develop a "logic of fringes." Unfortunately, again, McGilvary had no access to the relevant papers of Ch. S. Peirce, most of which were still unpublished at that time.

the interesting topic also lies, that is quite sufficient to make of it a relevant and appropriate portion of our train of thought.[51]

What does James mean by these two sentences? Peirce' more refined notions may serve as an interpretational scheme with which one can untangle James' conception.

The first sentence quoted refers to the question of when a "substantive conclusion" is being acceptable to our thinking. The second sentence refers to the question of relevance which is the major point of interest here. The tie, so to speak, between both questions is that the "quality of the fringe" implies "the scheme of relations."

1. When is a "substantive conclusion" acceptable to our thinking? What does James mean by his answer that its acceptance depends upon its fringe letting us "feel ourselves 'all right' "? The substantive conclusion refers to what Peirce called a state of belief: "As soon as a firm belief is reached we are entirely satisfied, whether the belief be true or false." [52] Every further interpretation including the whole pragmatic theory of inquiry depends, of course, upon this last qualifying phrase "whether the belief be true or false." Peirce' analysis of the different "methods of fixing belief" [53] is more or less a first elaboration of this phrase. James, on the other hand, whose interest did not turn in this direction, opened himself here to the most scathing criticism.[54] "*Any* thought the quality of whose fringe lets us feel ourselves 'all right,' " signifies *any* state of belief to be reached by *any* means. Peirce asked here carefully:

If the settlement of opinion is the sole object of inquiry, and if belief is of the nature of a habit, why should we not attain the desired end, by taking as answer to a question any we may fancy, and constantly reiterating it to ourselves, dwelling on all which may conduce to that belief, and learning to turn with contempt and hatred from anything that might disturb it? [55]

This simple method of "tenacity" cannot be ruled out easily with con-

---

[51] *Principles,* vol. 1, pp. 259f.

[52] *Coll. Pap.,* 5.375.

[53] See in the same volume the §§ 377–387. Peirce' four "methods" are called "tenacity," "authority," "a priori," and "science."

[54] One of James' most articulate critics has been Bertrand Russell. See, for example, the chapter on James in his *A History of Western Philosophy* (New York, Simon and Schuster, 1945). – But even Schütz judged pragmatism for the most part to be "just a common-sense description of the attitude of man within the world of working in daily life, but not a philosophy investigating the presuppositions of such a situation." (*Coll. Pap.,* vol. 1, p. 213n) My references to Peirce are an effort, if not to refute, so at least to question this judgement.

[55] *Coll. Pap.,* 5.377.

tempt: Considering also means of social control, which Peirce described in his "method of authority," it has at least a limited range of intersubjective validity. Peirce illustrates this point vividly in the same context:

When an ostrich buries its head in the sand as danger approaches, it very likely takes the happiest course. It hides the danger, and then calmly says there is no danger; and, if it feels perfectly sure there is none, why should it raise its head to see?

The ostrich "hides the danger" quite similar to a social group hiding the deviant behavior of some member. Taking this problem up in the context of the social construction of social objects, as I have to later on, James' notion of "a fringe letting us feel all right" will reveal itself to be rather useful. It is James' disinterest in the intersubjective validity of thought that makes his conceptions very vulnerable.

2. More important, however, for my present argument is James' second sentence quoted above. He states that the relevance of a thought depends merely on our feeling that the thought has "a place in the scheme of relations in which the interesting topic also lies." In most cases "this topic is a problem, a gap we cannot yet fill . . . but which . . . influences us in an intensely active and determinate psychic way." [56] One is immediately reminded of Schütz' notion of thematic relevance and of Gurwitsch' conception of a given theme (topic) before the background of a diffuse and undetermined thematic field.

For James, the topic of thought (theme) is given in a "scheme of relations," and its relevance is felt through its fringes. The fringe refers to the unexplicated and mostly vague transitive parts of the stream of thought establishing the continuity between one substantive conclusion and the other. The transitive parts compose every ongoing process of thought. The relations, however, between these transitive parts can either be vague and undetermined or they are definitely formulated, i.e. they are clear and distinct. Peirce referred to the same difference and distinguished:

An "Argument" is any process of thought reasonably tending to produce a definite belief. An "Argumentation" is an Argument proceeding upon definitely formulated premisses.[57]

He attacked "those current notions of logic which recognize no other Arguments than Argumentations." There are Arguments which are no Argumentations; i.e. Arguments characterized by a vague composition that

---

[56] *Principles,* vol. 1, p. 259.
[57] *Coll. Pap.,* 6.456.

nevertheless are apt to lead to conclusions. But their vagueness does not fore-close an analysis of their structure. This is an important insight of Peirce: any productive inquiry leading to an advancement of knowledge has to start from Arguments. One of the most "Neglected Arguments" in the history of logic is "abductive reasoning," as Peirce called it to distinguish it from induction and deduction.[58] Closely related to James' notion of fringes, Peirce' theory of abductive reasoning will be shown to offer essential con-tributions to the analysis of social types.

3.31 The First Stage of Inquiry: Abduction, which is Related to the Emer-gence of Incipient Events

Every inquiry, according to Peirce, is composed of three stages, of which the first is to establish familiarity with the object of interest.

Every inquiry whatsoever takes its rise in the observation . . . of some surpris-ing phenomenon, some experience which either disappoints an expectation, or breaks in upon some habit of expectation of the *inquisiturus* . . . The inquiry begins with pondering these phenomena in all their aspects . . . At length a con-jecture arises that furnishes a possible Explanation, by which I mean a syllogism exhibiting the surprising fact as necessarily consequent upon the circumstances of its occurence together with the truth of the credible conjecture, as premisses. On account of this Explanation, the inquirer is led to regard his conjecture, or hypothesis, with favor. As I phrase it, he provisionally holds it to be "Plausi-ble". . . The whole series of mental performances between the notice of the wonderful phenomenon and the acceptance of the hypothesis, . . . the search for pertinent circumstances and the laying hold of them, . . . the scrutiny of them, the dark laboring, the bursting out of the startling conjecture, the remarking of its smooth fitting to the anomaly, as it is turned back and forth like a key in a lock, and the final estimation of its Plausibility, I reckon as composing the First Stage of Inquiry. Its characteristic formula of reasoning I term Retroduction (or Abduction; footnote of editor), i.e. reasoning from consequent to antecedent. . . . In short, it is a form of Argument rather than of Argumentation.[59]

The propositional prototype of abductive reasoning[60] may be compared with the following syllogism: "All men are mortal; Socrates is a man; there-fore, Socrates is mortal." This is deduction *from antecedent* (all men are

---

[58] The explication of "abductive reasoning" (also called "retroduction" or "hypo-thesis") as the basis of all inquiry has been a leading theme of Peirce' work. Its succes-sive development is of no further interest here. I am quoting mainly from a very late formulation (1908) of his theory of abduction taken from the essay "A Neglected Argument," *Coll. Pap.,* 6.452–485.

[59] *Coll. Pap.,* 6.469.

[60] The following examples are not to suggest that abductive reasoning occurs *neces-sarily* in propositional form. To the contrary, the above quotes of Peirce show that "Arguments" do *not* proceed "upon definitely formulated premisses."

mortal; Socrates is a man) *to consequent* (Socrates is mortal). It is "necessary reasoning," as Peirce called it, or Argumentation, and contributes nothing new to the process of inquiry. Keeping the structure and the terminology of *this* syllogism in mind,[61] Peirce analysed inferences of the following kind: All men are mortal; Socrates is mortal; therefore, Socrates is a man. They are abductive.[62]

Of the same logical structure, though seemingly more plausible, is an example mentioned by Peirce:

A certain man had the Asiatic cholera. He was in a state of collapse, livid, quite cold, and without perceptible pulse. He was bled copiously. During the process he came out of collapse, and the next morning he was well enough to be about. Therefore, bleeding tends to cure the cholera.[63]

The abductive suggestion, i.e. the formation of an explanatory hypothesis by *reasoning from consequent* (next morning he was well) *to antecedent* (bleeding cures cholera) comes to us, as Peirce calls it, "like a flash."

It is an act of insight, although of extremely fallible insight. It is true that the different elements of the hypothesis were in our mind before; but it is the idea of putting together what we had never before dreamed of putting together which flashed the new suggestion before our contemplation.[64]

Abductive reasoning may become clearer by applying it to the example introduced before: Being invited to a party and being received by a young female, the situation is one of surprise and uncertainty. "Normally," the thematic field "being-at-a-party" presupposes and even requires the correl-

---

[61] This terminology will be retained throughout, for two notions can get easily confused here: The terms "antecedent" and "consequent" are taken from the *deductive* syllogism and do *not* signify "premisses" and "conclusions" of inferences in general! Thus, in abductive reasoning "from consequent to antecedent" (both terms referring to the deductive syllogism) the inference runs from the "consequent" (which is *as premise,* of course, antecedent to the conclusion) to the "antecedent." In order to avoid any confusion, I am using the terms "antecedent" and "consequent" *only* in reference to abductions.

[62] Already a short reflection on the "logic of everyday thinking" reveals an abundance of abductive reasonings. The most severe are those in legal proceedings: A man having blood type x was killed in the place y at time z; I was seen in place y at time z, and I have blood of the type x on my clothing; therefore, I am the killer. This inference based on "circumstantial evidence" is abductive. Significantly, the "authorities" confronting the suspect with such "evidence" pursue substantially a course of action similar to the theory I intend to present: They confront the suspect in incessant "plays-at-this-theme" of murder until he "breaks down," i.e. until the "incipient event" of "murder committed" breaks through in a confession. The "truth" of such a confession rests merely on a verbal transformation of an abductive statement into a deduction.

[63] *Coll. Pap.,* 5.271.

[64] *Coll. Pap.,* 5.181.

ative social objects "host" and "guest" to be constituted in the situation. But any typificatory attempt in the direction of these objects is stopped short by certain puzzling elements of the situation: the bearing of the young girl, especially her dress, her speaking French, my being asked to mix a drink and play a hand of cards, etc. What is the social object in this situation? Any of those puzzling elements may become a theme, but even all possible themes can lead only to "circumstantial evidence" (see the "murder case" in footnote 62 above) concerning the *only* social object being able to clarify this diffuse thematic field: A "host" and more specifically "Mr. L. as host." I am totally left go guessing "who is who" unless Mr. L. appears himself. (I am overdrawing this example in order to clarify the abductive structure. The theoretical interest is, of course, merely the constitution of *some* social object.) The only hold I have on this situation is one or the other theme (the consequent) from which I may attempt to reach the social object (the antecedent) thus trying to clarify the thematic field. The process is, using Peirce' terminology, abductive: I am "reasoning from consequent to antecedent," from the theme to the social object.

It becomes clearer now what Peirce meant by saying that "abductions may be mistaken for perceptions" and that "abductive inference shades into perceptual judgement without any sharp line of demarcation between them." [65] *If* the surprising phenomenon is finally not so surprising after all, i.e. if, for example, the host suddenly appears and introduces her as his "niece," then the whole sequence of my experiences with the young girl "most naturally" are taken as being perceptual affirmations within the current thematic field. In case these expectations are disappointed, in other words, should the thematic field "being-at-a-party" finally "explode," then the lines of demarcation between perceptual affirmations and abductive inferences relative to the (just abandoned) thematic field will be most clearly drawn. But, in both cases the processes are abductive, they are reasonings from consequent to antecedent. I contend that Peirce made a considerable contribution here to the problem of "understanding" social phenomena though he did not apply his theory explicitly to social contexts. He stated, however: "If we are ... to understand phenomena at all, it must be by abduction that this is to be brought about." [66]

The only sociologist who, to my knowledge, came close to Peirce' position was Pareto in his theory of non-logical actions. He proposed that "non-logical actions originate chiefly in definite psychic states, sentiments, sub-

---

[65] *Coll. Pap.,* 5.190 and 5.181.
[66] *Coll. Pap.,* 5.171.

conscious feelings, and the like." [67] And he explained arguments based upon sentiments: "In ordinary logic . . . the conclusion follows from the premisses. *In the logic of sentiments the premisses follow from the conclusion."* [68] Plainly, the logic of sentiments is what Peirce called the logic of abduction. But in difference to Peirce, who considered abductions to be constitutive for every inquiry, Pareto interpreted the logic of sentiment as being merely a source of ideological thinking. He continues the phrase quoted above: "In other words, the person who makes the syllogism, as well as the person who accepts it, is convinced in advance that A has the attribute B, and merely wishes to give his conviction an appearance of being logical." [69]

3.32 The Second Stage: Deduction, which is Related to Typification.

According to Peirce, the second stage of the process of inquiry requires testing of the hypothesis suggested previously by abduction. While abduction started with scrutiny of *phenomena,* it is subsequently necessary to *examine the abductive hypothesis.* One has to study "what effects that hypothesis, if embraced, must have in modifying our *expectations* in regard to future experience." [70] This procedure is deductive and it is thus an Argumentation: After explicating the hypothesis "as perfectly distinct as possible" the subsequent deduction implies demonstrating which predictions must be drawn from the hypothesis. This is the stage of "collecting consequents of the hypothesis" and "it invariably requires something of the nature of a diagram." [71]

3.33 The Third Stage: Induction, which is Related to the Formation of Types.

The third stage of inquiry is mainly inductive and has to ascertain "how far those consequents (resulting from deductive application of the hypothe-

---

[67] Vilfredo Pareto, *The Mind and Society* (New York, Harcourt and Brace, 1935), vol. 1, par. 161.

[68] *op. cit.,* par. 514.

[69] A critique of Pareto can be omitted here since it would not further my present argument. But it seems to be apparent that Pareto was led to his mistaken conception by accepting uncritically the classical notion that any scientific reasoning has to be either deductive or inductive. Peirce insists that it may also be abductive. – But this critique of Pareto shall not imply a rejection. To the contrary: His analysis of residues and sentiments has some facets which, due to their closeness to Peirce' argument, will be taken up later on.

[70] *Coll. Pap.,* 7.114.

[71] *op. cit.,* 6.471f. – The term "consequents" applies here, of course, not to an abduction but designates the *necessary* consequents of deduction. This possible confusion of terms has to be kept in mind while reading Peirce.

sis) accord with experience."[72] In this inductive stage of inquiry one has to show "that something actually is operative,"[73] i.e. that the hypothesis and its necessarily subsequent predictions are in accord with and operative in experience. Thus, Peirce suggests, "we make experiments, or quasi-experiments, in order to find out how far these new conditional expectations are going to be fulfilled . . . In so far as they greatly modify our former expectations of experience and in so far as we find them, nevertheless, to be fulfilled, we accord to the hypothesis a due weight in determining all our future conduct and thought."[74]

3.34 Summary:

This final sketch of Peirce' theory of inquiry served a threefold purpose which will be explicated more fully in the next sections: 1. Abduction as an important stage of inquiry has been presented in some detail. Its, so-to-speak, inverted inferential form, i.e. its reasoning from consequent to antecedent, can describe processes of guessing, of "circumstantial" inferences, which have some relationship to the "perceiving" or "understanding" of social objects. 2. James' "logic of fringes" and Peirce' "abductive reasoning" both try to achieve the "reinstatement of the vague to its proper place in our mental life." The notion of "vagueness" remains, however, exceedingly diffuse in James' formulation, while Peirce was able to show its abductive structure to be an important force in all inquiry. 3. The major theoretical topic of the next chapter is a further elaboration of the "tie" between theme and attentional object in a *social* situation. Gurwitsch has shown that James' notion of fringes can be used to reveal the manifold relations between theme, thematic field, and context. Some of these relations (which is to be shown in the following) are constituted in abductive processes.

---

[72] *Coll. Pap.,* 6.472.
[73] *op. cit.,* 5.171.
[74] *op. cit.,* 7.115.

CHAPTER 4

SOCIAL INCONSISTENCIES AND SOCIAL TYPES

THEME:

The intentionality of perceiving social objects has a multiple directional structure. This main hypothesis requires a redefinition of theme, thematic field, context, and social relevance. Subsequently, social types and typificatory processes are shown to be intrinsically related to social inconsistencies and their intersubjective solution by incipient events.

What determines the attentional grasp of social objects constituted in social interaction? Husserl's notion of interest, his distinction between theme and attentional object has been shown to be most fruitful for a theory of relevance both by Schütz and by Gurwitsch. But Husserl limited himself to the study of objects of "normal perception in the modus of naive certainty".[1] This does not allow an immediate application of his results to the perceiving of social objects. Every synthesis in an apprehending mental activity of immediate perception is based on the fact that its object is "over there". But social objects constantly come about and are apt to vanish. Their vague contours are due to their intersubjective constitution in social interaction.[2]

A conceptual frame now has to be developed in order to study the threefold relationship between interlocking intersubjective perspectives of rele-

---

[1] "Normale Wahrnehmung im Modus der naiven Gewißheit." See: *Erfahrung und Urteil*, p. 105.

[2] The vague contours of social objects are a central theme in poetry and literature. But descriptive studies in sociology (Goffman, Anselm Strauss, et al) have dealt with this problem, too. For example: *Glaser* and *Strauss* describe "the tendency to treat a recently deceased kinsman as if he were still alive," a tendency which takes into account "the deceased person's awareness." They illustrate: though the immediately attendable "living body" has vanished, it may still be constituted as a social object of extremely vague contours. B. G. Glaser and A. L. Strauss, *Awareness of Dying*, (Chicago, Aldine, 1965), p. 114.

vance, the subsequent (or antecedent?, or simultaneous?) arisal of the social object, and its typification. This frame obviously restricts social situations to face-to-face situations of social interaction. But only a study of the temporal structure of social inconsistencies in the next chapter will prove this restriction to be necessary: It is inadmissable to "abstract" a social situation from the immediacy of intersubjective events. Hence, I am using the term *situation* in this sense: it implies that human beings are present among a variety of objects available for manipulatory purposes or as objects of meditation or reflection.

4.1 The Structure of Social Relevance

In developing a conceptual frame for my problem at hand, I am going to keep close to Gurwitsch' notions of theme and thematic field. These will require, however, some alterations under the main hypothesis that the perceiving of social objects has a triadic structure. Furthermore, they will be applied in successive interpretations to intersubjective events arising in the situation referred to previously: Being invited to a party by Prof. L., who teaches philosophy at Z-College and whom I never visited at home before, I am received by a young, French-speaking lady who asks me into a bar-room for a drink and card game. Nobody else seems to be present.

The *thematic field* throughout this situation is "being-at-a-party". Some *theme* arrests my mental activity in the situation. It may refer to her dress or her French language, to Prof. L.'s recent visit to France or his interest in exotic birds, etc. "Tending toward an object qua theme and qua object," to quote Husserl, determines my prevailing interest in a definite manner: Though a situation like this one may be extremely vague and puzzling, I come to terms with it under the specific guidance of one or the other theme. Certainly, the theme as well as the thematic field might have to be abandoned if "inconsistent" situational elements emerge. This case, however, will be discussed later.

What is meant now by the phrase "tending toward an object"? In visual perception, for instance, of a tree, every perceiving can rely on immediate perceptual affirmations. In that case, a theme has no effect on the formation of the object as such. The object "is there". Can this be assumed to hold also for a social object, say for myself as "guest"? First of all, I cannot be a "guest" without there being some "host," and secondly, I cannot speak of either without reference to a thematic field like "being-at-a-party".[3] "Guest" and "host" are correlative formations in respect to the the-

[3] To avoid a possible misunderstanding: I am not talking here about reciprocal typifications in role-interaction. I am assuming a diffuse and undetermined situation which

matic field "being-at-a-party". The situation being vague and totally surprising, the few distinct contours are perceptual forms like the attractive
shape of the young woman and the setting of a comfortable room, further
her French language or some outstanding theme. But what is to be called
a "social object" in this situation?

The notion of theme as that upon which the inquiring subject concentrates his mental activity is sufficiently clear for further analysis. As to the
"object" I can, up to now, merely say it is that upon which the inquiring
subject concentrates his attention. In analogy to the Bergson-Schütz phrase
of "attention à la vie" one could say, the "basic regulative principle of our
conscious life" in the present situation is an *attention à l'objet social inarticulé*. The intentional structure of tending toward this still unarticulated
social object is definitely not the same as in visual perception in the modus
of naive certainty. If this were the case, the subsequent constitution of
social objects and of a social world based upon passive and active syn-
theses of conscious activity could be performed by a *solitary* individual
similarly to his constructing and constituting a meaningful visual or tactual
environment. No phenomenological analysis in this direction has been
successful, and no sociological theory accepts today such a Robinson
notion of social reality. The intentionality of perceiving a social object very
likely has a multiple directional structure. Clarification of this structure is
necessary before the constitution of social objects can be studied.

There is a second possibility of slipping into subjectivistic notions which
can be avoided. In "normal perception in the modus of naive certainty"
my perceptual interest gets stimulated first by some feature of the object,
then a theme may arise. If this order were abandoned in case of perceiving
social objects, that is, if the social object may be assumed to arise *subsequently* to the theme, then the notion of social reality gets a strictly subjective and even solipsistic status. It is the world of Don Quixote, where
any arising theme finds its appropriate object.[4] To avoid this consequence,
*the constitution of a social object as antecedent to the theme has to take
place in an abductive procedure* in precisely the sense given this term by
Peirce. Hence one may conclude that the social object as antecedent to
the theme is constructed intersubjectively in a situation becoming relevant
through a dominant thematic field.

The often rather vague conception of "intersubjective constitution of a

---

I am unable to typify. The vagueness of it is very difficult to preserve in a description
since the words I have to use in my description may seem to typify the situation.

[4] Schütz has written a most admirable paper on "Don Quixote and the Problem of
Reality," *Coll. Pap.*, vol. 2, pp. 135–158.

social object" has previously been made transparent by Schütz. He showed the social object to be a construct of meaning in the context of social interaction. My attempt, as has been pointed out in the beginning, is an effort to approach the problem from a study of the structure of relevance.

Aron Gurwitsch has shown that a theme is tied to a contextual background by the surrounding fringes of the theme. The theme is given in a "scheme of relations," as James used to called it. These are relations *within* the situation. The situation is to be called a *context*, if its relations are such that they unify the situation through an indicative scheme of reciprocal relations between the outstanding situational characters. This unity of the context thus comes about via the fringes of the theme, by way of the multitude of relations originating in the theme and bringing all "relevant" elements of the situation into relation with each other. For *relevance* is merely a correlate term to the notion of context. The unity of the context is a unity by way of its relevance.

The terminology might become clearer by referring to our example. Though the thematic field "being-at-a-party" was already in my mind before I entered Mr. L.'s residence[5] it is prevalent throughout the situation. Assume now that my interest gets focused upon the French language of the girl. The arising theme brings forth a multitude of relations between elements of the situation: I have recently spoken about French parties to Mr. L.; girls ought to talk French at Mr. L.'s parties; in France they do these things, of course, at most parties; etc. Again, one has to warn here of the implicit typifications of language I have to use in this description: those relations I am talking about are still merely feelings of some sort of affinity between elements of the situation, which "belong together," as one would say in everyday language. They are unifying the situation to a context as it presents itself under this theme. The situation has gained relevance for every participating actor whose "attention à l'objet social inarticulé" is guided by the prevalent thematic field.

But the notion of "relations between the elements of the situation" is still very ambiguous. The paramount "elements" are its inherently social constituents: the young woman and myself. Relevance is relevance of the context as it presents itself to and through the acting individuals: the total context presents itself first of all immediately to me, and secondly, it presents itself mediately to me through the actions, gestures and expressions of the

---

[5] It determined a scheme of anticipations; it has been constitutive for a multitude of projects, which I have either performed before or which I keep in stock, so to speak. But I am purposefully avoiding this line of argument at present, the problems of which have been clarified by Schütz.

girl. This last presentation I take as the major constituent of the *thematic field*. The whole bearing of the young woman, her alien language, her dress, her inviting me into the next room: every one of these situational elements I may take as indicating the total context; the diffuseness of the thematic field results from the puzzling incoherence of these situational elements. Every one of them may be taken up as germinal for a theme.

This definition of thematic field makes it immediately evident that a thematic field is "invariant" in a certain sense. The mediate presentation of context through the Other is not as easily subject to change as my possible shifting from one theme to the other. It is not that *I* have a thematic field, but *we* have an intersubjective thematic field as long as I am able to bring forth themes which successively clarify her presentation of context. Even in highly typified situations of social interaction the mediate presentation of context through the Other[6] is, of course, exceedingly vague and open to various "interpretations." Yet, this term cannot be used here. It is *not* that I *interpret* the context as it presents itself through the Other. This notion would lead to giving the Other and myself, and finally the individual, the *only* social status in the situation and reduce its other elements to mere things.[7] Such a sharp demarcation ends always in subjectivistic notions, which have to be *founded* on a theory of signification and signs. Hence, the whole argument would simply be transferred into a theory of symbols which is generally based on some ontological or metaphysical principles.

My approach to these problems does not allow such a transference into a constituent theory of symbols. *The Other does not represent, he presents the context of which he is a constitutive part himself.* Going back to our example: the girl speaks French and this is first of all an integral part of the situation. The thematic field "being-at-a-party" might bring this horizonal element into the context. It becomes relevant, if her presentation of the context (she speaks French under the situational circumstances) suggests formation of some theme. For instance, "Prof. L. has been lecturer of French literature," or "he has recently returned from France," "he is a bachelor," etc. Again, this is not to be taken as some form of propositional reasoning. It is more like the arisal of patches of related elements. Peirce

---

[6] This is a variation of Sartre's notion of "le regard d'autri." In Schütz' formulation: "I perceive the objects as not only perceived by me, but as perceived also by him, the Other." (*Coll. Pap.*, vol. 1, p. 188). I restrict myself, however, to saying that the composition of the thematic field is determined – and not exclusively – by the mediate presentation through the Other.

[7] This argument has at this point only methodological significance. It becomes sociologically significant especially in the later study of the notion of human body. (see *sect.* 6.3.)

described this style of "inquiry" as coming about in pictoral hunches and guesses satisfying for the moment the restless doubt. The thematic field had been diffuse at first, but the foreign language of the girl has induced a theme, which received a general orientation from and may lead to a clarification of the thematic field. The thematic field impressed thus a *positional index* upon the theme, i.e. the relations "party – Prof. L. – France" etc. come about through this indicative link between thematic field and theme.

Again, a further clarification seems possible. The positional index designates a directional sentiment within a diffuse and indeterminate thematic field. It has been pointed out before that all searching inquiry in the situation is guided by the theme under an "attention à l'objet social inarticulé," i.e. the inquiry is directed toward the constitution of an intersubjectively valid social object compatible with the given theme. This process has to be abductive: the antecedent object has to be gained abductively from the consequent, the theme. The "positional index" giving a "sentiment of direction" is simply another way of expressing this procedure. It is "the search for pertinent circumstances and the laying hold of them, the dark laboring, the bursting out of the startling conjecture, the remarking of its smooth fitting to the anomaly, as it is turned back and forth like a key in the lock."[8] Only in our case, which Peirce did not discuss in any detail,[9] not only the key but also the lock is socially constructed. The thematic field imposes a first contextual fixation upon the theme coming about mainly through the mediate presentation of context through the Other. This circumscribes a vague hypothetical locus of the social object which has to be abductively reached.

In concluding this section, I can tie the different notions developed above into a more precise *definition of social relevance*. Relevance and thematic interest cannot be analytically separated, and this might have been falsely suggested by the previous discussion. Relevance as "relevance of the context as it presents itself (immediately) to and (mediately) through the acting individuals" is established if some theme suggested through the presentation of context by the Other is compatible with the thematic field. This presupposes a complex intentional structure of perceiving social objects which I have previously called the "triadic structure of relevance": My tending toward the (possibly totally vague) social object has to imply the tending of the

---

[8] *Peirce*, Coll. Pap., 5.469.

[9] The problem of an intersubjective constitution of reality coming about in processes of inquiry is one of the major topics of Peirce' work. Though I do not intend to follow Peirce here into an exposition of his theory of reality because of its metaphysical implications, my presentation is, in my judgement, generally in line with Peirce' theory of reality.

Other toward the object and toward myself. Only through this interlocking of what one could call the *perspectives of relevance* is the mediate presentation of the context possible. Only subsequently the thematic field may become clarified, and finally the social object may be constituted.

4.2 The Rôle of Play in Processes of Typification

How does this "interlocking of perspectives" come about? Take, for example, a young child to whom I am pointing out a certain "object". The very young child will first look only at my finger, he may look also at the "object," but he does not yet grasp my tending toward the "object" and my tending toward him into his own tending to the·"object"; there is no relevance established yet. My thematic interest, i.e. my tending toward the object qua object and qua theme, has to be apprehended by the child within the frame of a relevant thematic field. This probably will be exceedingly vague in the beginning, but its clarification has a direction as soon as a theme arises. But how does this direction come about?

The problem has been dealt with on the level of scientific inquiry, for example, by Peirce. How is it possible, Peirce asks, that the hypothetical guesses on the abductive level of inquiry are usually very close to the later result?

Think of what trillions of trillions of hypotheses might be made, of which only one is true; and yet after two or three or at the very most a dozen guesses, the physicist hits pretty nearly on the correct hypothesis. By chance he would not have been likely to do so in the whole time that has elapsed since the earth was solidified.[10]

Peirce continues: Man seems to have acquired a "faculty of divining the ways of Nature," but he acquired this faculty "certainly not . . . by a self-controlled and critical logic . . . It appears to me . . . that man has a certain Insight . . . into the Thirdnesses, the general elements, of Nature . . . This Faculty is, at the same time, of the general nature of Instinct."

Man seems to have an *acquired* faculty which is of the *general nature* of instinct. In earlier writings Peirce called this acquired faculty a "rule of action" or a "habit,"[11] while later he referred also to "the Play of Musement" having a constitutive part in establishing this faculty. Only, he reminds the inquirer, "the Player should bear in mind that the higher weapons in the arsenal of thought are not playthings but edgetools".[12]

---

[10] *Coll. Pap.*, 5.172f.
[11] *op. cit.*, 5.397.
[12] *op. cit.*, 6.461.

Play is referred to in a similar fashion by Pareto. As I have shown before, Pareto's "logic of sentiment" circumscribes the same style of reasoning which Peirce has called abduction. However, Peirce carefully avoids falling back into biologistic notions, for example into a naive Darwinianism, which cannot be said of Pareto. He frequently uses the terms "instinct" and "sentiment" synonymously, talking about "certain instincts in human beings".[13] Sentiments or instincts find their manifestation in residues[14] which in turn are the origin of many social phenomena.[15] Play, in the opinion of Pareto, is one residue among others: "The little girl who dresses her doll and offers it food is not imitating her mother, she is expressing a spontaneous sentiment of her own, as is the case with the swallow that has hatched a brood".[16] Pareto conceives play, which he deals with only in a marginal manner, to have its root in the instinctual composition of human nature and to be constitutive for certain social and cultural phenomena. But another notion is more interesting here: Residues are "wanting in definiteness, in exact delimitation" but are often clarified and transformed into scientific facts and principles. Quite similar to Peirce, Pareto conceives the "residue of play" as having a mediary role in the process of inquiry.

This suggestion about the rôle of play in abductive scientific reasoning may lead also to a solution of the present problem. The "interlocking of perspectives of relevance" leads to a thematic field which is constitutive for any construction of the antecedent social object. The question of why our guesses, why our attempts to clarify a diffuse thematic field can usually be broken off after a few trials has a simple answer: because *we* play and we play the *same* games.

George H. Mead assigns to play a similarly fundamental rôle.[17] Children "organize . . . the responses which they call out in other persons and call out also in themselves." They are taking "the rôle of another" sometimes evoking an imaginary companion in their "play at something". Since assumption of rôles presupposes processes of typification, since, moreover, reciprocal responses presuppose already established thematic relevance and interlocked perspectives of relevance, I can rely on Mead's notion only insofar as it refers to "play at something" as an interactional means of

[13] Pareto, *Mind and Society*, par. 870.
[14] *op. cit.*, par. 875.
[15] *op. cit.*, par. 885.
[16] *op. cit.*, par. 1150.
[17] George Herbert Mead, *Mind, Self and Society* (Chicago, Univ. of Chicago Press, 1934), p. 150.

clarifying a thematic field in a given situation. With these restrictions in mind I want to call this kind of play *playing-at-a-theme*.

The difference from Mead has to be made still more explicit. I have defined relevance of a situation as a specific constellation of the context. My tending toward the "object" within its context as it presents itself immediately to me, has to imply the mediate presentation of the context through the Other, i.e., it has to imply the tending of the Other toward the "object" and toward myself. The problems of the theory of intersubjectivity are touched upon at this point. But they have to be left open for now.[18] Talking about "Other" and "myself" shall not presuppose more: we are part of the situation. The social constitution of Self is a problem mainly subsequent to, but in any case *not* preliminary to, the coming about of relevances and types.

Mead's theory of the social Self is, as far as I can see, within certain limits compatible with my presentation. For Mead defines: "The attitudes of the others constitute the organized 'me,' and then one reacts toward that as an 'I'."[19] The scheme of relations which Mead refers to here is comparable to the perspectives of relevance adopted above. But the analogy has to stop at this point. Presentation of the context through the Other is a much wider notion than Mead's "attitudes of the others," though it might happen that the context is reduced to mere attitudes and gestures of the Other, say, in a situation of making love to each other.

4.3 The Notion of Typificatory Scheme

But this discussion of Mead brings one point into the foreground which has been set aside until now. In every situation the interacting partners are already in possession of a more-or-less extensive stock of types and experiences of previous typifications.[20] Even the very young child, as soon as it is able to grasp the structure of relevance of a situation, experiences the presentation of context by the Other as a thematic field under typical aspects. However, available types are often inapplicable or inadequate, and

---

[18] See *sect.* 6.3.

[19] Mead, *Mind*, p. 175.

[20] This assumption is *practically* self-evident for any sociological study of major social problems. But *theoretically* it raises some important methodological questions. Husserl and Peirce both accepted that assumption. *Husserl* defended it with his basic notion of the horizonal character of every experience. ("Die typische Vorbekanntheit jedes einzelnen Gegenstandes der Erfahrung." *Erfahrung und Urteil*, pp. 26ff.) – *Peirce* developed the negation of his own question: "Whether there is any cognition not determined by a previous cognition?" (*Coll. Pap.*, 5.258), into a critique of the Cartesian notion of the priority of first and ultimate origins. (*Coll. Pap.*, 5.264–314, published in 1868).

this is the situation of vague uncertainty I have been discussing above. Thus at this point I have to take notice of an *iterative procedure in the constitution of types and social objects*. Every construction of type and every typification goes on before the background of and in intimate relation to already acquired types and presedimented typical knowledge of typical situations. But iteration implies still more. One has to avoid the misleading conception that the stock of typified experiences is something like the "memory" of a computer. Every sedimented experience refers to a typical solution of a typified problem lived through by the individual. This lived experience is still "living" in the sense of its potentially being "reactivated" in the process of further advancement of knowledge. But this implies an ongoing reconstruction of typical contexts encompassing typified social objects.[21]

The iterative constitution of types and social objects implies that every type carries, as Schütz has called it, an *index* referring the type to its constitutive context. This is a short form of saying that types have arisen in problematic contexts and that each subsequent arisal of a sufficiently similar context and of "its" type requires at least a very rudimentary reconstruction of the type. That this is being achieved "with ease" and – except in pathological cases – "without notice" can be explained by the arisal of types in playing-at-a-theme.

The interactional attempts to clarify a diffuse thematic field in a given situation have been called "playing-at-a-theme". One has to distinguish carefully the level of immediate social interaction in the situation from its context and theme. A *diffuse* thematic field indicates an *ambivalent* contextual relevance in a *vague* and disoriented situation. One could call this situation "dramatic" and all action in such a situation *dramatic action.*[22]

The notion of context in case of a diffuse thematic field has to be clarified first. Two modes of presentation of context have been distinguished: the context presents itself immediately to me and it presents itself mediately to me through the Other; the latter presentation is the major constituent of the thematic field. Speaking of a diffuse thematic field implies, therefore, a diffuse mediate presentation of context. Relevance has already been established, since otherwise the situation would not be unified into a context; this entails that *some* theme suggested through the mediate presentation of

21 For the rôle of language in this process of reconstructing social reality in marriage see: Peter L. Berger and Hansfried Kellner, *Marriage and the Construction of Social Reality,* Diogenes 46, 1964, pp. 13ff.

22 This is a notion of Anselm Strauss. See his *Mirrors and Masks* (Glencoe, Free Press, 1959), p. 66.

context has to be "compatible" with the thematic field. Consequently, diffuseness of the mediate presentation of context leads to a set of vague relations in the situation coming about because of the ambivalence of successively suggested themes.

The example of "being-at-a-party" may clarify this problem further. Assume that the French language of the young girl gives rise to some theme. Is it "compatible" with the given thematic field? I may be reminded that I have recently talked to Mr. L. about informal social meetings in France. Thus, relations between the types "France," "cocktail parties," "Mr. L." etc. arise. The types belong, of course, to my "stock of types". Now, assume I utter timidly "Monsieur L."? This utterance does not only become an immediate element of the situation, but it occurs in two modes of presentation, relevance being established, of course: it presents itself immediately to me as "my utterance"; it presents itself mediately through the Other as "my utterance tended toward by her". Only this last presentation may or may not reveal if the theme is "compatible" with the thematic field: She may neglect the utterance; she may show irritation; she may take it up and play-at-the-theme; she may respond affirmatively in a "typical" way.

These four cases show "different degrees of ambivalence". Except for the last "affirmative" case they have to be studied in detail later. Her last and typical response suggests a coincidence of both modes of presentation: the type "Monsieur L." is contextually relevant; it ties, so-to-speak, the immediate and mediate presentations of context together.

The following theoretical notions can be formulated now more precisely. 1. I speak of *compatibility between theme and thematic field*, if arising types, which are suggested through the relations the theme induces within the situation, bring about coincidence between mediate and immediate presentations of context. Since a theme is always induced by the presentation of context through the Other, since furthermore a theme is composed out of types itself, compatibility is only a question of degree: in any relevant situation, there are some types which tie the immediate and mediate presentations of context together.[23] 2. I propose to call the *relations between* all *those* available *types*, which "tie" the immediate and the mediate presentations of a given context together,[24] its *typificatory scheme*. In a similar

---

[23] Compare this statement with the later discussion of anomie (*Sect.* 6.21.): compatibility is *the* condition for a "nomic" situation.

[24] These are all types which have – according to Schütz – a common *problem-relevance:* "The well-circumscribed problem can be said to be the locus of all possible types that can be formed for the sake of its solution, that is, of all problem-relevant types." *Coll. Pap.*, vol. 2, p. 235.

sense, the term has been used by Berger-Luckmann,[25] though they derive their notion differently. Since a typificatory scheme is formed by the relations between all "problem-relevant" types, i.e. by relations induced by a prevalent theme, it is a phenomenon of context: the typificatory scheme ties a theme to a specific context.

4.4 Gaps and Social Inconsistencies

The notion of context in case of a diffuse thematic field has been clarified. The two modes of presentation of context do not fully coincide: the typificatory scheme, which circumscribes an "indicative scheme of reciprocal relations" unifying the situation into a context, is "short of types," so-to-speak. More specifically, the relation between the phenomenon of relevance and processes of typification has been clarified. Context and relevance are correlative terms, and correctly speaking, *social typifications occur only within a context.* The pregivenness of relevance in any process of typification is thus a simple consequence of my foregoing argument. Speaking of "typifications of a given situation" is imprecise and entails the danger of confusing typifications of social objects with those of visual objects.

Social typifications may be required, however, in an ambivalent context, i.e. in case of a diffuse thematic field. If typificatory attempts seem to fail in a dramatic situation, the context has a *hole* or a *gap:* the typifications available in a dramatic situation tie – to speak – only the outer fringes of both modes of presentation of the context together relating it thus with the theme; they leave an untypifiable or untypified *gap.* More precisely: The thematic field imposes a positional index upon the theme unifying the situation in a context; there is some sense of direction now in the dramatic situation, and playing-at-the-theme occurs in attempts to clarify the thematic field; the theme suggests a typificatory scheme for typifications of the context; the thematic field, however, is diffuse, i.e. none of the typifications by those available types is able to encompass the context; they are broken off at various points thus leaving within the typificatory scheme a set of *pragmatic differences,* as one could call them, localizing the gap in the context.

4.41 Permanent Gaps

The interactional mode of playing-at-a-theme may become clearer in those problematic cases, where the actors in a specific situation try to avoid

---

[25] Peter L. Berger and Thomas Luckmann, *The Social Construction of Reality* (Garden City, Doubleday, 1966), pp. 29ff.

an apparent inconsistency. This phenomenon may be illustrated at what would be called *permanent gaps*. They arise in dramatic situations which resist strongly any typification in lived-through experiences. These are situations of danger, of birth and death, of suicide and homicide, which are indicated by ritual, tabu and forbidden language.[26] A tropical storm at sea, for example, is still today a great danger for any ship and its crew; it poses ultimately a dramatic situation for anybody aboard. Assuming that a "point-of-no-return" has been passed not allowing the ship to find refuge anywhere, the thematic field "storm-at-sea" imposes itself upon all situations. Avoidance of the storm will determine most compatible themes, which refer to navigational skill and experience of the skipper. These themes relate, however, to extremely limited interactional efforts of avoidance, which I supposed in this case to be of no avail. But another mechanism of avoidance is inherently built into the process of constitution of type and social object. It is inherently given with the abductive procedure prevalent in dramatic situations in which, as I have shown before, the *antecedent* type and *social object* are abductively constructed out of the *consequent*, the *theme*. Initial typification proceeds from the given theme and takes part in the antecedent constitution of the object.[27] Thus by completely avoiding the thematic field "storm-at-sea" and also all possibly "related" themes, no theme arises and thus the social object and its type cannot come about.[28] Here lies one of the roots of "les jeux interdits," to refer to a

---

[26] To mention again the excellent study of Glaser and Strauss, *Awareness of Dying*, this book may be taken page by page as an illustration of the phenomenon of "permanent gap": the immediate presentation of context (the patient's view of his disease) and its mediate presentation through the nurse, the physician, the family, et al, are carefully described by the authors.

[27] This "mechanism" – a poor term – is at the basis of what one calls in sociological literature the "Thomas-Axiom." W. I. Thomas' so-called "definition of the situation" has its root in the pragmatic notions of Peirce. – But this insight is not limited to the pragmatic tradition. In pointing out the basic difference between "natural" and "historical" forces and constellations Plessner brings a very vivid example: "Ein Reservoir ist nichts ohne seine Staumauer and ohne seine Zuflüsse ... Historische Konstellationen sind grundsätzlich anderer Art ... Die Vorstellung von dem, was man will, und der Appell an die Phantasie, die ihrerseits schon an dem Bild der eigenen Geschichte sich vorgebildet hat, wirken zugleich nach vorwärts und rückwärts. Sie rufen die Quellen, sie rufen den Regen, sie schaffen den Stau." Helmuth Plessner, *Die verspätete Nation* (Stuttgart, Kohlhammer, 1959), p. 11.

[28] The second of Festinger's "basic hypotheses" for his theory of cognitive dissonance has thus been established *for the case of a permanent gap*. "When dissonance is present, in addition to trying to reduce it, the person will actively avoid situations and informations which would likely increase the dissonance." Leon Festinger, *A Theory of Cognitive Dissonance* (Stanford, Stanford Univ. Press, 1957), p. 3.

famous play of Cocteau, since playing-at-the-theme invokes the process of initial creation of type and social object.

Avoiding any play-at-the-theme would also be a rule totally "reasonable" in non-dramatic situations, since the typificatory schemes are adequate to clarify swiftly any diffuse thematic field. In other words, typification and constitution of social objects do not take place in non-problematic situations: the Egyptian does not need and does not have five different names to distinguish different types of snow from each other, just as the Eskimo would have some linguistic difficulty (of which he is not aware in his igloo) in classifying the gait of a camel.

Similarly, avoiding any play-at-the-theme is at the basis of what Peirce has called "the stage of tenacity" in the process of inquiry. To repeat his vivid illustration:

When an ostrich buries its head in the sand as danger approaches, it very likely takes the happiest course. It hides the danger, and then calmly says there is no danger; and if it feels perfectly sure there is none, why should it raise its head to see?

The sailor indeed tries to avoid the storm by "hiding the storm," i.e. by avoiding any related theme. (And he certainly would be more successful, if the storm were a social object.) This he tries to achieve on a mythological level: He not only avoids the thematic field "storm-at-sea" but also any theme which, in his opinion, is "related" to it; these are, for example, themes composed of the word "horse" or of the triple numbers "3 3 3". Thus he achieves two results: 1. Both themes are links to mythological thematic fields: the Germanic belief in Wotan riding his horse through the winds; the Christians associating it with the Holy Trinity. Thus, contexts are constructed which make the object "storm" quasi-social. 2. Avoiding, however, these "related" themes serves to make the pragmatic differences more distinct: the "hole" in the context becomes a clearly cognizable permanent gap thus indeed stabilizing the dramatic situation at least on its fringes.

4.42 Definition of Social Inconsistencies

The study of a permanent gap has been useful to clear up some general features of the notion of playing-at-a-theme. Avoidance of the thematic field, which is constitutive for the gap, as well as avoidance of any possibly related theme is the leading interactional goal in a dramatic situation. This reveals the especially intimate relatedness between theme and thematic field in case a gap occurs in the context.

The conceptual frame for a definition of social inconsistencies has been clarified sufficiently by the previously developed theoretical notions: A gap in the context occurs, if the mediate and the immediate presentations of context cannot be brought to coincidence by some typificatory scheme; the *mediate presentation* of context by the Other is the main constituent of the *thematic field*; the *immediate presentation* is the context as it presents itself to me. My attention is focused now on the gap: it becomes the prevalent theme itself; the mediate and immediate presentations come "closer" to each other by iteratively approximating theme and thematic field. In this sense, the notion of playing-at-a-theme has been introduced earlier as an "interactional means of clarifying a thematic field." This "closeness" between theme and thematic field in a dramatic situation justifies (besides terminological convenience) to speak of "playing-at-a-theme," though very correctly one ought to call it "playing-at-a-thematic-field." For clarification of the thematic field is its purpose: not only *I* am attempting to clarify the *Other*'s mediate presentation of context as it is presented by him (or her) to me, but also the *Other* tries to clarify *my* mediate presentation of context as it is presented to him (or her).

It is now possible to define the notion of inconsistency. A *social inconsistency* occurs in a situation, if a diffuse thematic field leads to an, at least temporarily, untypifyable gap in the context.[29] This definition implies:

1. A social inconsistency occurs in the situation: It is a phenomenon of context and constitutes a dramatic situation, in which the action patterns appear to be interrupted. Mutual hesitancy, shouts, crying or laughter, stuttering or "painful silence" may indicate an inconsistency.

2. A diffuse thematic field does not have to lead into an inconsistency. Clarification of a diffuse thematic field is achieved by successive typifications of the gap occurring in the context. If sufficient typificatory schemes are available, a gap can be bridged after a few typificatory attempts and an inconsistency does not emerge: social relevance does not even become ambivalent in this situation.

3. But what determines the arisal of an inconsistency? In this case, mediate and immediate presentations of context can be "tied" on the "fringes" only: there is no type available to bridge the gap in the context.

---

[29] A "logical inconsistency" in propositional logic is defined as a special "onefold relation" between two propositions p and q. They are said to be inconsistent, if and only if p and q cannot be "true" in the same context. See for example: Kemeny, Snell, Thompson, *Introduction to Finite Mathematics* (Englewood Cliffs, Prentice-Hall, 1956), p. 34; or any other introductory text in formal logic. – In other words, the realms of validity where p resp. q are "true" do not have any points in common. There is a "gap" between these realms, though *some* relations prevail.

The typificatory scheme is, as I called it before, "short of types:" the relations (between available types constituting the typificatory scheme) induced
by the theme do not fully unify the situation into a context; pragmatic differences occur in the typificatory scheme. The more types are available, the
more intermeshed is the net of relations within the typificatory scheme. But
also, of course, an increase of available types implies nothing but an extension of the field of social experience. Stated the other way around:
phenomena like "death" or "divorce" are untypifyable for a small child,
being outside of his experiential range. They do not even lead to a gap (not
to speak of an inconsistency) as long as there is no theme stimulating some
thematic interest. Since *with an increase of available types* the typificatory
schemes become more and more differentiated, the typification of phenomena becomes more problematic, and *the chance for the arisal of a gap
in the context increases*. But, as mentioned above, the more and more differentiated typificatory schemes lead also to an increasing chance that a
gap can be bridged after only a few typificatory attempts. Consequently,
the *arisal of an inconsistency in the situation* does not immediately and exclusively depend on the number of available types or the subsequent differentiation of the typificatory scheme. The relationship between available
types and possible inconsistencies cannot be studied further, before the
process of type-formation has not been clarified.

4. Since the gap is a specific formation of the context, social relevance
is prerequisite for an inconsistency. But relevance has become ambivalent
insofar as the perspectives of relevance are fixed upon the gap. My tending
toward that which is inconsistent implies the tending of the Other toward
it and toward myself. But this constellation of perspectives no longer entails the earlier problem of how the Other may "know" of the inconsistency
I am tending to: the mediate presentation of the ambivalent context by the
Other is what mainly composes the thematic field; his tending toward that
which is inconsistent for me means simply his diffuse presentation of the
context.

5. The intersubjective constitution of a thematic field must prevail in
case of a social inconsistency: A dramatic situation encompasses both myself and the Other, but the immediate and mediate presentations of the
context are mere intersubjective constructs. A child's touching a hot stove
and burning himself leads only to a social inconsistency if his mother
makes it thematic by a warning cry or some subsequent admonition.
Napalm in Vietnam or the gas-chambers in Ausschwitz become social inconsistencies beyond the range of the victims only within some thematic
field. Total separation of victims and executioners is an effective means to

control the arisal of inconsistencies. Every such effort to fragment the situation leads to an impoverishment or even dehumanization of social life.

4.5 The Arisal of Social Types

An inconsistency requires typification by a "new" type or a constitution of a whole "new" typificatory scheme. To make these generic conditions for the formation of social types as transparent as possible, the arisal of some inconsistency in the previously introduced situation of a party at Mr. L.'s residence will be discussed in some detail. The young lady, let us say, offers me some "cigarettes" having a peculiar taste. The difference between social and perceptual types in this situation has to be most clearly seen. To find out what type of *cigarettes* she has offered me is *not* a problem of *social* typification. I might even know immediately that she is offering me "pot," since I had experimented with narcotics before. The present typificatory problem: I never had been offered some at a party. The cigarettes as such are merely elements of the situation which can be perceived, typified, judged, appreciated, or rejected like that feminine shape in the other chair. Social typification has to come to terms with her *giving* these cigarettes. Her giving them to me is the mediary of social interaction in which a social object becomes constituted.

A more careful analysis of the situation is required. A unified relevant context had existed from the time of my entry due to the still prevalent thematic field "being-at-a-party." The density of types related to this theme is considerable: being invited and attending a party is no new experience to me, nor is it apparently to her, as her presentation of the context reveals. The conduct and behavior of both of us show a determined directedness in spite of the surprising theme "marijuana-at-a-party." To be more precise: The triadic intentional structure of the perspectives of relevance, encompassing our mutual deliberation to clarify the diffuse thematic field, composes the set of relations induced by the theme in the context. Thus, her "giving" can be reduced to her tending toward me and her tending toward the "object" revealing a twofold composition: "something to be given," which is implied in her tending toward the "object," and "something to be received," which is implied in her tending toward me. These two implications can be perceived as a unity only, if the two modes of presentation of context can be unified; i.e. some type has to be constructed (on the basis of some appropriate typificatory scheme) that ties these two presentations together. Thus, the type to be constructed in our case has to imply the twofold composition "something to be given" and "something to be received."

One may note three important consequences: 1. I showed before that the constitution of the social object is an abductive procedure starting from a given theme "retroductively" by clarifying the thematic field in typificatory attempts. "Type" and "object" have to be taken as being iteratively constituted, the one on the background of the other, the type becoming more and more schematic in the processes of its subsequent applications, the object becoming more and more unique and individual in every subsequent typification by "its" type.

2. The intersubjective constitution of a social inconsistency and the rôle of the thematic field in bringing about the unity of context limits severely the creation of totally "new" types of completely "new" social objects. In a biographical sense, individual creation of types and objects for the individual actor involved in the situation may take place. But mostly this is a re-creation of socially derived and socially transmitted types and objects. It may also be, and perhaps this has to be assumed in most cases, that an already constituted object previously experienced gains a totally new aspect in this situation. In any of these cases, the problem remains the same: The interactional context must be such to allow for a creation, a re-creation, or an "enlargement" of type and object. And this, I contend, is achieved by playing-at-a-theme.

3. The twofold composition "something to be given" – "something to be received" must also be a subsequent characteristic of the type and the "social object." The structure of social relevance becomes an inherent characteristic of the type and of the social object: Schütz' notion of "index" pertaining to each type and pointing to the related problem circumscribes this same situational state.[30]

4.51 The First Stage: Arisal of an Incipient Event

Since "type" and "object" are iteratively constituted as *antecedent* to a given theme, since, furthermore, theme and thematic field are most intimately interwoven in this process, one has to conclude that in the initial state of arisal of type a distinction between "type" and "object" is hardly possible. Thus, one may say: A social inconsistency in a given situation leads to an interactional "solution," which I propose to call an *incipient event*.[31] The incipient event emerges in the situation bridging, so to speak,

---

[30] See above *sect.* 3.13. Schütz' notion of "interpretational relevance" related the phenomena of relevance and typification: He describes essentially the same problem dealt with above. In my presentation, however, "interpretational relevance" belongs to the first stage in the arisal of social types.

[31] The term is close to G. H. Mead's notion of "emergent event." See esp. his *Philosophy of the Present* (LaSalle, Open Court, 1959), p. 23. Starting from this point, the notion of social temporality will be developed later.

the gap which indicates the inconsistency in the context. In other words, playing-at-a-theme brings about an incipient event, which will "separate" in subsequent typificatory attempts into a more and more schematic type and a social object. The incipient event is an element of the situation. But it is *also* a phenomenon of context, since it presents itself in both the mediate and the immediate presentations of context. It "ties" both presentations together, though only extremely provisionally, but it serves the purpose of removing, at least for the moment, the given inconsistency. However, not only does playing-at-a-theme bring the incipient event about, also conversely, the incipient event structures the interaction going on in playing-at-a-theme.

I may illustrate this process again at the previous example. The thematic field "being-at-a-party" is diffuse. The bold dress of the young female, her French language, her inviting me to a game, and finally her offering narcotics: any of these surprising elements of the situation may induce a theme. (One should observe that in case of a high density of types, as in this present example, only a whole syndrome of surprising elements will likely lead to a diffuse thematic field, since a single surprising fact may easily be neglected altogether.) Suppose her offering of marijuana has become the theme now. The thematic field immediately imposes a direction upon the theme. Invited to a party, and expecting to be a guest and to meet the host, narcotics are offered by "someone." Is she a "hostess," is she a "guest," am I a "barkeeper," or am I supposed to accompany her on a "trip?" The theme thus induces a set of relations within the context. Previously relevant *social* types like "cigarettes offered and taken," "guests being received and presenting themselves," "drinks to be mixed by hosts and not by guests," etc. etc., are interrelated one with the other in a typificatory scheme. It unites the situation into a context as long as the thematic field can be maintained. That is to say, relevance prevails as long as the *relations* between these types persist, though the types themselves may be enlarged or reduced in processes of subsequent typifications. But none of these types leads to a complete clarification of the diffuse thematic field; their typifications break off and leave pragmatic differences within the typificatory scheme. The context has a gap: Guests did not do it before and neither did hosts. Two possibilities are open now: either abandoning the thematic field or "taking a stand in the situation."

I assume, the latter is the case. Playing-at-the-theme is now a specific interaction going on between myself and the young girl. I act toward her offering these cigarettes by "accepting" them. But this "accepting" gains an all-circumscribing significance, which merges my attention toward the theme totally into the thematic field. In other words, to a certain degree, *all* types relevant in the situation have to be reconstituted under this new aspect: the types "drinks offered at parties" and "cigarettes offered at parties" are played at under the aspect "narcotics;" "girls and parties" may become related to such distant themes like "the report x in the Sunday Times on barbiturates and frigidity," etc. This does not mean that all relevant types have to be enlarged: they merely become ambivalent. But exactly because of this ambivalence they allow a "new" formation of the typificatory scheme (to which they belong) by an incipient enlargement of the central types "host" and "guest." This incipient event (she has given and I have taken *those* cigarettes) structures the passage of interaction: I may comment to her on the taste of the smoke; I may take up the pack and read aloud to her the notice "Smoking may be hazardous to your health" eliciting a smile or a "pooh, pooh" from her; I may also offer her later a cigarette from this pack myself; etc. There is no typical *pattern* of interaction in playing-at-a-theme in front of an incipient event, since the event structures the given situation.[32] But one may expect some limitations of possible interaction imposed by the situation.

A *first limitation* is imposed on the number of typificatory efforts leading up to a solution. Peirce had pointed out the astonishing fact that merely a few hunches and guesses in a vague situation of inquiry are usually sufficient to establish an abduction. If these guesses were dependent merely on chance, a child would never outgrow the mental stage of a small rabbit.[33] Depending on the density of types available, playing-at-the-theme can be broken off sooner or later. But why is that so? The thematic field being-at-a-party gives all playing-at-the-theme a definite direction. It is furthermore subject to intersubjective consent. To be more precise, the thematic field which ties the actors into a unified context can achieve this unification only through the schemes of relations prevalent in the context: these relations are constituted within the perspectives of relevance by an arising theme. "Something to be given," "something to be received" have been played at often before by myself and also by the young female. We are playing at it now: She notices my hesitation, my slight irritation, the kind of language I choose, or the gestures I make; and we are coming to terms with the situ-

---

[32] For instance, incipient events cannot be dealt with in a rigorous theory of ideal types (See *sect.* 4.53.) – An entirely different question is the *sequence* of interactions from playing-at-a-theme in front of an incipient event up to the final constitution of a social type. This sequence typically occurs in three major phases which I am studying at present.

[33] Psychological theories which try to "explain" the solution of social inconsistencies by a "theory of trial-and-error" fail at this point.

ation by a play we often played before. This is an intersubjective performance and is broken off as soon as a mutually agreeable clarification of the thematic field has been achieved. Its intersubjective validity is, of course, still severely limited.

The second limitation is imposed on a change of the thematic field. It is certainly not completely up to me to choose a new one. Since I am an integral part of the situation, my freedom to change the thematic field is limited. Only a few alternatives (having-gone-to-the-wrong-place, being-invited-to-a-love-in, etc.) are compatible with the previous one, i.e., they do not lead to dissolution of the context. Any adoption of an alternative thematic field depends, of course, also on the consent of my partner, if relevance is to prevail.

The third limitation concerns the enactment of the incipient event. I shall show later in more detail that this enactment is not preceded by a project: it is not a "social action." [34] For, every projecting is an anticipatory *typification* of the context in which the social action is to occur. A project is to assure success of action. It tries to anticipate possible inconsistencies and either *overcomes them in advance* through adequate typificatory means or designs a path of interaction which *avoids* them. – On the other hand, however, social inconsistencies are intersubjectively constituted. Thus, there also has to be some purposive construction of social inconsistencies under very specific circumstances. This intimate relation between project-formation and the arisal of inconsistencies will be analysed later. [35]

But what can be said "positively" about the incipient event and its enactment? A diffuse thematic field leading to a social inconsistency and to enactment of an incipient event cannot be studied by the common sociological device of the "disinterested observer," who sits on his solid rock of reflection and constructs a "model" of the situation. Every such construction is a construction by ideal types or some other typificatory means. Types and typificatory schemes are, however, constructions *subsequent* to the emergence of incipient events and arise – to use Peirce' notions again – on the deductive and inductive levels. They do not structure the whole pre-

---

[34] See *sects.* 5.11, 5.2 and 7.0. – I am aware that Schütz' *formal* concepts of social action and project circumscribe also limiting cases like an enactment of incipient events. A high degree of "emptiness" characterizes the anticipated state of affairs in front of a social inconsistency. I contend that the anticipatory typifications in a project of social action cannot be "empty" to such a degree that they delineate the contours of incipient events.

[35] Compare especially the later discussion of the symbolic type of "fool." Inconsistencies are purposefully created by some team. But the incipient event, which "someone" is to impersonate in making-himself-a-fool to bridge the inconsistencies, is *not* subject to his control or his projecting. See *sect.* 6.22.

liminary field of abductive inquiry where one may be "stumbling around" from one conjecture and guess to the other. But this cannot imply, of course, that description is impossible: the incipient event and its enactment are subject to a *mere* description. A hesitant word, an admonition or a shout, a joke or some witticism may indicate the incipient event, the mere hypothetical solution of the dramatic situation.[36]

4.52 The Second Stage: Typification by the Incipient Event

The first stage of arisal of types described above is mainly a scrutiny of the surprising phenomenon, i.e. in playing-at-the-theme the inconsistency becomes "localized" and leads to an incipient event. In the remaining second and last stages of the arisal of types the incipient event has to be "tested" to see if it can clarify the diffuse thematic field.

The incipient event itself demands all attention in this second stage. The incipient event has to be "explicated," it has to be "unfolded," and in some form or the other it has to be "demonstrated." These terms point all in one direction: Somehow relations have to be constructed which tie the incipient event into the context, relations which are given in case of an undramatic situation in a typificatory scheme. Hence, attention in this stage has to focus on the relationship between the incipient event and the prevalent typificatory scheme. By typifying the whole context by means of the incipient event, relations emerge pointing out necessary consequences of adopting the incipient event for incipient typificatory purposes. These relations indicate the necessary alterations of the typificatory scheme in case the

---

[36] On the predicative level one can find similar situations which may be taken as prototype of the "dramatic language" bridging an inconsistency. In papers of beginning students in mathematics, for instance, one often observes a "trick," where the "conclusiveness" of an argumentation is to be conveyed to the (hopefully inattentive) reader. Starting from a set of propositions the student argues correctly toward the theorem to be proved. But he does not quite get through to the required result. Then he starts from the other end, taking the theorem as starting point and tries to pull a few presuppositions out of it, which point in the direction of the unfinished business above. Not being able to tie the two strings together logically, the student places into the middle of the "proof" a dramatic "Therefore." (Terms like "therefore," "hence," "since," "entail," "imply" play a similar rôle. These terms are indicative for the attempt of the student to play at the logical sentiments of the reader. Better: He plays purposefully with the "tending of the Other toward him," thus trying to lull him away from his "tending toward the object.") But observe: the student is not simply "tricky." Not only have all his other operations been "correct," but also the conclusive "Therefore" *may* turn out later to be conclusive indeed. The student "invented" a solution by "jumping" over the gap. – In a social context this procedure will be much more successful because of the *antecedent* intersubjective constitution of the "object" in an abductive process. The dramatic "Therefore" may "create" the solution.

incipient event is to become a social type. I refer again to the previous example of a party to illustrate this stage.

After the incipient event (She – a "hostess" – has given and I – a "guest" – have accepted "those" cigarettes) has arisen as antecedent to the theme marijuana-at-the-party, it furnishes now "explanations" by which the surprising fact of being offered such cigarettes appears as being "necessarily so." These "explanations" arise in typificatory attempts: "Of course, one smokes this stuff at Mr. L.'s party;" "expansion of the mind by narcotics is the only way to enter new dimensions of experience;" etc.; etc. To be more precise: the whole context is being typified anew by this incipient event leading to a first clarification of the thematic field. The gap and its pragmatic differences vanish: The mediate presentation of the context by the young girl and the immediate presentation of the context to me "coincide," they are "tied" by the incipient event. This is another way of saying that the consequences of enacting the incipient event come to be considered as intersubjectively "necessary." [37] If the "host" offers narcotics, then the "guests" accept them. The surprising fact has become (for the time being) an old shoe: "Guests do it (here)," and "hosts do it (here)," also.

The highly typified context of this example is rather inflexible and typification by the incipient event has not become transparent enough. I may therefore refer to another example of my own observation. My son Georg (5; 6)[38] saw children with a kite and asked me to build one, also. I promised to do so, and after recollecting my long-past experiences concerning kite constructions and after buying some material we both considered to be appropriate, we set out on the job. I did the "groundwork" of simple mechanical construction; he did the more artistic part by painting a design on the paper. We waited for a nice windy day, went out with our kite, and – as may be expected by any expert in kite construction – the thing did not fly more than a few feet.

As it became evident by later events, this mutual enterprise created a dramatic situation for Georg. His perception of the context became ambivalent, since his tending toward the "kite-being-built-by-us" could not imply any more my tending toward the kite (which was most assuring, as long as we were at home) and my tending toward him (which has not

---

[37] Schütz developed his notion of "motivational relevance" (see *sect.* 3.12 above) to explain phenomena closely related to my present problem. I described them under the presupposition that an inconsistency has to be overcome in the given situation. Since a "definition of a situation" usually implies the solution of some problematic situation, the topics dealt with by Schütz and myself can even be considered the same.

[38] I am using the standard notation (5; 6) to give his age of 5 years and 6 months.

suffered assuredly because of this "drama;" – at least, I am sure he did not notice any ambivalence, since the adult is equipped with the protective mechanism "It is just play," [39] which indeed proves to be protective for the child at this point.) The thematic field became diffuse and the boy could not typify the context because of an inconsistency in the situation.

I sat down the next day alone, since he showed a remarkable disinterest in the kite for a while,[40] and I tried to recollect my knowledge of long-forgotten physics courses. After drawing some nicely colored parallelograms, which Georg glanced at occasionally, I said at lunch that the problem had been solved: "One has only to know how to string it in relation to its center of gravity."

This term "center of gravity" became for Georg an incipient event. While working in the garden after lunch, he asked me: "What is a center of gravity?" I picked up a long stick and balancing it explained what it meant. Then I took a shovel, balancing it also. I reminded him of a seesaw, and finally I remarked: "You have a center of gravity, too, and that is your navel." Next, he picked up a few sticks himself and tried to balance them, more or less successfully. His attempts to typify the whole context by means of the incipient event became unmistakably clear when he called me in for supper: "Supper is ready, you Center-of-Gravity!" Before sitting down to eat, he balanced his chair "explaining" its center of gravity to his mother. But after having eaten a few bites, he began to complain of "terrible" pains in his stomach. He mentioned "center of gravity" once more but never again all evening, wailing more and more realistically about a persistent stomach ache. Being questioned, if it hurt around the navel, he denied it pointing toward parts usually indicating appendicitis. We got slightly worried until he said: "We should ask a doctor, what is in there, what happened in there. *Are there any animals inside?* One has to look!" [41]

I suspected that his typifying the context by the incipient event had turned toward his navel, especially, since I had previously compared his navel to a center of gravity. Thus, in an effort to partly clarify the situation, I took a long bench and lay down swinging as if I were a seesaw myself.

---

[39] Compare the extensive discussion of this "protective mechanism" in *sect.* 7.2.

[40] In line with my theoretical presentation, I have to assume that the boy tried to overcome this dramatic situation first by a series of unsuccessful typificatory attempts. Since I did not suspect at that time the arisal of an inconsistency, I did not observe his actions and expressions carefully in that early stage. Thus, the whole first phase of playing-at-the-theme cannot be described here.

[41] For the occurence of animisms in processes of incipient typification see *sect.* 6.3.

He looked at me without comment, then went to bed crying about the pain and asking that we call a doctor. Soon afterwards he fell asleep.

One may object that the highly abstract notion of "center of gravity" can hardly be grasped by a boy five years old. But what does "not being able to grasp" mean? Any typification of this inconsistency depends on his being able to relate the incipient type "center of gravity" to *some* already existing typificatory scheme.[42] The typificatory scheme of theoretical physics is not, of course, available to him. But he had to establish *some* typificatory scheme in which our future mutual kite constructions would endure and "explain" also possible failures without threatening the unity of context. Georg's actions the next day (very healthy, very much alive) concerning the "center of gravity" illustrate those attempts. For he typified the following situations without any "playing-around" or similar expressions of ambivalence.[43]

1. During breakfast, two small boys in the neighborhood came in, one of whom had never visited us before. Georg got up, and about the first thing he did was take the small bench I had used the night before for my own demonstration: He lay down on it and addressed the two boys (whom I have to quote now in German since the equivocation gets lost in English): "Guck, dies hier ist ein . . ., dies ist ein schwerer . . ., wie heißt das noch mal?" My answer: "Ein Schwerpunkt." "Guck, das ist ein Schwerpunkt." But the two companions were totally unimpressed by his performance and turned away disinterestedly. Thus, Georg joined them also.

2. A few hours later he took the kite from the wall (incidentally the first time he related the problem to the kite) and said: "Look, Mommy, this is a point of gravity. Exactly in the middle!"

3. A few days later after another slightly more successful trial flight he commented after supper: "You have to work on the kite tonight. You have to fix the center of gravity."

These last events already anticipate some of the notions to be explicated in the following last stage of the arisal of types. The main purpose of this example was to show that "typification by an incipient event" leads to a typification of the whole context by means of this event and that the typificatory consequences appear to be necessary, even "painfully" necessary. The thematic field is thus being clarified and the gap vanishes. The incipient event "center-of-gravity" has solved the *social* problem.

[42] If this "dramatic" experience cannot be typified retroactively, then the incipient event will somehow "sink away in oblivion," very probably the state of very young children *after* they have grasped at some point the triadic structure of social relevance but have only few available typificatory schemes.

[43] We refrained, of course, from mentioning the incipient event at all.

4.53 The Third Stage: Type and Social Object

In typifying the context by an incipient event the consequences of enacting the incipient event are becoming intersubjectively "necessary". But
their validity is still restricted to the given situation in which the incipient
event arose. To some degree, the "necessary" consequences of enacting the
incipient event have to be compatible with previous experiences: they have
to fit into some typificatory scheme. In subsequent situations, therefore, an
iterative construction of type takes place, in which those earlier typificatory
results are "tested." [44]

The question might be raised, if this "testing" is an intersubjective process occurring in subsequent situations, or if it may take place in solitary
reflection. This alternative, I contend, is a false alternative and hides, by
its very formulation, important aspects of the constitution of social types.
Both Max Weber's notion of ideal types [45] and Husserl's method of eidetic
variation [46] (if applied to social experiences) presuppose that alternative
and decide for the individual actor or scientist, whose "testing" takes place
in solitary reflection either within a certain eidetic region or in the context
of some science. But Schütz has shown the consequence of both methods:
one must be able to describe the context of interaction in toto as a context
of meaning. [47] This raises several difficulties: 1. The first objection follows
from Aron Gurwitsch' contention that the phenomenon of context cannot
be analysed in terms of phenomenal time. But social phenomena are in-

---

[44] Again referring to Schütz, he called the relevance underlying this process "hypothetical thematic relevance" (see sect. 3.11). This type of relevance makes me "cling to
a certain theme explicitly for the purpose of testing the validity of some of its ingredients in specific situations." The explanation offered above would not have to rely on
a specific type of relevance. Rather, I "cling to a certain theme" in these subsequent
situations since they alone assure the arisal of intersubjectively valid social types which
are a prerequisite for any projected social interaction.

[45] His essay "Die 'Objektivität' sozialwissenschaftlicher und sozialpolitischer Er-
kenntnis" is one of his most concise presentations of the theory of ideal types. The
point I intend to make at present refers to the intrinsic difficulty, as far as social objects
are concerned, of distinguishing contexts of "things" (sachliche Zusammenhänge der
Dinge) from contexts of "thought" (gedankliche Zusammenhänge), the former being
intersubjectively constituted. Nevertheless, Max Weber states as a basis for his methodological approach: "Nicht die 'sachlichen' Zusammenhänge der 'Dinge,' sondern die
gedanklichen Zusammenhänge der Probleme liegen den Arbeitsgebieten der Wissenschaften zugrunde." Max Weber, Gesammelte Aufsätze zur Wissenschaftslehre (Tübingen, Mohr, 2d ed., 1951), p. 166.

[46] For a detailed presentation of this notion see: Husserl, Ideen, vol. 1, chap. 1. A
concise summary may be found in Schütz, Coll. Pap., vol. 1, p. 114.

[47] Schütz' theory of "finite provinces of meaning" (Coll. Pap., vol. 1, pp. 229–234)
is the result of that method.

trinsically temporal, a social context has temporal dimensions. Therefore, reducing the context completely to a context of meaning has to open it up to an analysis in terms of inner time. 2. Reducing the context *in toto* to a context of meaning reduces the gap to a phenomenon of individual consciousness. In this case, the solution of social inconsistencies becomes possible within a theory of "finite provinces of meaning." Two objections may be raised: The phenomenon of play can be dealt with in this manner only within a dualism between distinct realms of "play" and of "serious" social action. My paper is an effort to avoid and to question such a dualism. Secondly, the notion of relevance underlying such a theory of distinct provinces of meaning has to take the subjectivistic formulation given it by Schütz, which I previously criticized.

These difficulties arise, if *total* reduction of the context to a context of meaning is attempted. I contend that social contexts cannot be totally dealt with as contexts of meaning, if typification and formation of types occur in a generic state. These are contexts, as will be shown in the next chapter, in which a social dimension of time arises due to the structurization of the situation by the incipient event. Dramatic situations evade any reduction. They have to be lived through. These are the situations meant above, in which the consequents of enacting the incipient event are *first* to be intersubjectively "tested," *before* ideal typical or eidetic methods may be applied.

The final phase of type formation may be clarified again with the example of "being-at-a-party." In the previous stage the incipient event served to typify the entire context anew. The types "host" and "guest" have been tentatively enlarged by the incipient event. (The problem would have been quite similar, if a "new type" emerges as in the example of kite-construction presented before. The density of types in the present example makes such new construction improbable.) The "enlargement" or re-formation of types is reaffirmed in subsequent situations. Assume, for example, that Prof. L. suddenly enters the room smoking a cigarette and greeting me cordially. There is a new situation: Though the thematic field remains the same, my thematic interest concentrates immediately on "that" cigarette. Does he or doesn't he?

Does Mr. L.'s entry present an inconsistency according to the previous definition? Obviously not, since there is neither an untypifyable gap in the context nor a diffuse thematic field: His presentation of the context unified by the theme "marijuana" coincides with the immediate presentation; typificatory attempts are going on and at least rudimentary types are available. Some uncertainty prevails only as to the contours of the type "host" and its object.[48] The subsequent interactional clarification of these contours may be compared to "playing-at-a-theme" on the abductive level. However, this interaction occurs now in a totally typifyable context, notwithstanding that the earlier gap has been bridged only by typifying it by means of an incipient event. This event was used to typify the total context and revealed certain necessary consequences. They lead, on the other hand, to expectations (does he or doesn't he?) which have to be interactionally probed now.[49] Thus, "testing" occurs, just "playing around" in order to find out in what way Mr. L. can be typified also by the "incipient event." However, in this situation the "incipient event" is not incipient at all any more. No gap is apparent: typification occurs by a rudimentary type. This testing in an interactional effort to clarify the contours of the type "host" requires – and this is the important difference to playing-at-a-theme – a rudimentary strategy:[50] *I* am the one who is interested in clarifying the case, *I* have to elicit some reaction from the Other which is to reveal if also in this case the type "host" is to be enlarged. In this process, occurring also, of course, in later situations, the type becomes more and more schematic, its contours become less ambivalent.

Typification, of course, is always typification of a social object. The arisal of social types has been shown to proceed in three very distinct phases. But what may be said about the social object? Since some major concepts (interlocking perspectives of relevance; incipient event; etc.) have been introduced by referring to the notion of social object, a short summary of these references seems to be in order.

1. Social objects are intersubjectively constituted. Social objects are, of course, elements of the situation, but they are constituted in reciprocal interaction in the situation. Independently of a situational context, social objects do not "exist" at all. In other words, they are phenomena of context and presuppose relevance for their emergence. Due to their intersub-

---

[48] One should remark here that such uncertain contours are inherent and intrinsic to any social types due to their constitution in face-to-face situations of social interaction. Thus, the present study has to make clear how the uncertainty and ambivalence of social types becomes limited and reduced. "Sharp" contours are already typical for reified types, a problem which will be dealt with later.

[49] Peirce characterized the inductive stage of inquiry similarly: "We make experiments, or quasi-experiments, in order to find out how far these new conditional expectations are going to be fulfilled." (See *sect.* 3.33 above). A quite analogous procedure (similar as to its formal character) has to be pursued in eidetic variation and in the construction of ideal types, which are the two major processes of type-formation usually referred to.

[50] This "playing around" has some of the characteristics which G. H. Mead assigned to "game" in distinguishing it from "play." See the later *sect.* 7.0.

jective constitution, social objects have "vague contours;" they are apt to vanish as soon as the triadic intersubjective perspectives of relevance dissolve. Thus, two "polar degenerations" of the social construction of social objects are possible: A total dissolution of relevant structural contours in "anomie;" a hardening of these contours into thinghood, a process called "reification."[51] A partial dissolution of the contours of specific social objects is possible by not making them thematic: If "related" themes and thematic fields are avoided, the objects do not come about.

2. *Tending toward a social object has an intersubjective structure.* Perceiving a social object cannot rely upon immediate perceptual affirmations: I can perceive this book on my table as an *object* of the present situation and reaffirm myself by touching it or reading its title; but as a *social object* it has to be perceived in a relevant context, i.e., it has been written (sold, presented as a gift, etc.) by someone and has been read (bought, accepted, etc.) by someone else.[52] Tending toward a social object has to imply the tending of the Other toward it and his tending toward me, i.e. tending toward a social object has a "triadic structure" of intentionality.

3. *Thematic field and theme bring about the social object.* Social objects are constructed intersubjectively in a situation which is becoming relevant through the relations a theme induces in the context. This set of relations has been called a typificatory scheme. There are two modes of presentation of the context: an immediate presentation of context as it presents itself to me and a mediate presentation of context as it presents itself to me through the Other. The latter presentation is the major constituent of the thematic field. The two modes of presentation are simply correlates of the triadic structure of tending toward a social object. Thus, the immediate presentation has to imply the mediate presentation, has to "take account of" the thematic field, if the social object is to come about: both modes of presentation have to be "tied" together by a type. A *first consequence*: The theme, preceding the social object, leads to a type, and only *subsequently* the social object arises. Since this sequence entails, however, all the paradoxes of solipsism and would lead to a subjectivistic notion of social reality on the basis of *my* thematic interest in the situation, a way had to be found to explain this sequence (from a given theme to an arising

---

[51] For a discussion of anomie see *sect.* 6.21; for reification see *sect.* 5.4.

[52] Mead could solve the problem of the "correlative appearances" of an object only by imputing to the individual some inherent "tendencies": "Something that can be exchanged can exist in the experience of the individual only insofar as he has in his own make-up the tendency to sell when he has also the tendency to buy." (Mead, *Present,* p. 185) One tendency is "to call out" the other tendency in one's "nature": But how is this resonance to happen, if it is not based in the structure of social types?

social object), so-to-speak, "backwards": The social object had to arise as being *antecedent* to the theme. Playing-at-a-theme has been shown to be the interactional means going on in this abductive stage. A *second consequence:* Every social type has a twofold composition referring to the immediate and the mediate presentation of context. Every typification is rooted in typificatory schemes which relate to the situation. Since type and object arise iteratively out of some incipient event, this intersubjective structure of the type has also to be inherent in the social object.

This short summary has drawn a definitory frame for the notion of social object. But what *is* the social object? What is "left" of the incipient event after its typical "elements" have been iteratively "gathered" into a type? The closest answer, but still short of an outright "definition of social object," may be that a social object is that which is *in* the interlocking perspectives of relevance in a social situation. This formal answer may be hardly satisfying to a more analytically-minded critic. But any such critic attempting a more stringent definition has to take account of the multitude of contours a social object may take in spite of the relative constancy of the types being composed within a given language. Interaction between schizophrenics shows, for example, how bizarre the contours of social objects may become, while the types these patients employ are often indistinguishable from those in everyday life or even in science. Thus, in order not to limit the further studies too stringently by some "rash" definition of a social object, I would rather like to keep the question open and join Alfred Schütz in an answer he gave in a similar situation: "But to one who is not satisfied with such guarantees and asks for greater reality, I want to say that I am afraid I do not exactly know what reality is." [53]

4.6 Conclusion

In closing this section, I want to refer again to *Charles S. Peirce'* contention that understanding (social) [54] phenomena is possible only in abduction. Abduction is, on the other hand, at the basis of social typifications. It seems that a circle is closed here. *Max Weber* had entered it first in showing that "understanding" social phenomena is to be achieved on the

---

[53] *Coll. Pap.,* vol. 3, p. 88. – I am aware that I am shortcircuiting the discussion at this point. But any further questioning (besides not immediately contributing to the topic of this study) would lead into the most difficult problems of the theory of intersubjectivity. As far as I am acquainted with the work of Charles S. Peirce, his theory of reality as an intersubjectively valid reality emerging within the process of mutual inquiry would allow pursuing the questions much further than I am able to do here.

[54] I bracket the term "social," since Peirce' contention was more general, but never specifically applied to social objects.

basis of ideal types. One of *Alfred Schütz'* most important contributions to the social sciences was extending this Weberian notion in showing that "the individual's common-sense knowledge of the world is a system of constructs of its typicality."[55] Thus he was able to show that the process of understanding by types is both basic for scientific inquiry and for the common-sense orientation in everyday-life.

Schütz insisted that the constructs of social science are ideal types formed out of the common-sense-typifications of everyday-life.[56] He referred the genesis of these latter types to the vernacular of everyday language.[57] For it was less their genesis than the constitution of their meaning Schütz was interested in. On the other hand, the meaning of a type, as it is constituted by the activities of the mind, may be ascertained by the eidetic approach of phenomenological analysis. And this leads into the second major method, to the construction of types by "eidetic reduction" resp. "eidetic variation" already mentioned above.

This paper followed a different path which led to the question of the genesis of common-sense-typifications. For – by shifting the argument from the context of meaning in social interaction to an analysis of the structure of relevance – I tried to find an approach to several questions: In a situation of social interaction, how am I going to ascertain that typical goals and typical motives imputed to my partner are indeed his goals or his motives? Does some kind of play have a constitutive part in social typification and is it thus possible to distinguish play from social action? Does a genuinely social dimension of time arise in social interaction and in how far is it related to the emergence and subsequent typification of incipient events? The last question can be answered in the affirmative by approaching it from the notion of social time elaborated by G. H. Mead.

---

[55] A subtitle in his essay "Common-Sense and Scientific Interpretation of Human Action," *Coll. Pap.*, vol. 1, p. 7.

[56] He called them "second-order" resp. "first-order" constructs. See: *Coll. Pap.*, vol. 1, pp. 58f.

[57] *op. cit.*, vol. 2, p. 233.

CHAPTER 5

TEMPORAL TYPIFICATION AND SOCIAL TEMPORALITY

THEME:

The previously developed conceptual frame is further differentiated in a limited study of the temporal dimensions of social situations and contexts. Incipient events, which arise in typificatory attempts to bridge social inconsistencies, structure those temporal dimensions and are hence not separable from a study of social interaction.

Social inconsistencies lead to the arisal of social types. Social types, on the other hand, structure the passage of social action. The previous presentation has already shown that social inconsistencies and subsequently arising incipient events occur, so-to-speak, as "variations" or "transformations" of context. This phenomenon of "contextual variation" is an intersubjective process. Its mode of mutual interaction has been called "playing-at-a-theme." Has this mode been clarified sufficiently? To be more precise: What are the temporal characteristics of that intersubjective process?

Social action is intrinsically temporal and always constituted in a social context. But while social action is structured by "inner time," it is at least questionable, if the temporal dimensions of social context and of "contextual variations" relate also to "inner time." Aron Gurwitsch, for instance, showed with his much more refined conceptual frame[1] that *contexts* cannot be analysed in terms of phenomenal (or inner) time. Hence, I must ask if *social contexts* have a "temporal character" which is different from phenomena structured by "inner time."

Let me summarize the main notions developed previously. The term "situation" was introduced to indicate that human beings are present among a variety of objects available for manipulatory purposes and for meditation or reflection. The term "context" indicates the prevalence of

---

[1] *Field,* p. 329. – His studies of the organizational principles of theme, thematic field, and margin as constituents of the field of consciousness have only been touched upon in my presentation.

relations which are such that they unify the situation through an indicative scheme of reciprocal relations between the outstanding situational characters. This indicative scheme has also been called a "typificatory scheme"[2] in order to stress that all typification and formation of types take place on the basis of such a scheme. But not all typificatory schemes achieve a unification of context! This important qualification will be carefully discussed, since it seems to be the major structural discriminant bweeen "social temporality" and "inner time." It is a necessary consequence of taking the notion of context strictly in the sense of "context as it presents itself." Context and relevance are correlated terms: Unity of context comes about through *some* (not any!) typificatory scheme prevailing in a situation; the correlated unity of relevance is assured since this typificatory scheme achieves an interlocking of the perspectives of relevance by means of the triadic intentional structure of its social types.

5.1 Typificatory Schemes and Social Temporality

This conceptual frame limits, of course, the scope within which the problem of "social temporality" can be pursued. Its limits can be drawn by the following questions: Is "social temporality" also a phenomenon of the situation or only of the context? Does it constitute a typificatory scheme? Are social inconsistencies related to the emergence of "social temporality"? Does playing-at-a-theme contribute to such emergence?

These questions are guided by the hypothesis: "Inner time" (*durée*) may be distinguished from "social temporality."[3] The former is an intrinsic property of consciousness, the latter, I intend to show, is a phenomenon of

---

[2] See *sect.* 4.3.

[3] This distinction was also proposed by *Alfred Schütz*. On the one hand, the structure of social action has to be studied in terms of "inner time." Living in the ongoing process of my acting, i.e., being in action, I experience my acting *modo presenti;* in projecting, I look at the anticipated completed act *modo futuri exacti,* while the act itself can be grasped only in a past tense, in *modo praeterito. (Coll. Pap.,* vol. 1, pp. 214f). – On the other hand, in a face-to-face situation of mutual interaction the social experience of "growing older together" is constituted in intersubjective temporality: "My participating in simultaneity in the ongoing process of the Other's communicating establishes . . . a new dimension of time." (*op. cit.,* p. 219)

Berger-Luckmann make the same distinction: "Temporality is an intrinsic property of consciousness. . . . As we have indicated, however, intersubjectivity in everyday life also has a temporal dimension." (*Social Construction,* p. 26).

I am going to distinguish "inner *time*" from "social *temporality*," since I have to forego any discussion of the relationship between these two dimensions. Thus it would not be to the point, if some critics were to object that I am using incompatible notions of *time* here. I am restricting myself to a careful description of a specific phenomenon of context which I call "social temporality."

context. What may be said about the relations between the two "temporal" dimensions? One has to assume the possibility of a most intimate relationship, as long as this question cannot be pursued to any extent. For our present purpose it is merely necessary to clarify "social temporality" as a phenomenon of context in order to find some basis for the general contention that game and play constitute, and take place within, their own temporal boundaries.

5.11 Temporal Typification and Inner Time

Schütz analysed the "Time Structure of the Project"[4] and showed that it is intrinsically related to "inner time." The attitudes of reflecting (turning toward an accomplished act), of living (living within an ongoing action), and of projecting (phantasying the state of an accomplished act) are the basic dimensions of the consciousness of inner time and characterize distinct phases of social action. In projecting some future couse of action the actor "unifies" the situation in a peculiar way. He has to visualize in phantasy the future state of the situation which is to be brought about by his action. Only subsequently is he able to plan the intermediate steps to be taken in the course of his future action. A "unity of action" comes about and is constituted by the "span of the project":[5] *modo futuri exacti* the actor projects an imagined state of the situation; present situational elements are being related to their future constellation in later situations which are still to be brought about; the project "spans" a set of relations assuring "unity" of social action.

In other words, the project circumscribes a typificatory scheme. On this basis, the formation of "course-of-action types" and of "personal types" proceeds.[6] However, this typificatory scheme does not span relations *within one* situation thus unifying it to a context as it presents itself, but it relates a series of imagined situations *to each other*. Typification on the basis of the typificatory scheme of a project, i.e., projecting a typical course of action between typical partners who pursue typical ends by typical means, "induces," so to speak, a temporal dimension into the sequence of potential interactional situations. But this is a temporal dimension due to a specific process of typification.

This phenomenon may be called *temporal typification*. It is rooted exclusively in an actor's stock of available types and in his individual tending

---

[4] *Coll. Pap.*, vol. 1, pp. 68ff.

[5] The most explicit statement of the notion of "span" can be found in: A. Schütz, *The Phenomenology of the Social World* (Northwestern Univ. Press, 1967), pp. 62ff.

[6] See Schütz, *Coll. Pap.*, vol. 1, pp. 19–27.

toward these types. This process, however, is not a typification of context as it presents itself. If the temporal dimensions of a project also have an intersubjective aspect, then certainly not immediately by unity of context, but merely mediately because of the horizonal character of previous intersubjective experiences of the actor. Though temporal typification (based on "inner time") establishes typificatory schemes, it does not unify the situation into a context.

5.12 A Necessary Condition for Social Temporality

It proves to be reasonable, however, to posit that last phrase as a necessary condition: *Social temporality establishes typificatory schemes unifying a situation into a context.* This tentative definition of social temporality implies: 1. The term "to establish" may still be interpreted in various ways. A more stringent condition for social temporality will be given later. 2. Social temporality is related to the constitutive processes in which social types arise. Moreover, social temporality "establishes" social relevance, since its related typificatory scheme unites the situation into a context. I intend to show now that this "necessary condition for social temporality" encompasses both Schütz' and Parsons' notions concerning the temporal structure of situational social interaction. Both theoretical positions are sufficiently different to support the practicability of this notion of social temporality.

5.13 Schütz' Notion of "Vivid Present" and Social Temporality

Alfred Schütz referred frequently to a dimension of time he called "vivid present" which is to arise through synchronisation of the streams of consciousness of interacting partners.[7] In a study of the "mechanism of communication" he stated:

On the one hand, I experience the occurences of the Other's speaking in outer time; on the other hand, I experience my interpreting as a series of retentions and anticipations happening in my inner time interconnected by my aim to understand the Other's thought as a unit. – Now let us consider that the occurences in the outer world – the communicator's speech – is, while it goes on, an element common to his and my vivid present, both of which are, therefore, simultaneous. My participating in simultaneity in the ongoing process of the Other's communicating establishes, therefore, a new dimension of time. He and I, *we* share, while the process lasts, a common vivid present, *our* vivid present, which enables him and me to say: "*We* experienced this occurence together." By the We-rela-

---

[7] This is *one* of the ways Schütz used the term "vivid present." I am going to show in *sect.* 5.22 in detail the subtle changes in Schütz' conception of social temporality. However, they are not in conflict with the necessary condition his notion supports at present.

tion, thus established, we both – he addressing himself to me, and I, listening to him – are living in our mutual vivid present, directed toward the thought to be realized in and by the communicating process. *We grow older together.*[8]

Which typificatory schemes arise with Schütz' notion of "vivid present"? The "occurences of the Other's speaking" are major elements of the given situation. The Other is "addressing himself to me" and I am "listening to him," – but this last phrase easily tends to veil a twofold relation. My listening is a "participating in the ongoing process of the Other's communicating," i.e. my listening implies and takes in the Other's tending toward the occurences of his speaking, *and* his tending toward me. We are both "directed toward the thought to be realized" in this process, that is, there is a common thematic field. Thus, a reciprocal triadic scheme of relations prevails in the situation unifying it into a context in precisely the way in which this notion of context has been defined. *Communicating in "vivid present" establishes a unity of context by a typificatory scheme.* On the basis of this typificatory scheme, as Schütz shows in detail, the typical relations to contemporaries, predecessors and successors arise.

5.14 Parsons' "Pattern Variables" and Social Temporality

Turning now to Talcott Parsons, the search for support of my notion of social temporality becomes somewhat more involved. For Parsons did not, to my knowledge, state explicitly his conception of social time. Instead he distinguished in rather grand fashion "the systems of nature, action and culture" by their spatial and temporal characteristics:

The nature systems involve time in relation to space in the frame of reference, the action systems (involve time) in relation to the means-end schema. . . . Action is *non*-spatial but temporal.[9]

The standards of space and time are based on the "nature system." Thus "time" is for Parsons what Schütz has called "cosmic time."[10] As far as time is involved in action systems, it serves like the physicists' notion of time, as a "parameter of relation" by which the action system is related to its means-end schemata.

To some degree, this concept of time is compatible with Schütz' concep-

---

[8] *Coll. Pap.*, vol. 1, pp. 219f.

[9] Talcott Parsons, *The Structure of Social Action* (New York–London, McGraw-Hill, 1937), pp. 762f.

[10] *Coll. Pap.*, vol. 1, pp. 215f.: "What occurs in the outer world belongs to the same time dimension in which events in inanimate nature occur. . . . It is . . . objective or cosmic time."

tions. Though this agreement between the two otherwise often antagonistic theoreticians does not immediately relate to my line of argument, a short sketch of two concordant points can be inserted to make both notions of time more transparent.

1. Parsons simply *substitutes* the notion of space in the "nature system" and lets the means-end schema take its place. The notion of time remains unchanged. But the means-end schema itself is *not* conceived in temporal terms; time *relates* means-end schemata to action systems. In cases. where Parsons has to deal in the course of his analysis with "temporal dimensions" of the means-end schema he refers them back to spatial representations.[11] Both Schütz and Parsons insist that "time" as a notion of the "nature system," as "cosmic time," does not structure the project of action. It has no place in the means-end schema itself.

2. Parsons relates means-end schema and action system by his notion of time; time is a parameter. Of special import is the case of so-called "rational action":

Action is rational in so far as it pursues ends possible within the conditions of the situation, and by the means which, among those available to the actor, are intrinsically best adapted to the end for reasons understandable and verifiable by positive empirical science.[12]

In this case the actor is supposed to have "scientifically sound knowledge of the circumstances of his situation." The means-end schema tends to become a logically closed, scientific system itself. "Nature time" is penetrating the means-end schema, since "time" changes from a rational parameter *between* schema and system to a parameter *within* systems, merging action system and means-end schema. Such merger is, of course, conceptually inadmissable to Parsons. Thus, he avoids it by stressing rational action as an essentially unattainable limit case. In order to further enforce separation, he uses subsequently the term "rational" not so much in respect to the motivational structure of the means-end schema but in relation to the action system itself. "Rationality" becomes a relational notion similar to the temporal parameter linking action system and means-end schema. This becomes apparent in terms like "rational instrumental goal-orientation" within a system.[13] The notion of rationality is to bridge the conceptu-

---

[11] For example: The "temporal dimension of the actor's concern with the development of the situation may be differentiated along an activity-passivity coordinate." Talcott Parsons, *The Social System* (Glencoe, Free Press, 1951), p. 8.
[12] Parsons, *Structure*, p. 58. – Schütz' paper "The Rationality of the Social World," (*Coll. Pap.*, vol. 2, pp. 64–88) is mainly a discourse about this definition of Parsons.
[13] See, also for the following quote, *System*, pp. 42f.

al gap between motivational schemata and action systems, a gap which originates in his notion of time. This conceptual problem lies at the basis of his scathing attacks against Durkheim: It would otherwise hardly be comprehensible that "reduction of motivational dynamics to rational instrumental terms . . . is a reduction ad absurdum." The motivational sphere has to be kept apart from the realm of nature time. Time structures the situation of interaction between individual actors insofar as its interactional pattern is part of an action system. As Parsons puts it:

(Actors) are motivated in terms of a tendency to the "optimization of gratification," whose relation to their situations . . . is defined and mediated in terms of a system of culturally structured and shared symbols.[14]

Both Parsons and Schütz insist that the motivational sphere is not structured by nature time. As to the constitution of the motivational sphere, they differ completely.[15] But considerable agreement between Schütz and Parsons exists in respect to the relations between the motivational sphere and the situation of immediate interaction. This relationship as "a system of culturally structured and shared symbols" has been studied by Schütz in terms of appresentational references leading to symbolic social types:

I have to learn the typical social roles and the typical expectations of the behavior of the incumbents of such roles, in order to assume the appropriate corresponding role and the appropriate corresponding behavior expected to be approved by the social group. At the same time, I have to learn the typical distribution of knowledge prevailing in this group, and this involves knowledge of the appresentational, referential, and interpretive schemes which each of the subgroups takes for granted and applies to its respective appresentational reference.

And Schütz remarks in a footnote to this passage:

Readers familiar with Parsons' and Shils' monograph . . . ("Values, Motives, and Systems of Action") . . . will recognize in this statement an allusion to their theory of "role-expectancies". Although the approach of the present paper differs from these authors' in several respects, their treatment of a common system of

---

[14] *System*, p. 5. – His notion of "motivation" ties Parsons' theory of Social System interestingly close to the Theory of Economic Games. This is not so surprising since the notion of time in both theories is the same. See for more details *sects*. 5.4. and 7.4. – One may object that though I am talking of "time" in these contexts quoted from Parsons, he does not use the term. But neither does the physicist who talks about "movement," "acceleration," "processes of disintegration" etc. in *describing* his phenomena. Similar language is used by Parsons: His pattern-variables, as is to be shown next, are supposed to indicate temporal phenomena of social change.

[15] For Schütz' notion see *sect*. 3.12: "Motivational Relevance."

symbols as a pre-condition of the reciprocity or complementarity of role expectations is compatible with the view here suggested.[16]

It could be considered an additional argument for the compatibility of both theories of social symbols if Parsons' notion of time also were to support the necessary condition for social temporality stated before. This is the case, if the notion of time prevalent in Parsons' conceptions of "process" and "pattern" constitutes a typificatory scheme unifying the situation into a context.

Parsons states that a "situation" is "consisting of objects of orientation,"[17] a notion general enough to be included in my earlier definition of situation. Relations between actors in a situation form a "higher order unit," as he calls it, a "status role," which Parsons defines further, in his typical fashion of forming substantive elements, as "the participation of an actor in a patterned interactive relationship."[18] The status role *is* thus the structure of the relations between the actors in a situation which the actor assumes with his participation in *patterned* social interaction.

The stress lies here on the term "pattern."[19] Patterns are structured by "pattern variables," which grasp the "relational aspect of the role structure." Parsons lists five pattern variables: they are contraries called "universalism-particularism," "achievement-ascription," "private-collective," "specificity-diffuseness," and "gratification-discipline."[20] They are part of the action system and pattern social interaction. In assuming his status role the actor participates in the ongoing interaction. Thereby he "assumes" the relations between the actors (a notion reminiscent of G. H. Mead's concept of "taking the rôle of the generalized other") and with his assumption of rôle he internalizes the pattern variables.

Pattern variables bridge the conceptual gap between the motivational realm of means-end schemata and the action system, which came about as

---

[16] Schütz, *Coll. Pap.*, vol. 1, p. 351. – For the quoted monograph see: Parsons, T. and Shils, E.A., *Toward a General Theory of Action* (New York, Harper, 1962), pp. 47–243. Schütz cites esp. pp. 105, 162f, and 166.

[17] *System*, p. 5.

[18] *op. cit.*, p. 25.

[19] The notion of "pattern" itself remains less defined than any other of the major Parsonean terms like role, status, etc. Parsons even presupposes that notion in his essay *"Toward a Common Language for the Area of Social Sciences,"* a paper intended to clarify the conceptual chaos Parsons said existed in sociology: *Essays in Sociological Theory Pure and Applied* (Glencoe, Free Press, 1949), p. 42. – I contend that the notion of "pattern" can be defined or reduced to set-theoretical terms grasping a "patterned situation" like a specific set-structure. Parsons' notion of time supports such a contention.

[20] *System*, p. 67. See also: Parsons and Shils, *General Theory*, pp. 76–91.

a consequence of Parsons' notion of time. Thus, pattern variables have to have an intrinsic relation to the notion of time, if my interpretation of Parsons has been correct.

This can best be shown by turning to one of Parsons' papers dealing with applications of his theory. The "Sources and Patterns of Aggression"[21] are established in childhood, where "aggressive patterns develop when security in some form . . . is threatened." Parsons describes different dimensions of insecurity and orders them into his frame of pattern variables:

1. The *Gratification-Discipline Dilemma* may arise for the child "who has felt inadequate in the face of expectations beyond his capacity."
2. The *Private-Collective Interest Dilemma* comes about through conflicting "moral norms current in the family and society."
3. *Universalism* and *Particularism* are felt, for example, because of the "relative distribution of affection between siblings."
4. The gap between *Achievement* and *Ascription* occurs where one is "expected to do things one is unable to achieve."
5. *Specificity* and *Diffuseness* are felt first through ambivalence or inconsistency of maternal love.

There may be better examples among Parsons' writings to illustrate these notions. But this one suffices for my purpose. Pattern variables indicate the structural aspects of relatively irreversible and determinate changes of behavior patterns. These patterns do not have to be deviant or extrordinary, as in the example quoted here, but they always indicate processes of change. To be more precise: They do not merely "indicate" processes of change, but they give *thematic* dimensions of social change. Those five dimensions of insecurity are specific, irreversible and determinate structures of *temporal thematic fields*.

But processes of change are for Parsons either a maintenance or a readjustment of what he called the "equilibrium" of an action system in respect to the means-end schemata of the situation. These processes are structured by pattern variables. A readjustment of the system has to be immediately thematically relevant in the appropriate situation, since it would otherwise remain a merely formal notion. Hence, both thematic field and process are referred to in the notion of pattern variable. The temporal structure of process Parsons assumes without discussion to be based on "nature time."[22] Otherwise, Parsons could not declare consistently his interest in

---

[21] Parsons, *Essays*, pp. 253ff.

[22] I mentioned above that Parsons' notion of "motivation" ties his theory of action into a close relationship to the mathematical theory of strategic games. The "tie" can be clarified now as to its temporal structure:

finding a mathematical form for his theory of pattern variables.[23] For, this implies a study of change by one or the other form of differential equations which presuppose a notion of time at least isomorphic to "nature time."

To summarize Parsons' theory in my own terms: The status role circumscribes interaction in a (nearly) totally typified context, which is patterned according to certain types. The corresponding typificatory schemes exhibit structures induced by pattern variables. The latter determine temporal thematic field, which are often diffuse for the interacting partners, but always clear for the observing social scientist. The arising patterns are unifications of the situation which the actor assumes in taking a status role. His participation implies the reciprocal relations between the interacting individuals constituting relevance in the situation. Thus, the typificatory schemes arising on the basis of pattern variables unify the total situation into a context.

5.2 Social Temporality and Incipient Events

The notion of social temporality has been clarified in part. Typificatory schemes that unify the situation into a context are related with social temporality. One should note that this temporal notion has not been introduced by definition as were earlier notions like "theme," "thematic field," "context," etc. Rather, "social temporality" circumscribes a structural aspect of context which still needs further clarification. Parsons and Schütz can again be consulted for this purpose.

5.21 Social Inconsistencies in Parsons' Frame of Pattern Variables

Parsons' theories are loaded with a considerable conceptual ballast. This seems to be a consequence of his holding rigorously to the idea that social

1. The major component of "motivation" in social action is its "cathectical aspect": It is the pay-off, or what each individual "gets out of" some chosen path of action. (*System*, p. 7)
2. This "cathectical aspect" is being studied under the title of "preferences" and "utilities" in mathematical game theory.
3. The pattern variables structuring this cathectical aspect of social action common to both Parsons' and Von Neumann's theory relate at least to compatible notions of time.

Parsons indicates this "tie" himself: "The pattern variables have proved to form, indeed, a peculiar *strategic* focus of the whole theory of action." (Parsons and Shils, *General Theory*, p. 49. – My italics.)

[23] T. Parsons, *The Social System: A General Theory of Action*, in R. R. Grinker (ed.), *Toward a Unified Theory of Human Behavior* (Basic Books, 1956), pp. 55ff. – Parsons' earlier preoccupation with the theory of differential equations is most obvious in his *Structure of Social Action:* The "Note B" (p. 77–79) reads like a lecture note from an introductory course on differential equations.

temporality and related phenomena like "change" or "process" are based on the concept of time dealt with in natural sciences like physics. These sciences can study "natural events" only *more geometrico*, i.e., as situational and operational projections in mathematical coordinate systems. The "natural event" is reduced to an index of some numerical complex.

Parsons placed his "analytical science of action" on precisely the same formal level. He discarded a closer study of "incipient events" within their immediate situational context almost from the start of his work. After stating in his "Structure of Social Action," as quoted above, that "action is non-spatial but temporal," he added this crucial footnote:

Of course, every *concrete* event occurs in space, *too*. But this fact is an unproblematic datum to the analytical *sciences* of action.[24]

I contend that the question may still be raised, whether concrete events "occurring in space" are problematic data for the social sciences, more specifically, whether social inconsistencies and incipient events arising from them are related to the emergence of a social temporality. If the latter can be shown, then Parsons' analyses miss an important social phenomenon because of his choice of method.

Parsons neither grasps incipient events nor the arisal and constitution of social types with his "analytical" methods. However, to a certain degree he takes account of social inconsistencies and describes their situational vagueness. For instance, in the already quoted paper "Sources and Patterns of Aggression" this vagueness is implied in terms like "inadequate expectations," "conflicting norms," "insufficient achievement," "ambivalence of maternal love," etc.. Parsons attempts to grasp these social inconsistencies in his frame of pattern variables. What are the limitations of such an analysis? In macrosociological studies of social change, for instance, where situational inconsistencies can be approached in a highly typified ("strategic") manner, an analysis of typically recurring patterns of social inconsistencies in Parsons' frame seems possible.

An entirely different question, however, is a study of "Personality as a System of Action."[25] For every social theory of personality has to take account of *biographic* series of inconsistencies. Inconsistencies, which have been "solved," have left their imprint on the individual's typificatory schemes. They have led to social constructions of types, which relate (in retrospect) the series of "mastered" dramatic situations with each other.

[24] Parsons, *Structure*, p. 763n.
[25] Parsons and Shils, *General Theory*, pp. 110–158.

Here, Parsons' attempt to describe social inconsistencies within a frame of pattern variables seems to fail:

Finally, it should be emphasized that *the variables* as we have stated them *are* dichotomies and *not continua*. *In a series* of concrete actions, *a person may be partly "affective" and partly "neutral"*. But this series would be composed of dichotomous choices; no specific choice can be half affective, half neutral. The same is true of the other pattern variables. One who has carefully read the definitions and discussions will see that each concept sets up polarity, a true dilemma.[26]

Every biography consists of such "series of concrete actions": *In* a specific actional series, biographic elements are continuous (*partly* affective, *partly* neutral). But every series is constituted *between* dichotomous sets of pattern variables. Hence, *biographic inconsistencies*, i.e., the lived-through series of concrete actions in a "problem-solving" situation, can be formulated and grasped by Parsons in some intermediate position between the dichotomous poles of coexisting pairs of the five pattern variables. Scalability of inconsistencies is an immediate, though highly questionable, consequence of Parsons' position.[27]

5.22 Incipient Events in Schütz' Notion of We-Relation

Parsons discards incipient events as "unproblematic" to a theory of social action. With Schütz, this question is not so clear-cut. Rather, as I have to show now, his thinking underwent a considerable change as he became better acquainted with the studies of William James and, more important, with those of George Herbert Mead. Before I start a more careful analysis, two quotes from closely related contexts may indicate the span of these changes:

An analysis of the phenomenal experience of will, the peculiar "fiat," as James calls it, by which the project is carried over into action, is not essential for our purposes and will, therefore, be dispensed with.[28]

But (my action) remains mere fancying unless what W. James called the voluntative "fiat" supervenes and transforms my project into a purpose.[29]

This development of Schütz' thought is determined by his studies of social temporality which becomes most evident in the subtle changes in his

---

[26] *General Theory*, p. 91. (My italics)
[27] A reification of type-producing processes takes place. See *sect.* 7.4.
[28] "Voluntary Action and the Problem of Choice" (1932) in: Schütz, *Social World*, p. 66.
[29] "Choosing among Projects of Action" (1951) in *Coll. Pap.*, vol. 1, p. 67.

notion of "We-relation." Examining four major publications of Schütz may suffice to support my contention: Starting with his first work "Der sinnhafte Aufbau der sozialen Welt" (1932), which contains only the marginal reference to James (as quoted above) and no mention of Mead at all, his paper on Scheler (1942) reveals considerable appreciation of "the great G. H. Mead" and "his most excellent books."[30] References to Mead, especially to his social theory of self, became frequent for a while and then again marginal in his later writings. Among those, the essay "On Multiple Realities" (1945) and "Symbol, Reality and Society" (1950) will be studied under the aspect of Schütz' changing notion of We-relation.

  I. Der sinnhafte Aufbau der sozialen Welt. In the first two chapters Schütz presents a phenomenological analysis of the constitution of "Bewußtseinserlebnisse" in inner time. But in the subsequent, highly important three final chapters, Schütz dispensed with the transcendental phenomenological method and developed a theory of "Fremdverstehen" within the "natural attitude" to be based on the immediate and unquestioned experiencing of the Other in face-to-face situations. This change of method had one single reason: Phenomenological studies of intersubjectivity had not yet succeeded in presenting the constitution of the alter ego on the basis of the transcendentally reduced realm of ego's lived experiences. At that time, Schütz still regarded such a theory as possible. He expressed this view in a footnote concerning Husserl's Cartesian Meditations[31] which appeared in print after Schütz had completed his manuscript. Later on, he thought such a theory would be impossible, referring to his notion of We-relation presented first in "Sinnhafter Aufbau" as a step toward a possible solution.[32]

  The temporal dimension of Schütz' We-relation as "growing-older-together" in "vivid present" was already mentioned in section 5.13. The continuity of Schütz' *formal* notion of We-relation and his different attempts to deal with intersubjective events *within* the We-relation may be shown by focussing on three major points within the context of all four publications.

  1. Schütz' first concern is to explain how I am able to grasp experiences the Other has. "Keineswegs . . . muß ich die reflexive Zuwendung auf *mein* Erlebnis *vom* Anderen vollziehen, um das Erlebnis *des* Anderen in den

---

[30] *Coll. Pap.,* vol. 1, p. 172.
[31] *Social World,* p. 97n2. – I quote, as before, the English translation of "Aufbau."
[32] See his paper "Phenomenology and the Social Sciences" from 1940 (*Coll. Pap.,* vol. 1, pp. 118–139) and especially one of his last essays "The Problem of Transcendental Intersubjectivity in Husserl" from 1957 (*Coll. Pap.,* vol. 3, pp. 51–84).

Blick zu bekommen." [33] I do not have to "look" *from* the Other upon my experiences of him in order to grasp his lived experiences. Schütz reveals here a much simpler process and a much more fruitful, genuinely social phenomenon. Though my own experiences are not accessible to me in their emergence in a living situation (Erlebnissituation), the experiences the Other is making are: I have to "simply look at him" (im bloßen Hinsehen). I grasp his experiences in observing the expressive gestures of his body. Schütz called his phenomenon of "simultaneity," or "coexistence," or "intersection" [34] of two streams of inner time "growing older together": I am grasping the experiences the Other is making in their emergence.

2. Schütz proposes two generalizations of the notion of "growing older together" in his "general thesis of the alter ego": Referring to Max Weber's conception of "aktuelles Verstehen" he insists first that I can "understand" socially transmitted cultural artifacts and objects in a kind of "quasi-simultaneity" with the durée of the once producing alter ego. Secondly, I ascribe to the Other "an environment which has already been interpreted from my subjective standpoint." [35] In this notion of "ascribing a typical environment" to the Other one recognizes again the disputable process of "imputation" discussed before in the second chapter.

3. Observe that Schütz does not mention any "new" dimension of time in this first book! "Growing older together" is an intrinsically social phenomenon, but its temporal aspect is merely a *formal simultaneity* of two durées: I may live with some predecessors even in "quasi-simultaneity." However, the notion of the We-relation presupposes that I am immediately

---

[33] *Sinnhafter Aufbau*, p. 112 – The English translation is not quite correct: "By no means . . . need I attend reflectively to *my* lived experience *of* (?) you in order to observe *your* lived experience." *Social World*, p. 102.
On first reading, this statement of Schütz seems to conflict with my notion that tending toward a social object has to imply the tending of the Other toward it and toward myself. But such a conclusion would be false. I am talking about the intentional structure of tending toward a *social object*. – Schütz refers to the *lived experiences* the Other had made. They become part of his stock of knowledge and are not social *objects*, though they have a very important intersubjective horizonal structure.

[34] Especially the notion of "intersection" between two durées leads easily to spatial associations, since the term has topological equivocations. Remembering Schütz' reliance on Bergson's theory of inner time, which separated rigorously durée and spatialized cosmic time in order to avoid the fallacies involved in the traditional spatializations of inner time, one has to be careful not to introduce spatial notions "through the backdoor," so-to-speak, through a loose use of the term "intersection." –
Schütz pointed out the "inadequacy" of those terms, precisely because of their spatial connotations. But he remarked immediately following this warning that such references to the "spatial world" were inescapable, since ego and alter ego were to be considered as "psychophysical unities" within the "natural attitude." See: *Social World*, p. 103.

[35] *Social World*, p. 105.

face-to-face with the Other.[36] In tending toward the Other as he is tending toward me, a reciprocal social relation is established. This "pure We-relation" is, however, only a formal limit concept. It has to be "filled"[37] with concrete and actual experiences arising in mutual face-to-face inter-action. Thus, for example, if you and I observe together a flying bird, I can never have any certainty as to the sequence of your experiences in observing that bird. The only certainty I have of you, which you have of me of course also, is first that we have grown older together and secondly that the orientation of my body indicates to you, as your body does to me, "our" observing the bird. The important point: The concrete and actual experiences which "fill" the We-relation, i.e., the experience of the specific event "look-at-that-funny-thing-up-there," are *not* immediately and irre-ducibly tied to our bodily gestures indicating our observing the bird; our bodies *represent* something, and this "something" has to be revealed by an analysis of the specific kind of these representations, be it within a theory of signs, of marks, or of symbols, whatever the case may be. This notion of *representation* determined the core of his further studies: Schütz' changing approaches toward social temporality and the We-relation are all dependent on the development of his theory of representation.

II. In his paper on *Scheler's Theory of Intersubjectivity*[38] Schütz hints for the first time at *two* temporal dimensions. He distinguishes now, not only the phenomenal temporal structure of the field of consciousness, but introduces fundamental *attitudes* of "living in our acts" and of reflecting. He proposes "to glance now at the time-structure of both attitudes": In the first attitude we are directed toward the object of our action; in reflection we grasp a past act by other acts. Living in our acting we anticipate the immediate future and the object to be brought about by our expectations. "Living in our acts means living . . . in our vivid present." The three ques-tions singled out in (I) find in part new answers:

1. The basis on which I am able to grasp the experiences of the Other is considerably widened by Schütz. Hoe does not refer to my "looking at the Other"; nor does Schütz continue to employ his notion of "reciprocal tending" between ego and alter ego.[39] His references to James and Mead

---

[36] *Social World*, pp. 163–167.

[37] The notion of "Füllen" is central for phenomenological theory. See, for example: Husserl, *Ideas*, vol. 1, § 132.

[38] *Coll. Pap.*, vol. 1, pp. 150–179. For the following quotes see esp. pp. 172–175.

[39] This change is definitely grounded in Schütz' growing scepticism concerning Hus-serl's theory of intersubjectivity. It is hard to say if Schütz also became sceptical toward his own earlier theories of "Thou-orientation," "We-orientation," "They-orientation," etc. Certainly he never argued with these terms later on. In any case, Husserl remarked

in this context suggest that Schütz saw in the "vivid present" a genuinely social dimension of time: By simply equating "vivid present" with "growing-older-together," he tried to connect Mead's notion of present with his own earlier theories. But Schütz even went so far as to define the alter ego in terms of the vivid present: "The alter ego is that subjective stream of thought which can be experienced in its vivid present."

2. The subsequently stated "general thesis of the alter ego" is based now on "*vivid* simultaneity" of two streams of thought and does not allow including predecessors in some form of "quasi-simultaneity." The ascription of a "typical environment" to the Other is only referred to in passing. I can "seize" the activities of the Other "in their (vivid) present by my own simultaneous activities."

3. Finally, the relation between ego and alter ego is explained as a temporal phenomenon: "This (vivid) present, common to both of us, is the pure sphere of the We." Significantly, however, it is not the We-*relation* gained here, but the "sphere of the We." Since Schütz seems to abandon the constitutive notion of "reciprocal tendings," the We-*relation* as a *limit concept* cannot arise: Living within the vivid present, *we are directed toward common objects* of our mutual interaction; these objects are *not* to be abstracted from but are *integral parts of the "sphere of the We."* Common objects which are integral parts of the situation of mutual interaction: This phrase contains the kernel of Mead's imprint on Schütz' slowly changing notion of social temporality.

III. On Multiple Realities.[40] Schütz' scepticism about the philosophical profoundness of pragmatism has been noted before. Thus, it is not surprising that he tried to find a different basis for the "vivid present" by removing it from Mead's conceptual frame:

In and by our bodily movements we perform the transition from our *durée* to the spatial or cosmic time, and our working actions partake of both. In simultaneity we experience the working action as a series of events in outer and inner time, unifying both dimensions into a single flux which shall be called the *vivid present*. The vivid present originates, therefore, in a intersection of *durée* and cosmic time.

We are living in the vivid present "directed toward the objects and ob-

later: "Unser naives Vorgehen war in der Tat nicht ganz korrekt ... Die Epoché schafft eine einzigartige philosophische Einsamkeit ... In dieser Einsamkeit bin ich ... nicht *ein* Ich, das immer noch sein Du und sein Wir und seine Allgemeinschaft von Mitsubjekten in natürlicher Geltung hat. Die ganze Menschheit und die ganze Scheidung und Ordnung der Personalpromomina ist in meiner Epoché zum Phänomen geworden." *Die Krisis der europäischen Wissenschaften und die transzendentale Phänomenologie* (Den Haag, Nijhoff, 1962), p. 188.

[40] *Coll. Pap.*, vol. 1, pp. 207–259. For the following quotes see esp. pp. 212–220.

jectives to be brought about." The new notion is that of an "intersection of durée and cosmic time." Note: Schütz introduced the term "intersection" in "Sinnhafter Aufbau" to describe only the simultaneity of two streams of consciousness. At that time, Schütz warned against undesired spatial connotations of the term. In this paper, proposing an intersection of durée and cosmic time, the subsequently implied spatial notions are even invited:

> The wide-awake self integrates in its working and by its working its present, past, and future into a specific dimension of time (the vivid present); . . . it organizes the different spatial perspectives of the world of daily life through working acts.

Schütz assigns this new dimension of time to the "realm of working." Working is a narrower concept than social action. In working a projected state of affairs is to be brought about by "bodily movements." The spatial perspectives of the world of daily life are organized by bodily movements and become part of the arising social reality.

Most interesting is the sharp distinction between vivid present and growing older together. The vivid present is the temporal structure of the fundamental realm of working. In this realm arises communication, in the form of indicative gestures as well as in speech. Thus, Schütz takes up his earlier notion (I) that our bodily movements find representations which have to be revealed and deciphered. The representations are grounded on the realm of working and their vehicle is communication. The important difference to (I): Schütz introduces the temporal dimension of "vivid present" only as structuring the realm of bodily movements, of working. The We-relation comes about in *communication* in unison with the phenomenon of growing older together. Here, it is not the "sphere of the We," but again the We-relation established in reciprocal relations between ego and alter ego. But, in difference to (1), these relations are not merely *formal* reciprocal tendings, they are *communicative* relations.

> By the We-relation, thus established, we both – he, addressing himself to me, and I, listening to him – are living in our mutual vivid present.

His earlier "general thesis of the alter ego" is not mentioned any more: the universe of discourse created by communication is a system of typifications and types shared by all who are able to communicate. The major purpose of the "general thesis" was to ascribe to the Other a typical environment "identical" to my own. A shared universe of discourse forms the basis for such "identical" typifications in the realm of working.

IV. Symbol, Reality, and Society.[41] Schütz moved away finally from

---

[41] *Coll. Pap.*, vol. 1, pp. 287–356.

Mead's major positions with the publication of this essay. Among the introductory remarks he states that "for the purpose of the present discussion we wish to disregard the behavioristic thesis so ingeniously defended by George H. Mead, Charles Morris, and others." [42] But Mead had already left one significant imprint on Schütz' thought: the emergent event in intersubjective experience becomes a constitutive part of the situation of face-to-face interaction. As shown in (III), Schütz derived there his highly important notion of the We-relation from the representational realm of communication. His major efforts now concentrated on a study of symbolic interaction.

Schütz presents in this paper a theory too intricate to be sketched in a few sentences. Only major changes in respect to his earlier views can be presented. First of all, there is no longer any reference to the "vivid present." Rather, the temporal structure of the realm of working, which he calls "manipulatory sphere" instead, comes very close to Parsons' spatialized notion of "nature time":

This whole system "world within my actual reach," including the manipulatory area, undergoes changes by any of my locomotions; by displacing my body I shift the center 0 of my system of coordinates to 0', and this alone changes all the numbers (coordinates) pertaining to this system. [43]

Schütz described locomotions in terms which are reminescent of physical displacements in mechanics; the temporal dimension in this realm – though not explicitly stressed by Schütz – seems to be close to that in Parsons' "nature system." [44]

---

[42] *Coll. Pap.*, vol. 1, p. 291. – Mead's theory of signs and gestures deserves this label "behavioristic" only, if one accepts Morris' interpretation of Mead in his introduction to "Mind, Self, and Society." The following sections on Mead will question that interpretation in several ways.

[43] *op. cit.*, pp. 307f.

[44] Piaget imputes a notion of time to the child which is also exclusively related to this manipulatory sphere. He deduces his notion from experimental observations: After "rediscovering" the algebraic structures of sets and groups in the child's developing notions of number, set, movement and displacement, Piaget applied "the same hypotheses to the development of the child's notions of time." Hence, it is not surprising that the problems of duration and temporal order "appeared now in a considerably more simple form." But Piaget even reduced the manipulatory sphere to a much narrower scope than Schütz: 1. Piaget asked the child to react to specific physical displacements in experiments comparable to those studied by students in mechanical physics. 2. The *social* relevance structure in all experiments is that of child-adult. Thus it is not surprising that the observing adult notes the child reporting a temporal dimension which the adult assumes to prevail in the experiment: The child's tending toward the intersubjective "object" *implies* the twofold tending of the adult. – Piaget grasps in his experiments the temporal dimension of "nature time" and *not,* as Piaget assumes in his

Having suspended the notion of vivid present, Schütz stresses again some of his earlier formulations in "Sinnhafter Aufbau." But significant changes are to be observed. The quasi-simultaneity occurs now in *written* communication.[45] The *face-to-face relationship* – taken in a purely formal sense[46] – is introduced to explain the phenomenon of growing older together. In (II), Schütz simply equated "growing-older-together" with the "vivid present," in (III) he distinguished one from the other by referring the "vivid present" to the realm of "bodily movements" and by taking "growing older together" as a communicative dimension. In this paper, the "face-to-face relationship" implies all the formal essentials the "We-relation" had in (I); "growing older together" becomes, furthermore, the temporal dimension of this face-to-face relationship:

While the face-to-face relationship lasts we are mutually involved in one another's biographical situation: we are growing older together. We have indeed a common environment and common experiences of the events in it: I and you, *We* see the flying bird. And this occurence of the bird's flight as an event in outer (public) time is simultaneous with our perceiving it, which is an event in our inner (private) time. The two fluxes of inner time, yours and mine, become synchronous with the event in outer time (bird's flight) and there-with one with the other.[47]

The most significant change in Schütz' conception: the intersubjective event becomes part of and remains inseparable from the synchronisation of the two fluxes of inner time.[48] Consequently, of course, his earlier conception of a purely formal, reciprocal We-relation "melts away under his pen," so-to-speak, while its formal, structural aspects have already been

attacks against Bergson, the dimension of "inner time." Piaget's contention that he refuted Bergson's notion of "inner time" as constitutive for social action is as questionable as his generalization of having found *the* constitution of *the* notion of time for *the* child. His studies of time fit perfectly into Parsons' largely equivalent notions. But Piaget touches nowhere upon the *social* basis of social temporality. – See: Jean Piaget, *Die Bildung des Zeitbegriffs beim Kinde* (Zürich, Rascher, 1955); for the above quotes see pp. 9f. and chapter 10 for his critique of Bergson.

[45] *Coll. Pap.*, vol. 1, p. 324.

[46] *op. cit.*, p. 315n33. Schütz introduced the "face-to-face relationship" as a *formal concept* only in this paper. Its structural phenomenon of reciprocal relations between actors in one and the same social situation had been studied, though under another label, from the start (I): Schütz called it first "We-relation." By introducing a new terminology, the notion of We-relation becomes free for other interpretations.

[47] *Coll. Pap.*, vol. 1, p. 317.

[48] Apparently convinced that the intersubjective event had to be taken into his notion of We-relation, Schütz used the theory of appresentations as the basis for a theory of signs and symbols: "By the intermediary of events in the outer world, occurring on or brought about by the Other's body . . . I may comprehend the Other by appresentations." (*op. cit.*, p. 315.)

referred to the "face-to-face relationship." The We-relation is no longer an immanent part of the face-to-face situation:

The We-relation itself, although originating in the mutual biographical involvement, transcends the existence of either of the consociates in the realm of everyday life. It belongs to a finite province of meaning other than that of the reality of everyday life and can be grasped only by symbolization.[49]

The We-relation "transcends" the face-to-face relationship. The notion of "transcendence" implies here the penetration of one "finite province of meaning" by relations pertaining to another finite province; this penetration can be described as an appresentational process.[50] Thus, the We-relation penetrates the paramount reality of the face-to-face situation: The immediate reciprocal relations, for example, between myself and my friend are elements of the reality of everyday life, but "our friendship surpasses our individual situation"; there is a "joint interest" which makes us partners, and "the idea of *partnership* is perhaps the most general term for the appresented We-relation."[51]

Summary: Unlike Parsons, who thought "concrete events" to be no subject for an "analytical social science," Schütz' changing notions of "vivid present," "growing older together," and especially of the "We-relation" indicate that he tried different approaches to deal with intersubjective

---

[49] *Coll. Pap.*, vol. 1, p. 318.

[50] *op. cit.*, p. 329.

[51] *op. cit.*, pp. 353f. – A critique of this later theory of the We-relation is not essential for my present study. But perhaps I may state some objections:

1. "Friendship" as a prototype and "partnership" as the most general term for the "We-relation" are highly respectable notions of a humanistic perspective of social relations. However, both notions – in my opinion – represent syndroms of cultural and ethical orientations which have to be disentangled in sociological analysis, but are much too complex to be acceptable as fundamental terms for a theory of social reality.

2. If the "situation" can be "co-determined by the performances of our predecessors" (*op. cit.*, p. 352), it loses the precise distinctness otherwise characteristic of Schütz' terminology.

3. The earlier theory of "finite provinces of meaning," which also stipulated a duality between play and seriousness, seems not to be quite compatible with its later interpretation of Schütz. Transfer from one finite province to the other was supposed to be experienced as a shock. Each finite province has a peculiar cognitive style and a correlated "tension of consciousness." Different finite provinces may "merge" into each other: but *only* as "enclaves" within a province of meaning. (*op. cit.*, p. 233n). The cognitive styles pertaining to different finite provinces and enclaves are not transferable from one to the other. But mutual penetration of two finite provinces by appresentations introduces *formal* means of transformation bridging and possibly erasing this fundamental "gap."

events emerging in social interaction. The import of these changes for the whole of Schütz' work has to be seen in the right perspective. They shall not veil the remarkable consistency in Schütz' formal presentation and conceptual frame.

To be more specific: What Schütz called "We-relation" in his first writings is not *the same* interrelational social structure as in his later work, where it is called "face-to-face relationship." But the "We-relation" in its last formulation still *implies* the face-to-face relationship in its "transcending" the immediacy of the situation.[52]

I shall now relate the presentation of Schütz to my earlier argument. The "realm of working," the "manipulatory sphere" and the "sphere of the We" are specific situations. The relevant relations unifying each of these situations into a context are referred to by Schütz' We-relation. However, the specific kinds of these relations are diverse. In (I) the relations are merely a reciprocal tending between ego and alter ego; in (II) they are tendings toward common objects of interaction; in (III) the relations are those of mutual communications; and in (IV) they are appresentational references. In (I) one or the other intersubjective event may "fill" the purely formal "We-relation"; in (III) the intersubjective event – some common topic talked about – is an inherent part of the situation; in (IV) the event becomes explicitly synchronized with the fluxes of inner time of ego and alter ego.

5.23 A More Stringent Condition for Social Temporality

The "necessary condition for social temporality" required merely that social temporality as a phenomenon of context constitutes typificatory schemes uniting the situation into a context. Both Parsons' and Schütz' notion of "nature time" resp. "vivid present" fulfill this condition.

But the critique of Parsons, who avoids the study of intersubjective events, and the presentation of Schütz' preoccupation with this problem suggest a more stringent condition for social temporality. I previously distinguished intersubjective events in general and "incipient events" in par-

---

[52] This late notion of We-relation seems to be compatible with the "immediate" and "mediate" presentations of context I have introduced, if one "twists" Schütz' theory somehow: Since the mediate presentation (constitutive for the thematic field) and the immediate presentation of context as it presents itself immediately to me have to be "tied" (by some arising or available type), one could speak also of the immediate presentation as the "appresenting member" and of the mediate presentation as the "appresented member" forming a pair of presentations, the latter never coming into the same immediacy of apprehension as the former does. – The "twist" of Schütz' notions in such interpretation lies in one basic difference: I do not consider the context to be "represented" in some symbolic manner, but I have spoken from the outset about the context *as it presents itself.*

ticular, the latter coming about in typificatory attempts to "bridge" social inconsistencies. Social temporality was said to establish typificatory
schemes unifying a situation into a context. The rather ambiguous term in
this notion is the term "establishes." How does this occur? Can this be said
more precisely? *If the arisal of an incipient event leads to a structurization
of the passage of social interaction, thus bringing about a typificatory
scheme unifying the situation into a context, then this process is structured
by "social temporality."*

The new terms in the notion "structurization of passage" have to be
clarified. "Structurization" is to be understood as a phenomenon of context and not merely of the situation. Two examples may indicate the difference.

1. As a mere character of the *situation* one finds a "structurization of
passage" in prototypical form in the famous Kepler Laws. Sunrise, high
noon and sunset impose a "periodicity" on man's daily life. This is the
"periodicity" of "cosmic time," as Schütz called it, or of "nature time" in
Parsons' terms. Its deviations (differences in consecutive sunrises) show a
periodicity again and lead to the notion of yearly cycles, other deviations
to the notion of leap years, etc. Kepler's ingenious work culminated in his
describing successfully the differently observed deviations of the planetary
cycles into one grand periodicity of the solar system: cosmic time became
"absolutely" periodical, neither beginning nor end could be extrapolated
any more from deviations or excentricity.[53] Cosmic time allowed now
theoretically an absolute measurement of every "structurization of passage"
in which it has a part: from the sun-dial to the pendulum, from the fre-
quency of the quarz-cristall to the alphaline of the H-spectrum, these are
technical refinements to measure the ordering of natural events into the
passage of their occurence.

2. The "structurization of passage" as a phenomenon of *context* has
been discussed in Schütz' notion of growing-older-together. The synchronisation of two streams of thought within the passage of life is structured by
the fundamental events of birth and death. These events as such are, however, not incipient events constituted in an interactional context, as I am
using these terms at present; they are "natural events" comparable to sunrise and sunset despite all their social significance. They are permanent

[53] This is the reason for Kepler's terminating any classical basis for astrology of any
kind – and for Einstein's (apparently!) reopening it again with his notion of "Weltzeit."
Only modern astrology is clothed slightly more sophisticatedly with labels like "Theo-
logical Thought and the Theory of Relativity," etc. This misinterpretation slips through
by disregarding that the notions of the theory of relativity are only generalizations of
the Newton-Kepler laws.

gaps and can be played at in multiple ways, but they do not lead to incipient events unifying the situation into a context. They do not lead to
social temporality. This problem needs further clarification.

5.3 G. H. Mead's Notion of the Present and Social Temporality

The last two examples indicate, though only roughly, the major starting
points of George Herbert Mead's reflection about the phenomenon of
time.[54] Mead confronted the theories of Whitehead and of Bergson with
some ingenious intuitions he gained from studying the Einstein-Weyl
notion of time employed in the theory of relativity.[55] Mead's critique of
Whitehead aims at the latter's method of "extensive abstraction":

(Whitehead) finds in the mere happening the event, the substance of that which
becomes. He transfers the content of what becomes to a world of "eternal objects" having ingression into events under the control of a principle lying outside
of their occurence.[56]

Whitehead abstracts mere passage from the time within which events
happen, a notion which had already been criticized by Bergson:

There are movements, but there is no inert or invariable object which moves:
Movement does not imply a mobile.[57]

Mead rejects Whitehead here and goes along with Bergson for a while:

If, in Bergson's phrase, "real duration" becomes time through the appearance of
unique events which are distinguishable from each other through their qualitative
nature, a something that is emergent in each event, then bare passage is a manner
of arranging these events.[58]

---

[54] See George Herbert Mead's *Philosophy of the Present,* esp. pp. 1–31.

[55] Mead "extrapolated" one basic intuition into the field of sociality: Spatial and
temporal orientations (coordinates) are *constituted by* specific distributions of events
(matter and mass). However, this "extrapolation" is less artificial as my remark may
suggest, if one remembers Mead's intention "to present mind as an evolution in nature,
in which culminates that sociality which is the principle and the form of emergence."
(*Present,* p. 85) If one substitutes in this last quote the term "nature" by "typificatory
processes," one comes close to Schütz' intention, which I am also pursuing in this paper.
But again, such "substitution" does not diverge essentially from Mead's thought: He
conceived "nature" as an evolutionary process which "proceeds by reconstruction in the
presence of conflicts." (*op. cit.,* p. 174).

[56] *op. cit.,* p. 20.

[57] Henri Bergson, *The Perception of Change,* in: *The Creative Mind* (New York,
Wisdom Library, 1946), p. 149. – Bergson saw the basis for such "unjustified abstraction" in the predominance of visual perception: "The eye has developed the habit of
separating, in the visual field, the relatively invariable figures which are then supposed
to change place without changing form." (p. 147).

[58] *Present,* p. 22.

He agrees with Bergson that the structurization of passage and the emergence of events are a closely intertwined process. But is the structurization of passage simply a consequence of "the appearance of unique events," as Bergson assumed it to be? Structurization of passage, Mead argues, would become in such a case merely a "manner of arranging events" – in a *typical* manner – one has to add. Structurization of passage would imply merely an ordering of events into already existing typificatory schemes similar in structure to the typificatory schemes of counting.

Schütz' notion of "growing-older-together" is but one scheme of ordering daily events into passage: We are "counting time together." But Mead warns:

We are subject to a psychological illusion if we assume that the rhythm of counting and the order which arises out of counting answer to a structure of passage itself, apart of the processes which fall into order through the emergence of events.[59]

This statement may be generalized: It is a psychological illusion if we assume that typificatory processes and the relations induced in a context by means of typificatory schemes lead to a structurization of passage itself apart from the emergence of an incipient event. Time arises, according to Mead, not merely through the *appearance of events*, but through the *ordering* of passage *by these events*.

Mead called the temporal structure of the situation a "present." In a present, not only the passage of interaction is structured by emergent events, but the present is also the locus of all forms of arising sociality. Let me quote a decisive passage from Mead in detail to clarify this important point:

A present then, as contrasted with the abstraction of mere passage, is not a piece cut out anywhere from the temporal dimension of uniformly passing reality. Its chief reference is to the emergent event, that is, to the occurence of something which is more than the processes that have led up to it and which by change, continuance, or disappearance, adds to later passages a content they would not otherwise have possessed. . . . Given an emergent event, its relations to antecedent processes become conditions or causes. Such a situation is a present.

It marks out and in a sense selects what has made its peculiarity possible. It creates with its uniqueness a past and a future. As soon as we view it, it becomes a history and a prophecy. Its own temporal diameter varies with the extent of the event. . . . The past as it appears with the present and future, is the relation of the emergent event to the situation out of which it arose, and it is the event that de-

[59] *op. cit.*, p. 22.

fines that situation. The continuance or disappearance of that which arises is the present passing into the future. Past, present and future belong to a passage which attains temporal structure through the event.[60]

The passage of social interaction in a situation "attains temporal structure through the event," but this "passage" is always a more-or-less typified process. If the *event* can be readily typified, its "relations to antecedent processes" are relations between types: the notion of typificatory schemes was introduced earlier to circumscribe exactly this case; some typificatory scheme prevails, unifying the situation into a context. But a *typified event* acted upon within the passage of *typified social action* is grasped within the temporal dimension of the project, i.e. in terms of "inner time." This is *no* temporal structure of the situation, it is no social temporality, as I have introduced the term before. It is a process of temporal typification. Thus, Mead's notion of *emergent event* can be applied within my conceptual frame only to the case in which typificatory processes fail. There is to be some inconsistency leading to the emergence of an *incipient event*.

This restriction of Mead's notion of "event" has still another aspect. An inconsistency is not simply a "natural" phenomenon, no eruption of the *situation,* as Mead allows for in his "emergent event." The inconsistency indicates a non-typifyable gap in the *context* and presupposes relevance: It is intersubjectively constituted.

With these minor reservations as to Mead's theory, the long passage quoted above can be interpreted within my conceptual frame. It is easy to see that for any given incipient event, "its relations to antecedent processes become conditions and causes." Since relevance is to prevail, there is always some thematic field, however diffuse and vague, which imposes a direction upon any arising theme. In "playing-at-this-theme" a set of relations is induced in the context which are relations "to antecedent processes"; i.e., the incipient event and finally the social object are constituted as antecedent to the theme.[61] This *abductive process of constitution,* which has been germinal for the pragmatic theories of Peirce, is also basic for Mead's notion of "emergence." Mead calls a situation a "present" in which an event emerges: "It marks out and in a sense selects what has made its peculiarity possible." In other words, the dramatic situation "marks out" the gap in the context by a set of pragmatic differences resulting from "unsuccessful" typificatory attempts. The incipient event, intersubjectively

[60] *Present,* pp. 23f.
[61] See *sect.* 4.5.

constituted and thus an element of the situation, "selects what has made its peculiarity possible" by its "selecting" those types "sufficiently close" to the gap-to-be-typified. The incipient event structures the passage of social interaction in a dramatic situation: the interaction going on has been called playing-at-a-theme. Thus, in referring to the notion of social temporality derived before, one may conclude, that *playing-at-a-theme in face of an incipient event constitutes a genuinely social dimension of time.*

This conclusion is in line with Mead's notion of present save for one important qualification. I had to distinguish between those cases, in which the *emergent event* can readily be typified by some available typificatory scheme, and the genuinely *incipient events* which lead to the arisal or enlargement of types and typificatory schemes. Social temporality had to be restricted to the latter, while the former process is structured by inner time and leads to temporal typifications.[62] But in playing-at-a-theme we are intersubjectively engaged in clarifying a diffuse thematic field. This activity has a temporal structure different from the temporal typifications prevalent in the realm of social action. The often postulated "duality" or "dialectic" between play and serious action also seems to result from an unjustified extrapolation of these temporal differences. In the next chapter I shall study this problem further. But first, I would like to turn to some notions of Jean-Paul Sartre which are closely related to my present topic.

5.4 A Comparison with Some Notions of Sartre

Sartre's notion of temporality is to reveal the relations between consciousness and Being. It is intrinsically tied to his ontological premises concerning the dialectic of Being and Non-Being. Man's temporality is the signification of his freedom and irreducible to any natural order. The distinction I have drawn between "inner time" and "social temporality" finds no support in Sartre, unless one tries to modify and then to interpret my notions as expressing the fundamental differences Sartre assumes to exist between the realms of *pour-soi* and *en-soi.*[63] Though Sartre's notion of temporality must be taken into account in any careful study of the relations between inner time and social temporality, the present scope of this paper does neither allow nor necessitate such an analysis.

I wish to restrict my consideration of Sartre to two points. His notion of

---

[62] See *sect.* 5.11.
[63] See for example: Maurice Natanson, *A Critique of Jean-Paul Sartre's Ontology* (Lincoln, Univ. of Neb. Studies, 1951). This study of Natanson is a remarkably clear introduction to Sartre's earlier positions in "Being and Nothingness."

"event" and the related "Project" [64] are immediately reminiscent of Mead's theory presented above. I intend to point out where Sartre's presentation is in line with the previous arguments concerning social temporality and at which points he diverges basically from the positions of this paper. [65] Thus, this section on Sartre will serve mainly to clarify and draw distinct lines for my own presentation.

In spite of the ontological basis of Sartre's thought, he conceives philosophy as being one with the "movement" of society. Philosophy is alive in "praxis," in a continuous dialectic adaptation "by means of thousands of new efforts, thousands of particular pursuits," [66] by men "in need" [67] going beyond their situation and cutting across their social milieu. This central notion of "praxis" forces Sartre constantly into a confrontation with the "facticity" of everyday social life. As may be expected, however, this confrontation is based on an encompassing interpretational scheme: Human interaction takes place in "objective situations" which become "objective" by taking all situational relations into the focus of historical "ends" of action.

The simple inspection of the social field ought to have led to the discovery that the relation to ends is a permanent structure of human enterprises and that it is *on the basis of this relation* that real men evaluate actions, institutions, or economic constructions. It ought to have been established that our comprehension of the other is necessarily attained through ends. [68]

But does a "simple inspection of the social field" establish that result? No doubt, relations to ends in social interaction play a significant rôle in sociological theory; Sartre refers here to a central notion of its theory of "social action." But is social action and its frame of means-end schemata indeed *the* fundamental category constitutive for comprehending social phenomena? [69] In other words, is Sartre's "simple inspection of the social

---

[64] To distinguish Schütz' notion of "project" from Sartre's concept, the latter will be capitalized as "Project."

[65] This limited interest in Sartre allows me to refer mainly to the rather broad presentation of his later position in *Search for a Method* (New York, Knopf, 1963). This book is the prefatory essay to *Critique de la Raison Dialectique* (Paris, Gallimard, 1960).

[66] *Search*, p. 7.

[67] *op. cit.*, p. 91.

[68] *op. cit.*, p. 157.

[69] Compare also my earlier critique of Schütz' notion of "motivational relevances" and of Parsons' "means-end schemata." Both indicate a strictly Weberian point of view in their assigning "social action" *the* fundamental place in all social theory. Both positions, as well as Sartre's, do not allow an adequate grasp of the phenomena of play and game. I contend and propose to show that typificatory processes play a more fundamental rôle in social theory than the notion of "social action."

field" perhaps not a tremendous reduction of social phenomena, a reduction which he would consider to be incompatible with his own method? [70] The extent of these reductions becomes apparent, if one looks at Sartre's studies of phenomena of social play within his reduced frame of "relations to ends." For Sartre has to rely on existential psychoanalysis to comprehend all states of human play as well as "to discover the whole man in the adult." [71]

Thus, I contend, a critical appraisal should start with *Sartre's notion of "relations to ends"* in social situations. Are "relations to ends" constitutive *for* social contexts or are they constituted *in* them? There are "relations in a situation," as I have already shown, which unify the situation into a context, and these relations become indeed *the* "structure of human enterprises." But it is questionable if these are *necessarily* relations to ends. If one allows for a wider notion of relations unifying a situation into a context, Sartre's claim still holds that "real men evaluate actions, institutions, or economic constructions" on the basis of these relations, i.e. *on the basis of their social relevance.* These relations are, however, relations between types, and the unity of such a set of relations has previously been called a typificatory scheme.

Sartre's notions of "alienation" and "reification" can also be "translated" into such an enlarged frame of situational relations. Taking those terms in the Hegel-Sartre adaptation by Berger-Pullberg [72] one may read these notions in the following sense: 1. *Alienation* is the specific mode of intersubjective activity in a situation, in which the "unity" of the producing of types and the types already produced is "broken," i.e. it is a mode in which incipient events no longer emerge, and thus no social temporality can arise. 2. *Reification* is a specific mode of tending toward social objects in an alienated state: relations (not merely to ends, but more generally between types!) are now considered to be types themselves, they are "hardened" into the character of things. Typificatory schemes cease to be merely relations between types, but become "types of types," so-to-speak, and interaction in a reified state is totally typified.

These somehow more general notions do not distort Sartre's conceptions

---

[70] "The dialectical method . . . refuses to reduce." (*Search*, p. 151).

[71] *op. cit.,* p. 60.

[72] "By alienation we mean the process by which the unity of the producing and the product is broken." "By reification we mean the moment in the process of alienation in which the characteristic of thinghood becomes the standard of objective reality." Peter L. Berger and Stanley Pullberg, *Reification and the Sociological Critique of Consciousness,* New Left Review, 35, 1966, p. 61.

as he exemplified them, for instance, in the relations between buyer and seller in a situation of economic bargaining:

The stabilization of prices in a competitive market *reifies* the relation between seller and buyer. Courtesies, hesitations, bargaining, all that is outmoded and thrust aside, since the chips are already down.[73]

The price is, of course, *the* social object par excellence tended to by seller and buyer in the situation of bargaining. Stabilization of prices means the existence of typificatory schemes, the relations in which become subject to mathematical analysis.[74] They are totally typified. There is no "playing-at-the-price" going on, no "courtesies, hesitations, bargaining" etc., as Sartre circumscribes these modes of interaction. The "chips are down," since commodity, price, situations of buyer and seller are all totally typified.

Sartre's notion of social relevance is rather limited, if relevant relations are to be "objective" unifications of the situation by historical ends of action:

The structure of a society which is created by human work defines for each man an objective situation as a starting point.[75]

Thus, for Sartre, intersubjective events are constituted within the realm of this narrow notion of relevance:

The event is not the passive resultant of a hesitant, distorted action and of an equally uncertain reaction: it is not even the fleeting, slippery synthesis of reciprocal incomprehensions. . . . The event in its full concrete reality is the organized unity of a plurality of oppositions reciprocally surpassed. Perpetually surpassed by the initiative of all and of each one, it surges up precisely from these very surpassings, as a double unified organization, the meaning of which is to realize in unity the destruction of each of its terms by the other. Thus constituted, the event reacts upon the men who compose it and imprisons them in its apparatus. . . . We view (the event) as the moving, temporary unity of antagonistic groups which modifies them to the extent that they transform it[76]

Sartre's notion of "event," cast into a rather narrow frame of social relevance, allows nevertheless penetrating studies of macrosociological problems of social and historical change. In such situations interaction and playing-at-relevant-themes occur between "teams" and "audiences" both struggling to impose their definition upon the situation: Competing groups

[73] *Search*, p. 158.
[74] The so-called "games" played in economic theories are examples for the degree to which typificatory schemes of social interaction can be reified.
[75] *Search*, p. 92f.
[76] *op. cit.*, pp. 128f.

struggle to install one's own group as team and all others as audience, and vice versa.[77] Dominance of a team implies a successful imposition of its thematic field upon the situation. All arising themes for the team as well as for its audience have henceforth a specific direction and unify the situation into a context. The thematic fields of "the others" have to be "destroyed," and in this sense, indeed, a unity of context is being established by "destruction of each of its terms by the other." The incipient event as an "organized unity of a plurality of oppositions" unites the mediate and immediate presentations of context into a "unity" of team and audience, of "antagonistic groups" in Sartre's terms. The incipient event thus constituted does not only "react upon the men who compose it," but it structures the total situation in subsequent typifications: It "imprisons them in its apparatus." But this "apparatus" is a typificatory scheme, which Sartre, as a consequence of his narrow notion of social relevance, assumes to be *necessarily* reified. Obviously, such typificatory schemes are inadequate to grasp the "totality" of living beings, to grasp man in his desire to fulfill his reach for freedom.

The reification of all typificatory schemes in team-audience formations is a consequence of Sartre's narrow notion of social relevance. Hence, man's alienation in social interaction is of equal necessity, though, as Sartre insists, it inflicts only accomplished ends of action: "Alienation can modify the *results* of an action but not its profound reality." [78] Its "profound reality" rests in *man's original temporality,* in the tie between consciousness and Being, and alienation cannot modify this realm. However, *alien temporalities* may arise in man's producing and working in social institutions. Capitalistic economy, for example, rests on monetary circulations constituted by the notion of infinitely divisible "compound interest." Thus, an infinitely divisible continuum is created which measures and orders all economic events and action. This phenomenon Sartre recognizes clearly as "nothing other than the 'time' of Cartesian rationalism." [79]

To cope with such "alien temporality" encroaching upon man's original temporalization, man has to "cut across the social field" in *Projects.*[80]

---

[77] See in *chap.* 8: "Team and Audience," a comparison between Goffman's and Sartre's concepts.

[78] *Search,* p. 91.

[79] *op. cit.,* p. 91n3. – Parsons' notion of "nature time," which pervades his theory of pattern variables, has the same characteristics of "Cartesian rationalism." (See *sects.* 5.14 and 5.21) In this respect, but *only* in respect to Parsons' notion of time, one can argue that the Parsonean System is a reflection of the Cartesian structure of capitalistic economy.

[80] *Search,* pp. 111ff.

Sartre defines this mode of action as a dialectical relation between "the given" and "the object aimed at": "the given" defines "an objective situation as a starting point," the "object aimed at" is part of a "field of possibles" depending "strictly on the social, historical reality." [81] The central notion of "relations to ends" in social action is again stressed here:

The most rudimentary behavior must be determined both in relation to the real and present factors which condition it and in relation to a certain object, still to come, which it is trying to bring into being. This is what we call a project. [82]

Those objects "still to come" are seen by Sartre in a wide historical perspective. Only the dialectical "crossreference" between biography and historical period [83] allows for the original temporalization of man in his "personal Project":

A personal project . . has two fundamental characteristics: first, it cannot under any circumstances be defined by concepts; second, as a human project, it is always comprehensible. [84]

The untenable consequences of Sartre's reduction of social relevance into a frame of "objective" ends of action become obvious especially at the *second* characteristic of the personal Project. But first I want to show how far the *first* characteristic is in line with the previously developed theory.

1. Where relevant relations are always *specific* relations to *specific* ends, arising events and "objects still to come" in a "field of possibles" take on a definite shape of purpose. An important possibility for the *construction* of social inconsistencies and incipient events becomes apparent here. Situational relations, as well as relevant themes, are subject to social consent. Social control can most effectively be exercised by teams determining for their audiences which objects to tend toward and which not to. Major limitations to any such exercise of social control obviously arise from the triadic structure of any such tending: I may be forced to look at some puppet, I cannot be forced to "look" at a social object. But I may *consent* to such impositions by submerging into team or audience, and it is the "alienated man" who does. [85] However, in "the human act," in a Project, he may cut across those imposing reified typificatory schemes and may even destroy them. The Project is a mode of interaction in face of specific incipient events: The basic inconsistencies are constructed out of

[81]   *Search*, pp. 92f.
[82]   *op. cit.*, p. 91.
[83]   *op. cit.*, p. 135.
[84]   *op. cit.*, p. 170.
[85]   Heidegger's "inauthentic" mode of existence in the anonymity of "Man" is close to this conception. See *sect. 8.1.*

the *purposive* rivalry of competing groups; playing-at-a-theme is to bring about clarification and dominance of one thematic field, and the Project is just a specific mode of it. Since social temporality arises in playing-at-a-theme, the same holds for the Project: the event structures the Project, as Sartre called it. Hence, in line with Sartre's result, one may conclude: the Project "cannot under any circumstances be defined by concepts," i.e. defined by types, as I have called it, since typifications and types arise only subsequently to the incipient event.

2. Difficulties arise with the second characteristic Sartre assigns to the Project: It is always supposed to be comprehensible. As long as the Project is limited to purposive rivalry between competing groups, comprehension always seems to be possible. The purpose directs the situational relations to specific ends which are open to inquiry and interpretation, more often to propagation and demonstration. However, Sartre would not consent to such limited interpretation of the rôle of ends in social interaction:

The permanent possibility that an end might be transformed into an illusion characterizes the social field and the modes of alienation.[86]

Thus, it is the task of existentialism to recognize "the existence of ends wherever they are found" and to declare "that certain among them can be neutralized at the heart of the historical process of totalization." This neutralization is a dialectical movement:

(It) enables us to understand that the ends of human activity are not mysterious entities added on to the act itself; they represent simply the surpassing and the maintaining of the given in an act which goes from the present to the future.

The ends *represent* the dialectical movement of the given and the object aimed at, and comprehension consists in deciphering these representations. But are these ends always clear and distinct? What about "illusory" ends? As a last resort these ciphers have to be read in psychoanalysis. Sartre contends that the time has passed that one can deprive oneself much longer of the "one privileged mediation which permits . . . to pass from general and abstract determinations to particular traits of the single individual":

Psychoanalysis . . . is a method which is primarily concerned with establishing the way in which the child lives his family relations inside a given society.[87]

Recent autobiographical "child-o-grams" in existentialist literature[88]

---

[86] See: *Search,* pp. 158f, for this and the following quotes.
[87] *Search,* p. 61.
[88] For example: J. P. Sartre, *The Words* (Greenwich, Fawcett, 1966).

attest precisely to this point: the relations tying a child into its family context are taken throughout as representations of certain social ends which are deciphered by the author in retrospect. The total absence in these reports of references to free and ambivalent play, of playing-at-themes in purposeless interactions, is symptomatic for these interpretations.

Apparently, if I may venture a guess in closing this section, existentialism does not dare to admit that intersubjective events may be constitutive for genuine creativity *independent of* the purposive ends of subjective consciousness. For Sartre, creativity has to be tied to a Project, by which man cuts across the social milieu, but nevertheless, it remains *his* cutting across out of his *own* revolt against institutional repressions. Does the dignity of man suffer at all, if genuine creativity is to be tied to the *intersubjective* arisal of incipient events? These events lead to typifications and finally to the arisal of types. Perhaps man's creativity lies in his taking part in mutual playing-at-incipient-events, perhaps it is nothing more than a taking part in the constitution of types, which he leaves behind after formulating them once, since types are necessarily inadequate to grasp fully the social reality.[89]

5.5 Summary

This study of the structure of social inconsistencies and of subsequently arising incipient events was carried out to the point at which a discrimination between major modes of social interaction like play, game, and social action seems to be possible. This discrimination, as I maintained from the beginning of this study, ought to rely on typical differences in the immediate context of social interaction.

Social temporality, as a specific phenomenon of context, has further clarified the notions of social inconsistency and of incipient event. Social inconsistencies are strictly phenomena of context: they occur in typificatory schemes which are "short of types." Incipient events, on the other hand, arise in the "ambivalent margin" between context and situation. They are, so to speak, in a potential state of becoming phenomena of context: they are constitutive for the arisal of social types. The structure of this "ambivalent margin" can be described in terms of abductive processes.

---

[89] Such a notion of creativity is corroborated by a remark of a notable modern mathematician: "Obviously the schematical execution of a given general procedure is (after a few tries) of no special interest to a mathematician. Thus we can state the remarkable fact that by the specifically mathematical achievement of developing a general method, a creative mathematician, so to speak, mathematically depreciates the field he becomes master of by this very method." See: H. Hermes, *Enumerability, Decidability, Computability* (Berlin–Heidelberg–New York, Springer, 1965), p. 2n.

It may also be explained by the differences between "social temporality" and "temporal typifications."

Both temporal phenomena constitute typificatory schemes. In temporal typification, however, which is structured by "phenomenal" or "inner" time, the arising typificatory scheme does *not* unite the situation into a context. Temporal typification structures, for instance, social action in its various aspects of project formation, performance of project and accomplished act. It is a process *not* composed of social inconsistencies; it is marked by a purposeful avoidance of expectable inconsistencies. In other words, the unity of context, which has to prevail if temporal typification is to proceed at all, is maintained by the multitude of typificatory schemes already prevalent in every social situation,[90] but it is not constituted in a project of action.

Social temporality, on the other hand, constitutes a unity of context. It is the temporal dimension of processes which are intrinsically related to social inconsistencies and which are structured by subsequently arising incipient events. All arisal, enlargement or variation of social types starts with incipient events. Hence, playing-at-a-theme, as the mode of social interaction in these processes, is structured by social temporality. Whether or not other modes of social interaction, for instance, play or game, also have this temporal dimension will be studied in the next chapter.

These modes of interaction are to be discriminated by structural differences in their respective contexts, by means of a conceptual frame which has been derived in its *temporal* aspects from two directions. The theory of relevance developed by Aron Gurwitsch gave the major frame for the notions of context and social typification.[91] George H. Mead's theory of the present, which is intricately interwoven with the thought of Charles S. Peirce, determined the direction for formulating the notion of social temporality.

My presentation, I believe, is compatible with *Gurwitsch'* analyses in

[90] Language as an "envelope" of every social interaction is the major source and "store" for these typificatory schemes. See, for instance, the section on "Language and Knowledge in Everyday Life" in: Berger-Luckmann, *Social Construction,* pp. 33–43.

[91] Some major changes follow from applying Gurwitsch' theory of "The Field of Consciousness" to *social* objects. The structure of *social* relevance has been described not merely as reciprocal, indicating relations between that which is given in a situation, but the "reciprocal indicating relations" have been interpreted as having a specific triadic structure. I have to admit that I do not clearly see at present how far this change is consistent with or affects the more detailed analyses of Gurwitsch, which I could not pursue in this study. To name only a few problems: I did not discuss in any detail his studies of "marginal consciousness," of the specific organizations of theme and thematic field, and especially his theory of the "unity by Gestalt-coherence."

respect to the point of major interest in this chapter: the notion of social temporality. For he concludes his own study of temporality:

Phenomenal temporality is not a sufficient condition of relevancy, since relevancy is absent from certain act-structures, whereas phenomenal temporality is involved in all acts and act-structures. Every act of consciousness occurs in phenomenal time and thus is subject to the laws of phenomenal temporality, that is it must necessarily exhibit the essential structure of phenomenal temporality. In this sense, *phenomenal temporality is a necessary condition of every act of consciousness* and of whatever exists in and for consciousness, hence, also of relevancy.[92]

That "phenomenal temporality" is a *necessary* condition for *social* relevance was stated early in our investigation: Relevance in a social situation implies the "interlocking" of the mutual tendings toward some common social object. The intentionality of perceiving social objects has, I assumed and tried subsequently to show, this triadic structure. And this intentionality is, of course, temporally structured by "inner time," by "phenomenal temporality." – But, on the other hand, this temporal dimension is no "sufficient condition of relevancy," since it does not constitute a typificatory scheme uniting the situation into a context. It merely structures "temporal typifications."

Finally, I should state again the differences between the notion of "social temporality" and Mead's theory of the present. The distinction between "temporal typification" and "social temporality" could not have been clarified merely within Mead's theory. Inconsistencies are for Mead eruptions of the situation; events are "natural phenomena"; both are moments in processes of change. But Mead's reflections about the structure of these processes and their "nature" are already so far removed from a naive biologistic evolutionism that they lend themselves immediately to transference into typificatory processes.[93] Hence, Mead's notion of "emergent event" was easily discriminated more sharply: the latter is in an incipient state and induces social temporality, if it arises from an inconsistency in the context and leads to the constitution of a typificatory scheme, which unites the situation into a context.

[92] Gurwitsch, *Field,* p. 347.
[93] This "transference" has its root, again, in Peirce' logic of abduction. It has been developed on the one hand to criticize logical implications of Darwin's and Spencer's theories, but is also basic for the constitution of social types.

CHAPTER 6

SOCIAL INCONSISTENCIES AND
SYMBOLIC TYPES IN PLAY

THEME:

Playing-at-a-theme as the interactional mode of solving social inconsistencies has to be analysed more carefully. For two important social phenomena, anomie and alienation, seem to be related to typificatory processes and especially to the arisal of symbolic types. Three sociological characteristics of play can be distinguished.

One may be tempted to distinguish "play" from "social action" by the differences between social temporality and temporal typification. A reduction of the interactional mode of playing-at-a-theme to the mode of play and of all typified modes of interaction to that of social action would follow. Hence, play would become *the* interactional mode for the arisal of social types and all typical social constructs would be constituted in play. This would be the argument of Caillois, Huizinga and Schiller: play is a total phenomenon at the basis of social life. Furthermore, contrary to the intentions of his work, G. H. Mead's theory of social self would be related by such a reduction to a total theory of play.

The interactional differences between play and social action are obviously not to be clarified by such a simple procedure. The structure of social inconsistencies still has to be studied more closely. A twosided approach will be taken. On the one hand, theoretical notions of play and game ought to be closely related to common-sense phenomena like children's "hide-and-seek" and adolescents' "playing ball." As many empirical examples as necessary will be referred to in this process of concept-formation. On the other hand, social inconsistencies and the interactional mode of playing-at-the-theme already have certain structural characteristics of play which will be studied now more systematically.

I am starting with the last set of problems. They may be grouped under three aspects which seem to be typical also for the interactional mode of play:

1. Clarification of an ambivalent context takes place in mutual playing-at-the-theme. My attempt to clarify the Others' mediate presentations of context occurs with their trying to clarify my mediate presentation of context. This intersubjective process is dependent on typificatory schemes. If it implies, for example, interaction between adult and child, the differences in available types is tremendous. Is it possible to distinguish action from play by a *reduction of available types*?

2. "Coincidence" of the *mediate* presentations of context has not been discussed up to now. The mediate presentation of context is the major determinant of the thematic field, which is supposed to be intersubjectively maintained in the situation. But my mediate presentation of context to my partner and his mediate presentation to me have to "coincide" in some manner, if the thematic field is to be an "invariant" characteristic for the constitution of social types. Hence, I must at least ascertain the limits between which such "coincidence" can be assured. *How are such social limits to be constituted*? Do these limits contribute to a distinction between action and play?

3. Clarification of a diffuse thematic field by interaction implies that *the body* plays some rôle in this process. In which ways is the reduction of types and the positing of social limits related to the body and its physical presence in the situation?

6.1 Reduction of Types in Play and Social Action.

Mutual attempts to clarify a diffuse thematic field presuppose a mutual reduction of relevant types to some common level. Take, for instance, the case of kite-construction studied before.[1] My son was sure I was going to build a kite that would fly. Hence, my mediate presentation of context to him had been perfectly assuring. My son presented the context to me in an equally affirmative manner. I was going to build a kite and I *knew* how to do it. The thematic field was clear. But after the unsuccessful trial-flight, we *both* began to overcome the inconsistency by tentative typifications. Theoretically, there were two possibilities for subsequent interaction in our attempts to typify the situation, though only one was discussed above: either the gap was to become permanent or not. In the first case a total *rupture of the context* ("Nothing works with the Old Man any more these days" and "forget that stupid kid's stuff") or an *avoidance of this specific theme* by "small talk," by some common "fidgeting around" would have followed.[2]

---

[1] See *sect.* 4.52.

[2] Most of the games studied by Berne in his *Games People Play* are such games of avoidance. Permanent gaps, if arising as idiosyncratic behavior patterns, are important origins for neuroses and Berne studies them from this perspective. See *sect.* 1.3.

Actually, however, the *second* case occurred: playing-at-a-theme took place first in typifying the context by the incipient event and then in iteratively separating typical and unique characteristics of the incipient event.

But a *mutual* reduction of types occurs in both cases: *In case of avoidance,* everyone shies away from any theme or type possibly related to the inconsistency. Since the inconsistency cannot be typified and many types could easily turn out to lead to the gap, interaction (if it is not broken off totally) will be restricted to an absolutely safe stock of types: small talk, polite gestures, little jokes, etc. *In case of mutual type construction,* typification of context by the incipient event would be extremely hampered, if one of the participants would "flood" the situation forcefully with ever new and unrelated types.[3]

6.11 A First Characteristic of Play: Reduction of Types in Play

This reduction of types is also a first characteristic of all play. This simple fact is often overlooked in studies of play and quite frequently the authors refer to most complex interpretations instead. For instance, Huizinga introduces the following example to support his theory of reality: a father meets his four-year-old son, who is playing train; he kisses his son and the boy reprimands him for kissing the locomotive, since otherwise the coaches might think it were not real.[4] Huizinga's assumption that the very young child *knows he is merely acting out of fun* and his conclusion that there is a feeling of *inferiority in play* is not so immediately evident as he assumes. Huizinga presupposes with this most complex interpretation that the child already has a fully developed social self which allows him to set himself apart from and over against his object of play. One could as well argue in opposition to Huizinga that the child identifies himself with the locomotive

---

[3] The notion of "flooding out" is introduced by Goffman similarly: "Transformation rules of an encounter oblige the participant to withhold his attention and concern from many potential matters of consideration. ... The matter in which he has been affecting disinvolvement suddenly becomes too much for him and he collapses ... he floods out." (*Encounters,* p. 55) Only, I am enlarging Goffman's notion: One may "flood" a situation, also, with a most eloquent "sea of words." Every teacher, preacher and politician often uses that device.

[4] Huizinga, *Homo Ludens,* (p. 15). – Roger Caillois, too, rejects this interpretation of Huizinga: "Das Kind, das Eisenbahn spielt, kann sehr gut den Kuß seines Vaters zurückweisen und ihm klar machen, daß man eine Lokomotive nicht küßt; es will ihm deshalb keineswegs vortäuschen, eine wirkliche Lokomotive zu sein." (*Die Spiele und die Menschen,* p. 30) – Caillois, on the other hand, takes this example as typical for a mode of playing he calls "mimicry." But Caillois does not discriminate between "being a locomotive" (a perceptual type) and "riding a locomotive" (a social type constituted in a context of interaction).

in playing, still better, that the child, being submerged in his context, differentiates and typifies the total context in terms of the thematic field "riding-a-locomotive."

But one can avoid all these complications. Instead, this small example shows a most significant trait of all play. Playing "train" allows only for certain typical actions and types. Whoever saw his father kissing a train? Such an interactional relation upsets the permissable types and creates an inconsistency. The "no-nonsense" attitude, or even the "seriousness" of the child in playing is due to his purposefully reducing the stock of relevant types. This reduction of types may also be found in all theories of play. Notions like play having its own "spatial boundaries," play being restricted to a "field of play" and being "separated from real life" all refer to its limitation as to permissable types.

From football and tennis to the small boy's playing train or hide-seek, the social types employed in these activities are extremely limited. The two most influential theories of play, those by Huizinga and Caillois, both present definitions of play, in which the reduction of types is acknowledged by way of negative definitions: play is "not really meant that way," it is "outside" of real life and entails no practical interests or advantages (Huizinga); play cannot be forced upon the player, it is not related to "ordinary activities," it has no determinate outcome and is economically unproductive (Caillois). And one of the first inceptions of theories of play already recognized its reductive element. Schiller insisted that man should only play with beauty, and if he has to deal with beauty, he only should play with it. Aesthetic notions of social and political life, aristocratic conceptions of communal existence have freely taken their legitimation from these reductive constituents of play every time, when play has been postulated as a total social phenomenon.

6.12 Reduction of Types as "Entlastung" in Social Action

But reduction of types, as has been shown above, must also prevail in all playing-at-a-theme. Since we cannot accept play as a total social phenomenon, i.e., since play is not a *necessary* mode of interaction in the incipient phase of the arisal of types, the reduction of types cannot be an exclusive, sufficient characteristic of play. Every typified social interaction between typical partners in typical situations can proceed along typical lines of expectations only, if "permissable" action types and personal types are also strictly limited. Every interaction within social roles, for instance, presupposes such a reduction of types. The general custom among sociologists to speak of "roles being played between role-partners" reminds one especially of this reduction. Reciprocal roles are enacted with relative ease, where interaction is limited to a "safe" stock of relevant social types. The reduction of types in all social interaction is a purposive and necessary device to avoid the arisal of social inconsistencies. Berger-Luckmann recognized the same problem and have taken some notions from Arnold Gehlen's anthropological theories to explain the reduction of types in processes of institutionalization.[5] Institutionalization, in their terminology, is a most elementary intersubjective process and occurs "whenever there is a reciprocal typification of habitualized actions by types of actors." Thus, reciprocal typifications *presuppose* "habitualization," in which the multitude of possible lines of actions is narrowed down, in which man is freed "from the burden of all those decisions." As they put it:

The background of habitualized activity opens up a foreground for deliberation and innovation.

Producing a background of habitualized activity is considered to be an anthropological necessity, grounded "in man's undirected instinctual structure": habitualization provides an "Entlastung" of man's "Handlungskreis";[6] it produces a stable environment for the "inherent instability of the human organism."

Questions concerning this line of argument arise, I contend, in respect to the "anthropological necessity," to the supposed cogent causality of these processes. Undoubtedly, the rôle of the body in typificatory processes[7] leads to many aspects, which Gehlen has described excellently within the conceptual frame of "Entlastung" in man's action-circuit. But does this conceptual frame have an anthropological basis, which precedes reciprocal typifications in social interaction? Are *social* phenomena, which are considered to be "anthropologically necessary," not necessarily already *typical* phenomena? In other words, is it possible to conceive of social necessity prior to or independent of the arisal of social types? At least within the conceptual frame developed up to this point, the question cannot be affirm-

---

[5] *Social Construction*, pp. 50f.
[6] A very concise presentation of the notions of "Entlastung" (unburdening, facilitation) and "Handlungskreis" (action-circuit) may be found in A. Gehlen, *Die Seele im technischen Zeitalter* (Hamburg, Rowohlt, 1957) pp. 17f. Gehlen developed these theories first in *Der Mensch* (Bonn, Athenäum, 6. Aufl., 1958). The first edition is from 1940. – Heidegger (1927) introduced the notion of "Entlastung" before Gehlen in a similar sense: "Das Man *entlastet* . . . das jeweilige Dasein in seiner Alltäglichkeit." See: Martin Heidegger, *Sein und Zeit* (Tübingen, Niemeyer, 10. Aufl., 1963), § 27, esp. p. 127.
[7] See *sect.* 6.3.

ed. On the abductive level of type-formation, no "necessary consequences" for social interaction may arise or have to be presupposed. Social necessity is posited only with the arisal of typificatory schemes, i.e. in processes of typifying the context by means of incipient events.

I have purposefully "blown up" a single argument in order to be able to state the present problem more clearly: It appears to be necessary to distinguish more sharply between the processes of "habitualization" and "institutionalization" than Berger-Luckmann were interested in doing at that time. Their reliance on Gehlen's anthropological theories has been stressed beyond their theoretical intentions and their dependency on Schütz' theories of relevance and social type has been overly neglected.

For, Schütz and certainly also Berger and Luckmann consider social relevances and typificatory processes to be at the basis of the construction of social reality. But Gehlen considered man's active appropriation and final dominance of a world, in which he has been thrown inadequately equipped with an altogether "undirected instinctual structure," to be based on *play*.

(Der Mensch) schafft eigentätig um sich einen "Leerraum" einer übersehbaren, andeutungsreichen und dahingestellt-verfügbaren Welt. Er baut sich diese auf im Zuge der Erfahrungsbewegungen, in denen ohne Triebdruck und Trieberfüllung – "spielend" – die Dinge in Erfahrung gezogen, kommunikativ aufgeschlossen und abgestellt werden, bis endlich das Auge allein eine geordnete, neutralisierte Welt beherrscht.[8]

Gehlen takes, like Schiller und Huizinga, play as a *total* social phenomenon, which is constitutive for social life *per se*. The distinction between play and the "seriousness" of social actions is then later introduced by means of the notion of "discipline" (Zucht):

Es ist nicht . . . die bloße Funktionslust der Bewegungen, die das Spiel ausmacht, sondern zuletzt das Sicherfahren der Grundeigenschaften der menschlichen Antriebsstruktur, die überschüssig, plastisch, weltoffen und kommunikativ ist, übrigens aus denselben Gründen dann der Z u c h t bedarf, wenn ernste Aufgaben herantreten.[9]

Gehlen's theory of play, I contend, deserves criticism because he does not discriminate sufficiently different interactional modes from play: the ambivalent mode of playing-at-a-theme, though described in detail,[10] is called "Spiel" together with the play of animals, children, and adults.

---

[8] Gehlen, *Mensch,* p. 49.
[9] *op. cit.,* p. 223.
[10] *op. cit.,* pp. 220ff, for instance, and at various other places.

Gehlen's notion of play as *the* vehicle in which man's "undirected instinctual structure" may come to terms with his world, is, I contend, not implied in Berger-Luckmann's reliance on Gehlen. They refer to Gehlen's theory of institutionalization which I would propose separating more clearly from processes of habitualization. Man's "undirected instinctual structure" determines significantly man's notion of body and thus also all typificatory schemes.[11] But producing a "background of habitualized activity" takes place, I contend, with the constitution of social types. The arisal of social types implies in its very process a "habitualization" of social interaction. Action patterns constituted in those processes reduce the permissable types effectively to those of the relevant typificatory scheme. "Entlastung" is a constitutive phenomenon in these processes, but its most significant aspect is a reduction of types.

6.2 Social Limits and Symbolic Types in Play

The processes of habitualization and institutionalization in Berger-Luckmann's theory cannot simply be separated, however, by equating the former with the formation of social types. For both processes are also supposed to have a nomic and identity-preserving aspect for the individual living within social institutions, "stabilizing" so-to-speak his "undirected instinctual structure." This peculiar socio-psychological impact of social institutions both regulates and protects the human self. This is, however, a quite original interpretation of the phenomenon of "Entlastung": Gehlen's notion, on the other hand, is closely dependent on Heidegger's ontology and on Schiller's theory of play. Its similarity with Berger-Luckmann's conception does not go very far.

This becomes even more apparent, if Schiller's notion of play is examined closely. For "undirected instincts" in human nature have already been assumed by Schiller, for whom "culture" was then to institute the limits balancing and directing man's natural impulses.

Briefly, this is Schiller's argument:[12] A formal and a natural impulse are constitutive for man's "dual nature."[13] Man tends to exceed all bounds and limitation, if one or the other of these impulses becomes dominant. "Über diese zu wachen und einem jedem dieser Triebe seine Grenze zu sichern, ist die Aufgabe der Kultur."[14] The human condition (Zustand), in which

---

[11] See *sect.* 6.31.
[12] First published in 1795. I quote: Friedrich Schiller, *Über die ästhetische Erziehung des Menschen in einer Reihe von Briefen* in: *Schiller's sämtlichen Werke* (Stuttgart, Cotta, 1889) vol. 12.
[13] For details: see *Ästhetische Briefe*, 15th letter, ("Seine doppelte Natur").
[14] *op. cit.*, 13th letter.

culture can realize the essential "task" and man can unfold his dual nature, is play. Only in play is human progress and change possible: Man may become a Self *and* man may become an Other. *Mutual limits come about* which save man from being a "Zero" *(eine Null),* from becoming a non-entity. In other words, play enables man to avoid both total isolation as well as total loss of identity.

The subjectivistic implications of this theory of play are evident. The arisal of social limits in play is to take place in a human condition, which is *totally* dependent on man's decision to play or not to play. *Durkheim* was the first sociologist to recognize clearly the consequences of raising such a notion to a regulative principle of social life. His concept of anomie was to relate man's "dual nature" [15] intrinsically to the potential degeneration and destruction of sociality. Man as a "homo duplex" may lapse into mere egoism, into an a-social Self, or he may become merely a social representation in a state of extreme altruism. Only by an all important voluntary effort he *may be able* to save his precarious dual nature. But this voluntary effort is *structurally* impossible, where either societal functions, originating in organic solidarity, or where individual drives, for instance toward individual totality, forestall voluntaristic cooperation: in both cases a state of anomie occurs. Durkheim – and this is the important conceptual link to Schiller's theory of play – describes the state of anomie also in terms of "limits."

Anomie occurs in society as a whole in the form of an unlimited, excessive change of integrative societal functions.[16] It manifests itself in the individual's sphere in the form of excessive drives beyond all limits set by the collective conscience: "Qu'elle soit progressive ou régressive, l'anomie, en affranchissant les *besoins de la mesure qui convient,* ouvre la porte aux illusions et, par suite, aux déceptions." [17] And also on the methodological level, the notion of limit holds a very central place:

---

[15] Durkheim's "homo duplex" is an essentially social notion, while Schiller adhered to an individualistic concept of "human totality" characteristic for German idealism. The differences are best seen in Durkheim's passionate defense of his anthropological position: "We distrust those excessively mobile talents that lend themselves equally to all uses, refusing to choose a special role and keep to it. We disapprove of those men whose unique care is to organize and develop all their faculties, but without making any definite use of them, and without sacrificing any of them, as if each man were sufficient unto himself, and constituted an independent world. The praiseworthy man of former times is only a diletante to us, and we refuse to give diletantism any moral value; we rather see perfection in the man seeking, not to be complete, but to produce."
Emile Durkheim, *The Division of Labor in Society* (New York, Macmillan, 1933), p. 42. – For a morally less "engaged" statement see Durkheim's "Individual and Collective Representations" in: *Sociology and Philosophy* (Glencoe, Free Press, 1953).

[16] *Division of Labor,* preface to the 2nd edition.

[17] E. Durkheim, *Le Suicide* (Paris, Presse Univ. de France, 1960), p. 322.

Our method has ... the advantage of regulating action at the same time as thought. If the social values are not subjects of observation, but can be and must be determined by a sort of mental calculus, *no limit,* so to speak, can be set for the free inventions of the imagination in search of the best. For how may we assign to perfection a *limit?* It escapes all limitations, by definition. The goal of humanity recedes into infinity, discouraging some by its remoteness and arousing others who, in order to draw a little nearer to it, quicken the pace and plunge into revolutions.[18]

The limitation of man's individualistic drives and the structural conditions for positing such social limits are seen by Durkheim in close relation to man's general approach to social phenomena. For anomie may arise, as the last quote reveals, also from sociological methods, which become detached of and independent from the objects they are intent to study. In other words: If social objects are constituted in social interaction, their tools of study have to be questioned, if they do not distort their constitutive interactional context. For the social context is always precarious and subject to imminent anomie. Only definite social limits, restricting the tools of analysis and their range of validity, as well as delimiting the destructive subjectivism of man (who has to cooperate in order to constitute social objects at all), may shield man from "anomic terror." Durkheim's main theme, which runs through all his work, may be stated in one sentence: Though the individual is not capable of constructing a social state on his own, he is very well able to destroy it.

6.21 Anomie, Social Relevance, and Symbolic Types

I contend that one should reject Gehlen's notion of play and its subsequent implications for his theory of "Entlastung" in favor of the Berger-Luckmann interpretation of this theory in processes of habitualization and institutionalization: it would otherwise lead to a paradox. For, *on the one hand,* Gehlen's notion of play is in its main aspects in accordance with Schiller's theory. That is to say, play as a total social phenomenon rests in and constitutes the individual's realm of *subjective* decisions leading to an autonomous existence. Durkheim has shown (and I assume here, as do Berger and Luckmann, that this theory of anomie is of undisputable significance for social studies) that social anomie is an imminent consequence of these a-social notions of individual autonomy, which can be countered only by *social limits* and boundaries situated in the social context. *On the other hand,* Schiller argues that it is precisely in play that social limits arise

---

[18] E. Durkheim, *The Rules of Sociological Methods* (Chicago, Univ. of Chicago Press, 1938), p. 74.

which are able to contain the otherwise destructive "natural impulses" of man.

The paradox is resolved if one abandons the notion of play as a total social phenomenon. The processes of habitualization and institutionalization must be placed directly in the context of the formation of social types. The phenomenon of anomie seems to be immediately linked with the problem of maintaining social relevance in a situation.

Social relevance can be constituted and maintained in its triadic structure only by an intersubjective effort. But even an individual refusal or incapability to take into one's own tending toward the Other also his tending toward oneself leads to a disruption of social relevance. This fundamental asymmetry of the perspectives of relevance limits the individual's part in constructing social reality, while it is also the source of the extremely destructive power of man's subjectivism. Durkheim saw clearly that even the *voluntary* effort to limit this destructive power may become structurally impossible.

Let me state the problem more precisely. In a state of anomie, socially significant structural contours become blurred, vague, and finally, entirely elusive. Mutual clarification of thematic fields and reciprocal constitution of types and social objects, which had been possible before, no longer succeed. The problem is reminiscent of the arisal of inconsistencies in those cases, where a permanent gap separates the mediate and immediate presentations of context. But there is an important difference: While inconsistencies are intersubjectively constituted and presuppose relevance and a common thematic field, in the case of anomie the situation cannot be united into a context. There is no common relevance. The mediate presentations of context do not "coincide." This implies that the typificatory schemes have "lost" their most potent and essential function: their relations no longer tie a theme to the situation.[19]

Berger-Luckmann have dealt with the same problem under the heading "legitimations of institutional processes."[20] Their main argument is: "first order objectivations," constituted in habitualizations and institutionalizations of immediate social interaction, must be made "objectively available and subjectively plausible"; this takes place in "second order objectivations" in which legitimating complexes of meaning are produced, these legitimations serve to integrate institutional processes and make them plausible, while at the same time the individual biography of the actor is being en-

---

[19] A sharp distinction can already be drawn here between "anomie" and "reification": The latter was described as a state ,in which relations between types (the typificatory scheme) are taken as types themselves. See *sect.* 5.4.

[20] *Social Construction*, pp. 85–96.

dowed with a socially coherent meaning. Legitimation takes place on four levels: 1. Incipient legitimation occurs with the acquisition of the vernacular of one's own social group. 2. Theoretical propositions, tales and proverbs determine the next level. 3. Consistent theories of social intercourse and 4. symbolic universes, which encompass the entire institutional order into a symbolic totality, are the final levels of legitimation. The nomic and identity-preserving rôle of second order objectivations is most important:

> The legitimation of the institutional order is also faced with the ongoing necessity of keeping chaos at bay. *All* social reality is precarious. *All* societies are constructions in the face of chaos. The constant possibility of *anomic terror* is actualized whenever the legitimations that obscure the precariousness are threatened or collapse.[21]

The institutional order, which is supported by processes of legitimation, "represents a shield against terror. To be anomic, therefore, means to be deprived of this shield." But how does this shield come about? How is anomie to be avoided? Despite their lucid description of the four levels of legitimation, which is based upon, but goes far beyond, Durkheim's notion of collective representation and Schütz' theory of finite provinces of meaning, Berger-Luckmann do not analyse further the constitution of "second order objectivations" in their relation to processes of typification. But they supply some valuable hints: 1. Legitimations are *representations;* i.e. they are assigned a symbolic or at least a semi-symbolic status. 2. The all-encompassing symbolic universe provides the "delineation of social reality" and sets "the *limits* of what is relevant in terms of social interaction."[22] 3. These delimitations are drawn by assigning rank and status to *specific types* of social objects. 4. The four levels of legitimation exhibit an *increasing degree of reification:* the typificatory schemes of the vernacular ("That's the way things are done") become rather set in proverbial form ("You can't have your cake and eat it, too."), they indeed become "sheltering canopies" in the definiteness of theories ("Act as if your acting is to establish a general law of nature") and turn sacred within symbolic universes ("Thou shalt not kill.")

The problem has to be reduced to a narrower scope here. Neither the boundaries of the social world, the delimitation of the relevant social reality as a whole, nor the continuous "maintenance" of a symbolic universe concerns us at present. But the peculiar structural conditions for anomie can hardly be understood without relating them to the *nomic,* to the relevance-

[21] *Social Construction,* p. 96.
[22] *op. cit.,* p. 94.

preserving character of specific processes of typification. Typificatory schemes, which tie a theme to a specific situation, inducing its unification into a relevant context, serve such "nomic" purpose. This process, as was shown in detail before, is abductive: the constitution of types and social objects starts with a given theme; type and object have to be brought about as antecedent to the theme. This general process has to be reviewed now under the specific conditions which, as Berger-Luckmann have pointed out, are constitutive for nomic legitimating processes: Specific types arise within typificatory schemes of increasing degrees of reification; they set limits for social interaction especially on the abductive level, i.e., they delimit the range of relevance; they are taken as representations, i.e., depending on the degree to which these typificatory schemes are reified, they assume a more-or-less symbolic status. For the sake of convenience only, I want to call the types arising in the processes described above "symbolic types." [23]

6.22 The Symbolic Type of the Fool

Symbolic types arise in nomic legitimating processes, in which social relevance is threatened. Unity of context "normally" comes about through some typificatory scheme: it is maintained, for instance, by a dominant team or typical role partners. Ambivalent relevance implies, therefore, that typificatory schemes "fail" to maintain unity of context. The situation is threatened, as Berger-Luckmann call it, by "anomic terror." Extrapolating their description of nomic legitimating processes, we may say that symbolic types are constituted to maintain relevance as types. Symbolic types come about in precarious situations and "tie" the mediate presentations of context together so that a common thematic field can be maintained.

Where typificatory schemes fail to maintain relevance in a situation, there cannot be any reciprocal role-typification in role-interaction. *Symbolic types are therefore typified formations "below" the level of social roles.* In other words, symbolic types like strangers, playboys, fools, villains, heroes and the like have a twofold characteristic: 1. They cannot be assigned a relative social prestige, and 2. they do not fit into the usual descriptions of a social role.[24] The latter may be explained also by the highly individual

---

[23] The notion of "symbolic type" shall neither suggest nor presuppose that these types are symbols in the usual meaning of this term.

[24] In contradistinction, for instance, to Parsons' notion of social role, I am stressing here the *necessary* role-condition of *ongoing reciprocal typifications* in role-formation. Social roles are correlative formations (student-teacher, father–son, etc.) coming about in face-to-face situations of interaction. The fool, for instance, has as a correlate the "non-fool," but that distinction is based on a formal, predicative judgement (like "non-tree") and induces merely an abstract, dual partition of the total situation. See *chap.* 8.

character ascription in symbolic types, which seems paradoxically to be accompanied by extremely stereotyped action-patterns; the former characteristic of a missing *relative* status points at a very interesting function of these types: they serve as social limits. The symbolic type of "fool" may help to make these characteristics more transparent.[25]

The fool as a personal type. Both an excess or a deficiency of "normally" anticipated conduct may lead to the typification of "fool." Conversely, the type of fool may serve to define and enforce the propriety of "normal" conduct. The most popular children's books of a social group contain a wealth of such types.[26] Excess of pride or a lack of competence, an extreme impulsiveness as well as submissiveness, the reckless daredevil, the unpredictable maverick, the battered dignity of a hobo: these are some typical attributes of a fool.

The process of character ascription to a fool becomes transparent, if one observes that my own tending toward a fool has to imply also the Other's tending toward the fool and toward myself. I am tending toward a fool as a socially relevant personal type by rejecting the possibility of being perceived by Others as a fool, too. Thus, the typificatory scheme encompassing the multitude of relations between fool, myself and all others in the situation is intentionally reified: mutual relations are pre-typified and do not arise ad hoc in face-to-face typifications.

The fool as an action type. The typificatory schemes are highly reified in situations, where interaction with a fool takes place. Klapp described this process:

"The creation of a fool is accomplished by ascribing characteristics of the fool to a person through situations which 'make a fool'. . . . Fool-making situations are so constantly presented to the average person that he may by unable to avoid occasionally falling into the role.[27]

---

[25] I quote in the following a study by Orrin E. Klapp, *The Fool as a Social Type*, Am.J. of Soc., 55, 1949, pp. 157—162. Klapp called "social type" what I have termed "symbolic type" above, since my usage of the term "social type" is much wider. – Klapp later tried to extend his observations into a theoretical frame calling his approach "Neo-Durkheimian," but his elaborations of the theory of collective representations do not go far beyond Durkheim. See: O. E. Klapp, *Symbolic Leaders, Public Dramas and Public Men* (Chicago, 1964).

[26] See, for instance, *English:* Raymond Briggs, *The Mother Goose Treasury* (New York, Coward–McCann, 1966); Hank Ketcham, *Dennis the Menace* (New York, Fawcett, 1966). *German:* Heinrich Hoffmann, *Der Struwwelpeter* (Stuttgart, Loewe, no date); Wilhelm Busch, *Max und Moritz* (München, Braun-Schneider, 1965). *Swedish:* Astrid Lindgren, *Pippi Langstrumpf* (Hamburg, Oetinger, 1968).

[27] *Fool as Social Type*, pp. 158f.

The fool's conduct is strictly patterned in fool-making situations. In other words, a specific theme (like "the-dignity-of-this-court-requires-your-getting-a-hair-cut") will unite the situation into a context imposing inescapably rigid action patterns.

The latter day revolutionary student, for instance, who intentionally invokes a fool-making situation by defiantly urinating in front of the judge in court, exposes by his antics the structure of social controls dominant in that situation. As social roles (judge-defendant) "degenerate" into reified symbolic types (like "tyrant" or "fool"), reciprocal typifications in role-interaction no longer operate; relevance structure and context (the so-called "definition of the situation") are dominated by the action patterns of the fool.[28] This phenomenon will be studied further in the chapter on team-audience formations.

The fool as a symbolic type. The highly reified typificatory schemes of fool-enactment posit social limits for all interaction, which become represented in specific stereotypes ascribed to the fool. "The fool," says O. Klapp, "represents values which are rejected by the group: causes that are lost, incompetence, failure and fiasco." Klapp closes this paper with the remark:

Chiefly, the social type of the fool functions as a device of status reduction and social control. Reduction of persons through the fool's rôle is a continuous collective process of status adjustment. . . . Fool ascription acts as a purging device, eliminating upstarts, pretenders, and incompetents from positions of influence.[29]

However, one ought to add that this "purging device" may also serve to "reduce" the fool's audience.

The limit-character of a symbolic type still has to be worked out more clearly. Why is a fool on the one hand depreciated in status and on the other hand socially valued? Depreciation of the fool constitutes him as a social "purging device." But how does this device work?

My tending toward the fool and toward anyone else in the fool's audience implies a deliberate attempt to reduce the Others' tending toward me: the Others are not to tend toward me as if I were a fool myself. Since, however, I cannot control the Others' tending toward me, the "safest" way is to totally typify their tending toward me and – for their own sake – also my tending toward them. Thus, all mutual relations within "the audience of the fool," all mutual tendings toward each other are reified: these relations are considered to be types themselves; interaction is totally typified. The indi-

---

[28] More often, however, and to the delight of the defiant student, the "judge" turns "tyrant" and takes upon himself the task of imposing a reified action pattern upon the situation.

[29] *Fool as Social Type,* p. 162.

vidual being pushed into the rôle of fool is alienated: the "unity of the producing of types and the types already produced is broken."[30] The perspectives of relevance have been stereotyped insofar that they exclude any reconstitution and reemergence of incipient events possibly leading up to this type for anyone within the fool's audience.

The symbolic type of a fool *determines* in its typicality my tending toward him, the tending of a typical Other toward him and toward a typified Me.[31] In this situation, social relevance does not simply come about in an unrestrained interlocking of the triadic perspectives of relevance. *Social relevance is "limited" by the symbolic type.* This limiting property induces, on the other hand, the social appreciation of the fool: Every delimitation of social relevance and every reduction of possibly relevant types unburdens the process of social interaction. An "Entlastungseffekt" occurs, if a symbolic type like a fool is once socially defined. The reification of some social relations in enactment of fool-creating situations serves, so-to-speak, to "de-reify" all other social interaction within the fool's audience. The audience gains a certain "tolerance" in interaction. Its relations appear to be less typified, appear to be merged with expressive gestures and bodily movements. The resulting ease and vagueness of social interaction can unfold on the latent background of symbolic types, which delimit the range of relevance.

6.23 Social Limits: Anomie and Alienation

Though the relations in a fool-making situation are reified, still, the constitution of this symbolic type occurs in mutual playing-at-the-theme. The symbolic type serves to legitimate the contextual order and delimits by way of its reified status the interactional realm of relevance. Hence, one may conclude: *Enactment of a symbolic type posits social limits.* This generalization may be further supported by studies of other symbolic types like heroes or villains,[32] rebels,[33] playboys,[34] or strangers.[35]

---

[30] See *sect.* 5.4.
[31] Compare this statement with an earlier formulation in *sect.* 3.0: In case of a typical project, the reciprocal tendings are "indicated," in case of a symbolic type they are "determined," i.e., from the outset reified.
[32] See Klapp, *Symbolic Leaders.*
[33] In Albert Camus' social philosophy the symbolic type of "rebel" holds a central place. A rebel is a man "who says no, but whose refusal does not imply a renunciation. ... He confronts an order of things ... with the insistence on a kind of right not to be oppressed beyond the limit that he can tolerate." (Camus, *The Rebel*, p. 13). The rebel's action is not egoistic and is not based on resentment: "When he rebels, a man identifies himself with other men and surpasses himself." (p. 17) The symbolic and representative

The compatibility of this notion of "social limits" with the earlier definition of anomie still has to be shown. In a state of anomie, some "structural condition" leads to a dissolution of socially significant contours. Durkheim suggested describing this "structural condition" by using the notion of limits: unlimited structural change leads to anomie. The "structural conditions" referred to were linked earlier to the notion of context: In an anomic state, the situation cannot be united into a relevant context; i.e., arising typificatory schemes cannot tie a theme to the situation any more. Apparently those themes are especially significant here, which posit social limits, i.e., themes related to symbolic types. Where the enactment of symbolic types is hindered, social limits do not come about and anomie is the consequence. Two closely related aspects of this phenomenon must be seen: 1. some structural condition may hinder the constitution of a symbolic type; 2. some individual incapability may prevent its enactment. The locus of this whole process is the abductive level of type formation, the level, on which relevance and its triadic perspectives come about.

The differences between alienation and anomie may now be drawn clearly. In a state of *alienation,* "the unity of the producing of types and the types already produced is broken"; the *abductive level is totally separated* from the realm of interaction which proceeds along completely typified lines and makes the arisal of incipient events and of social temporality impossible. Alienation may have a constructive function as, for instance, in the process of constituting symbolic types. It is always at least a latent situational phenomenon and can always be overcome. *Anomie,* on the other hand, signifies a *destruction of the abductive level.* Type formation and enactment of symbolic types do not succeed. There are not only permanent gaps in the context, but the mediate and immediate presentations of context are so much apart that they "atomize" the situation into total incoherence.[36]

character of rebellion leads Camus to an interesting notion of intersubjectivity which culminates in the brilliant phrase: "I rebel – therefore we exist." (p. 22)

[34] In recent years, magazines, posters, clubs and the like have succeeded in creating the symbolic types of "playboy" and "bunny." Whereas the symbolic type of playboy remains relatively close to the socially approved male-role, the "bunny" exhibits a strong "degeneration" of the female-role to a symbolic type. This becomes most obvious, for instance, in the totally reified patterns of a "bunny-calender." The symbolic type of "bunny" serves, of course, to delineate by contrast the otherwise rather vague contours of socially relevant masculinity, which – according to this argument – is much more threatened than the female-role.

[35] See, for example A. Schütz, *The Stranger,* in: *Coll. Pap.,* vol. 2, pp. 91—105, and his references to the extensive literature on this subject.

[36] At present, I cannot pursue this problem of "incoherence of the situation." I must

6.24 Play and Symbolic Types (Second Characteristic of Play)

The most interesting question as to the nomic rôle of play can be raised now: Do social limits arise in play? In other words, does the enactment of symbolic types take place in play? Is the constitution of symbolic types perhaps limited to play?

Play and game are for G. H. Mead distinct forms of social interaction, typical for two distinct phases in the development of a social self. While "play" is that earlier stage in which "the individual's self is constituted simply by an organization of the *particular* attitudes of other individuals toward one another," in "game" the individual self finds a more definite formation "by an organisation of the *social* attitudes of the generalized other or the social group as a whole to which the belongs." [37]

Clearly, Mead introduces the notions of "play" and "game" as labels for distinct phases in the genesis of a social self:

The child is continually acting as a parent, a teacher, a preacher, a grocery man, a policeman, a pirate or an Indian. . . . The child is continually exciting in himself the responses to his own social acts. In his infant despendence upon the responses of others to his own social stimuli, he is particularly sensitive to this relation. Having in his own nature the beginning of the parental response, he calls it out by his own appeals.[38]

As mentioned before,[39] Mead understood "nature" as a process which "proceeds by reconstruction in the presence of conflicts." "Having in his own nature the beginning of the parental response" is called by Mead elsewhere and in more detail "the internalization and inner dramatization, by the individual, of the external conversation of significant gestures which constitutes his chief mode of interaction with other individuals." [40] The child dramatically enacts the acquired social types of parent or teacher, of pirate or Indian.

But is Mead correct in limiting play only to an early phase in the child's development? I contend, one can safely generalize Mead's notion that a child's "infant dependence upon the responses of others to his own social stimuli" stimulates the child's play. This "dependence upon the responses of

turn back to the phenomena of play and their *nomic* role in the constitution of symbolic types.

[37] G. H. Mead, *Mind*, p. 158.
[38] G. H. Mead, *Present*, p. 186. – Mead's notion of game will be studied later. See *chap.* 7.
[39] Compare *sect.* 5.3.
[40] *Mind*, p. 173.

others" may be explained as an inherent characteristic of the constitution of *all* social types: social types refer to the triadic perspectives of relevance constitutive for these types; man's "dependence upon the responses of others" implies the triadic structure of man's tending toward social phenomena. With such a generalization of Mead's notion of play, his rather questionable equating of "primitive men"[41] and children loses its discriminative aspect: We are all children depending on what kind of inconsistencies arise in front of us.[42]

The reifications in children's play may be shown in a typical example. Quite frequently, one may observe that a child "plays mother" and "serves supper" – on completely empty plates. Is this play an "imaginative conduct" with "imaginary companions," as G. H. Mead would describe it? Or does the child even exercise in this play its imaginative power? [43] Or is the child, as Huizinga believes, acting just out of fun, while being fully aware that the "reality" is something quite different from the present situation? [44] One may argue any of these interpretations just so far; they all miss a significant point for a sociological understanding of this example: "peas being served" and "potatoes being taken" are *social* types constituted in a context of interaction; they are quite different from the *perceptual* types of "peas" or "potatoes." [45] In play, these social types are reified to such a degree that

---

[41] "They are children crying in the night." *Present,* p. 187.
[42] *Mind,* p. 370.
[43] Karl Groos, *Die Spiele der Menschen* (Jena, Fischer, 1899), p. 168.
[44] *Homo Ludens,* p. 15.
[45] *Preyer* already explained this play (drinking from an empty cup) by the child's diffuse concepts, by "an incapability to unite constant characters into distinctly limited concepts." He sought the origin of such play in a confusion between immediate perceptions and the memory of similar situations: "Diese Erinnerungsbilder werden förmlich substanziirt, wie die Hallucinationen der Verrückten, weil die sinnlichen Eindrücke dem werdenden Gehirn sich unmittelbar, ohne Reflexion, einprägen, daher die Erinnerungsbilder derselben von den Wahrnehmungen selbst, ihrer Frische wegen, nicht immer sicher unterschieden werden können."

This interpretation is questionable. Preyer admits (a few sentences later) that his explanation is only partly consistent with the general psychogenesis of the child. "Drinking-from-an-empty-cup" is preceded by plays which already require a more rigorous separation of immediate perceptions and memory: "Das Versteckspielen . . . bildet dagegen schon einen intellectuellen Fortschritt. Denn das Wiedererkennen eines bestimmten Gegenstandes unter ganz veränderten äusseren Umständen erfordert eine starke Abstraction vom unmittelbar Wahrgenommenen." The first playing of hide-and-seek was observed by Preyer about 6 months *before* the child started to play with empty cups. If Preyer's opinion were correct that immediate perceptions and memories are confused in these plays, one could not expect to find the high coordination between speech and action in this phase of the child's development.

Rather, I contend, immediate perceptions and social contours are in conflict here. Preyer's careful "book-keeping" about the development of his children supports this

they may even stand for perceptual objects themselves: they are representations. What is being "learned" here by the child is only in the very end an iterative approximation of the social to the perceptual reality, but at the outset it is an invoking of the interactional context constitutive for these social types. Said more simply: the child "learns" how to form projects for social action, he enacts in his play sequences of interaction, which will be constitutive for typificatory schemes of projects.[46]

Symbolic types *represent* a certain state of the situation, the relations in which are totally typified and taken as types themselves. Enactment of a symbolic type posits social limits. The boy, who is riding his train, or the girl, who is serving supper, are alienated in a specific sense: for certain social types, i.e., for the symbolic types of their play, the unity of the producing of these types and the types already produced is broken.[47] An ongoing reconstruction of symbolic types cannot occur, while typical sequences of interaction are constantly arising, being enacted and typified. "Riding a locomotive" or "serving supper" are reified, while the "discharge of passengers" and the "fueling of the engine" are enacted and typified similar to the "washing of vegetables" and the "cutting of meat" by the young girl preparing her dinner. Until these latter sequences of interaction can be typified and become part of a typificatory scheme, *symbolic types have to maintain relevance* in the situation. As soon as a certain "completeness" or "closure" of the typificatory scheme has been achieved,[48] *relevance may be maintained by a typificatory scheme*. In this phase, symbolic types and play become marginal and are largely replaced by social actions based on the typificatory schemes of projects.

The question remains: Is enactment and constitution of symbolic types

---

contention in many instances: 1. The child's notion of body is still vague. The child offered cookies to his own feet; at another occasion, he gave first a lost shoe to his parent and – upon request – tried then to give his foot also. 2. These "givings," as well as the earlier "servings" on empty plates or cups are *social typifications*. The child's tending toward his foot implies the adult's tending toward the child and toward the foot. The adult's "omnipotence" still governs the child's "giving." Yet, the first discriminations between the perspectives of relevance occur exactly in this phase. Simple projects occur and the child insists on "doing-it-alone."

Preyer's rich material is unfortunately only of limited use, since he did not distinguish systematically the child's immediate actions from their social context. See: W. Preyer, *Die Seele des Kindes* (Leipzig, Grieben, 4. Aufl., 1895), p. 238 for the above quotes, and pp. 413–445 for the chronological data.

[46] See *sect.* 7.2.

[47] It is most interesting for the theory of social roles, in which ways and under which conditions this state of alienation in play does later break up in reciprocal typifications and type-formations in adult role interaction.

[48] See *sect.* 7.3 for the notion of closure.

limited to play? Again, Mead's notion of play may serve as a first guide to an answer. In spite of his unacceptable limitation of play to a sociogenetic phase of the child, Mead would answer affirmatively. Though he speaks of a child's "taking the rôle of particular others" in play, Mead does not assume an enactment of social roles on this level. Only on the level of "game" a formation of social roles occurs and it presupposes the "generalized other." Reciprocal typifications in role-enactment presuppose the generic level of play. For Mead, therefore, social types *in general* arise in play.

The distinction between playing-at-a-theme and play proper may now be drawn clearly. The incipient *constitution of social types* was described earlier as taking place on the abductive level in a mode of interaction called *playing-at-a-theme.* Hence, in a more narrow sense, the *constitution of symbolic types* may be limited, by definition, to *play* as it is properly called in common-sense. *If one is engaged in play, symbolic types are due to arise, and if symbolic types arise in some mode of interaction, some play is going on.*

6.25 Summary: The Nomic Rôle of Play

While reduction of types is not an exclusive characteristic of play, this mode of interaction was defined as the constitutive realm for symbolic types. Enactment of symbolic types establishes social limits. This arisal of symbolic types in play can now immediately be linked to the discussion of anomie. Play has an important nomic rôle in processes of habitualization and institutionalization.[49] By positing symbolic types, play delimits the range of social relevance. More specifically: If reciprocal perspectives of relevance are to come about on the basis of a common thematic field, a coincidence within certain limits between my mediate presentation of context to the Other and his mediate presentation of context to me has to prevail.[50] Symbolic types serve precisely this purpose. The relevance structures concerning the prevalent symbolic types of a social group have been played through by everyone during socialization into a social group. A dramatic situation, in which relevance is threatened, may be "saved" by inducing a theme referring to some symbolic type. This, however, does not mean that any problem has thus been solved or any inconsistency overcome. On the contrary: It serves only the purpose of "saving" the situation by maintaining its relevance. But it *creates,* on the other hand, social incon-

---

[49] Psychotherapy has recognized this fact and employs play and games on this basis. See especially Thomas S. Szasz, *Ethics of Psychoanalysis.*

[50] This problem is obviously different from the "coincidence" between mediate and immediate presentation of context, which is achieved by constituting a social type.

sistencies by confronting the acting individuals with a highly reified symbolic type. In team-audience formations this is an important means of social control.

6.3 The Rôle of the Body in Play

Until now, I was guided by three general assumptions: 1. Clarification of diffuse thematic fields goes on in "playing-at-a-theme," in which interaction by gestures, by bodily movements, possibly also in direct bodily contact, is predominant. 2. A basic triadic intentionality structures all social intercourse and becomes the inherent characteristic of social types. 3. The body as a social object comes about as antecedent to some appropriate theme in abductive processes. In other words, the problem of intersubjectivity is not to be considered as *preliminary* to the arisal of social types and the constitution of social relevance.[51]

6.31 The Body as Incipient Event

The notion "body as a social object" means that my tending toward the body implies the tending of the Other toward it and toward myself. Immediately, the question may be raised: Is this "my" body or "his"? This alternative, however, is empty. It is based on the false assumption that perceptual bodies "over there" and bodies as social objects are the same.[52]

The body as a social object is constituted in social interaction and does not exist at all independently from a situational context. A still more significant aspect of this problem must now be established: the body as a social type is a constitutive part of all typificatory schemes which unite a situation into a context. One cannot speak of a social context without at least

---

[51] In his *Cartesian Meditations*, Husserl assumes that the realm of the alter ego and of sociality has to be constituted in the consciousness of the "pure ego." Any eidetic (i.e., roughly speaking: typical) forms of sociality arise from this fundamental intersubjectivity of ego and alter ego. – In a very interesting paper, Luckmann has proposed to reverse Husserl's argument by adhering, nevertheless, closely to Husserl's terminology and phenomenological method. See: Th. Luckmann, *On the Boundaries of the Social World*, in: *Phenomenology and Social Reality. Essays in Memory of Alfred Schutz*, (ed.) Maurice Natanson (The Hague, Nijhoff, 1970).
A "reversal" with similar consequences is implied in my presentation: the structure of abductive processes is shown to be constitutive for the arisal of social types and thus also ought to be basic for a study of the phenomenon of intersubjectivity.

[52] Recent experiments with hallucinatory drugs, like LSD, have shown, for instance, that the *perceptual* contours of one's own body may become entirely vague or distorted. The subsequent shock has even led to sudden suicides. – The dissolution of *social* contours, accompanied by no impairment of the perceptual abilities of the individual in a state of anomie finds in those cases a curious reversal: perceptual coherence explodes and the discrepancies with one's own stock of typified *social* experiences becomes unbearable. Durkheim's notion of fatalistic suicide comes close to this case.

a rudimentary typification of the body. But, on the other hand, social typifications are always typifications within a context, i.e., relevance must prevail. This apparent paradox finds an immediate solution on the abductive level of type-formation.

The notion of body arises as an incipient event within a diffuse thematic field. Becoming an incipient event implies constitution of the triadic perspectives of relevance. The incipient event "body" is *in* the perspectives of relevance. My tending toward "it" implies the tending of the Other toward "it" and toward me. Typification by this incipient event achieves a unification of the situation into a context, though this typification of "everything" by the incipient event "body" is extremely crude. Most important, the incipient event "body" lacks all differentiation; it is neither "my" body nor "your" body, neither "human" body nor "animated" body. However, the incipient event "body" has a *relation* to my own perceptual body and to that of the Other, and were it only because of my typifying *also* my perceptual body and that of the Other by this incipient event. The crude typificatory scheme "body-as-incipient-event" becomes enlarged, reconstructed, changed, etc., in subsequent typificatory attempts. The typifications of "my" body or "human" body arise in processes analysed before. They clarify, so to speak, the initial relation between the incipient event "body" and the immediately perceivable, physical bodies of the Other and myself.[53]

The propositions "Social contexts presuppose typifications of body" and "Typification of body presupposes a context" are neither paradoxes nor

---

[53] In the earlier example of mutual kite-construction (*sect.* 4.52) my son typified the total context by the incipient event "Center-of-Gravity." In a later phase, the boy complained about stomach pains and asked, pointing to his stomach: "Are there any animals inside?" Consistent with the argument given above, one may interpret this incident as follows: For the boy, the contours of the social object "my body" are still vaguely drawn and not yet reduced to the notion of "human body." Incipient events like "center of gravity" become "animated," when they are merged in typificatory attempts into a typificatory scheme of "body," which has not yet sufficiently lost its incipient character. – *Luckmann* argues in a similar way: Neither a distinction between inanimate and living bodies, nor an identification of the social with the human can be assumed as irreducible facts for sociological theory. The humanness of the human body is *constituted in* and *not constitutive for* social processes. "The sense 'living body,' which is originally transferred to all things in the life-world, receives additional and specific support whenever perceptible transformations of the outside of the object are directly and consistently apprehended as changes of expression." This original sense-transfer is later reduced, its "plausibility is weakened" on the basis of the experience that "some of the bodies to which the sense 'living body' was originally transferred do not move." But this subsequent reduction of the realm of "living body" does not have to coincide with the boundaries of the "human body." Ethnological studies of "animism," "totemism," "shamanism" and "fetishism" have presented data to the contrary. (Quotes from *Boundaries of the Social World*)

equivocations: in both cases, the term "typification" stands for very different phases in the complex process of typification. The rudimentary typification of body on the abductive level of type-formation leads to a typificatory scheme and to the unification of context on the basis of an "universal" typification of the situation by the incipient event "body." To be more specific, type formations (*my* body, *her* body, *human* body, etc.) are subsequently based on already prevailing contexts and typificatory schemes, each of which is composed of relations referring to the incipient body as a social type. Hence, the notion of "body" is a constitutive part of all typificatory schemes that unite a situation into a context.

I have shown before that playing-at-a-theme in face of an incipient event constitutes a genuinely social dimension of time.[54] Social temporality arises, where incipient events structure the passage of social interaction leading to an arisal or enlargement of types and typificatory schemes. Paramount among all incipient events is the "body," since its type becomes part of all typificatory schemes that unite a situation into a context. Thus, *the bodies of interacting partners in a social situation have to be considered as a paramount source of social temporality.*

In discussing Schütz' notion of "vivid present" I have shown that he took a similar position:

In and by our bodily movements, we perform the transition from our durée to the spatial or cosmic time.[55]

This "transition," which I had to criticize especially because of its spatial connotations, is constitutive for the "vivid present," for a *social* dimension of time. It rests in our bodily movements, in our "working actions" by which some projected state of affair is to be brought about. I take Schütz' notion of "transition" as a conjecture that a study of the relations between "social temporality" and "inner time" could start at this point: the bodies of interacting partners as the paramount source of social temporality.

6.32 The Body in Play (Third Characteristic of Play)

Reduction of types and constitution of symbolic types as social limits take place in play. What is the rôle of the body in these processes? To what extent are bodily movements and expressive gestures, disguise and presentation of the body in play constitutive for these processes?

Typificatory schemes and types arise on the abductive level of type-formation, where the body is paramount among all incipients events. The abi-

---

[54] See the end of *sect.* 5.3.
[55] *Coll. Pap.,* vol. 1, p. 216. – See also *sect.* 5.22.

lity of the individual to construct social types cannot be considered as an irreducible "natural" quality, either based in his biogenetic constitution or in some ontological existentials. The social phenomena of anomie and alienation are examples to the contrary: the abductive level may become totally separated or even destroyed. Correlative to that statement, one has to recognize that typification of social objects is a social achievement of man. The infant, who has to "learn" focussing his sight in order to become capable of an attentional grasp of visual objects, also has to "learn" constructing social context. The triadic intentionality of perceiving social objects is a *composite* phenomenon of consciousness and its composition arises in social intercourse. Young children's playing gains immediate significance if seen from this perspective.

I. Give and Take. When visiting a family with a small child, the visitor is often greeted by the young child's bringing him a toy or some other small object. I made this observation so frequently that I am inclined to consider it as a "normal" form of interaction between child and adult visitor. In addition, only a short glance into any nursery reveals the immense rôle of giving and taking in children's play. What happens in these interactions?

The child's "gift" induces a double reaction on my side: I tend toward the "gift" and I tend toward the child. Most important, though, the child apprehends this double tending as a simultaneous process, as soon as he does not merely "throw" the object at me, but starts to "give" it.[56] In earlier phases of mere physical displacement I simply avoid being hit, for instance, or I try to catch it, after which I turn to the child in subsequent reactions. If both my tendings can be grasped as one, the "gift" leads to an incipient event: "something to be given" and "something to be received" establish by bodily interaction a social relevance *for the child*. To be more precise: the child unifies the situation into context by its giving some object. The gift determines a thematic field; mediate presentation of context through the adult is established by the adult's taking the offering of the child as a "gift."

As I have shown earlier, relevance is maintained in this latent stage of social interaction by means of symbolic types. The "gift" has the status of a symbolic type, — but by means of which typificatory scheme? The incipient event "body" is paramount in the situation and leads to primary typificatory schemes of the child. The incipient event "gift" leads, there-

---

[56] Charles S. Peirce interpreted this act of giving as one of the most fundamental forms of "conduct," of "thirdness." See his *Coll. Pap.*, 1.345 and 1.475; also the excellent presentation of Richard J. Bernstein, *Action, Conduct, and Self Control*, in: R. J. Bernstein (ed.), *Perspectives on Peirce* (New Haven, Yale Univ. Press, 1965), p. 75. – In this context one should also mention Marcel Mauss, *The Gift* (London, Cohen, 1966).

fore, also to an enlargement of the typificatory scheme "body." The sequence of subsequent playful interactions between child and adult is, indeed, composed of various bodily performances: the child touches the toy and "fools around" with the adult, he jumps on him, turns around in showing off, etc. etc. In these various bodily movements, the child brings up a variety of themes in his effort to clarify the thematic field. The "gift" is here a symbolic type: reification of the typificatory scheme becomes apparent, if the child takes the toy back and hands it over again, etc. The adult reacts *as if* this created an inconsistency for him. How can he avoid insisting that one cannot take a "gift" back? The adult has but one answer: he takes the child's performance under a "protective cover," he calls it "just kid's play." To be more precise: the mediate presentation of context by the child to the adult is typified by the latter as "just play." [57]

Sociological insight into the significance of play is hampered by extending this typification to the total interaction between adult and child. Mead, for example, stated categorically: "You cannot count on the child," who *is* (!) "one thing at one time and another at another, and what he is at one moment does not determine what he is at another." [58] It is highly questionable, I contend, if interaction among adults is more predictable than interaction with children. Variety in social interaction depends on the availability of typificatory schemes, and one should not forget, that the child's store is still sparingly furnished. In other words, the earlier conclusion,[59] in which Mead's *limited* notion of play as a phase in the genesis of social self was criticized and rejected, finds new support from a different angle. Circumstances which lead someone to be "one thing at one time and another at another" may arise for the adult and the child alike.

To summarize the major points: What is being typified under the adult's perspectives of relevance as "just-playing-to-give-me-a-present" implies a reification of the relations child–adult. This reification reaches a turning point, when even the child says: "Oh, never mind, I am just playing." This interesting stage will be studied shortly. But before the child is able to pronounce it, the child's giving achieves merely a fixation of social relevance. His rudimentary typificatory schemes are all still closely related to the paramount incipient event of "body." The correlative social objects "something to be given" and "something to be received" still have sufficiently vague contours to be permeated by the notion of body. – One might call this phenomenon a "giving of the body" within "the gift."

[57] See the next section for more details.
[58] G. H. Mead, *Mind,* p. 159.
[59] See *sect.* 6.24.

Beyond an interlocking of the perspectives of relevance for the child, the constitution of the symbolic type "gift" serves also to clarify the child's notion of body. Inconsistencies are created by the child in order to be overcome. He takes the given object back, he builds bodily barriers and obstacles between giver and receiver in order to test the range of relevance at the limitations imposed by his and the Other's physical body. A series of games, which will be discussed later, immediately relate to this stage: they start with a simple throwing and catching of balls and culminate in games like tennis and baseball. This line of argument could reverse one traditional notion of play which assumed that a child is merely imitating and preparing for the roles of the adult.[60] With equal force one may argue that an adult playing tennis or golf is performing and "reviving" action patterns of childhood experiences, in which symbolic types have been enacted in rudimentary typificatory attempts.

II. Hide and Seek. An increasing awareness of the basic difference between visual and social objects arises in the playing of give-and-take.[61] To be able to grasp the "double intentio of the Other"[62] as bound to one's own giving is the first major *social* achievement of the child – or of the psychiatric patient.[63] The child becomes aware of social objects by means of the only "instrument" available to him, by means of his body. The child "tests" now subsequently the contours of the first social objects he has ex-

[60] Herbert Spencer and Karl Groos have established that tradition, and G. H. Mead and also J. P. Sartre defended it later.

[61] An excellent example is the following give-and-take I played with a neighbor's son, Daniel (4;6), who came into my study 3 weeks before Christmas presenting me with 3 buttons:

Daniel: "Here, a present from Santa Claus."
I: "Thank you, Santa Claus. Here, I also have a present for you." (I gave the buttons back)
D: "Thank you. – Where do you have them? Are they (the buttons) in there?" (He points to a basket.)
I: "I gave them back to you!"
D: *"No. You have to say: They are in there."*
I: "All right, they are in the basket."
D: "Bye, bye."
Visual and social objects are so tremendously different for children of this age that mutual play between adult and child is most precarious.

[62] See *sect.* 3.0.

[63] See, for the latter case, Goffman's report on "barter" among the patients of Central Hospital: Erving Goffman, *Asylums* (New York, Doubleday Anchor Books, 1961), pp. 274–286. – Goffman, however, interprets this phenomenon merely functionally as an "unofficial social exchange." I would argue that these patients are desperately trying to grasp social relevance with their giving and taking of cigarettes and nickels. Their position is much more precarious than that of children who are taken – in case of failure – under the protective cover of an "It-is-just-play."

perienced. The child will be especially baffled by the discrepancies between visual and social objects. Since visual and social contours do not coincide, what about the social object, if the visual disappears, if it is hidden?

The various forms of the play "hide-and-seek" presuppose already established relevant contexts. Mutual perspectives of relevance prevail in spite of one's hiding oneself. But, again, this is a stage not reached in a single step. The young child (my son, for instance, was 3;2) covers first only his face, calls out "Here-I-am," and wants his hands to be removed by the Other. A few weeks later, he crawled into a cupboard calling out all the time "Here-I-am" until he was "found." Finally, (at 3;10) he knew "correctly" how to play it by closing himself into some room and avoiding any noise or conspicuous movement. – In these phases, a significant development of the typificatory schemes relating to "my body" is evident. Earlier, covering one's face is taken as a hiding of oneself; "my-body-to-be-hidden" and "my-body-to-be-looked-for" are rather crude correlative aspects of an incipient event bridging the inconsistency created by the child's diffuse notion of body. "Correct" play – as an adult would call it – is achieved when finally immediately perceivable contours of the body coincide with the social contours of "my-body-to-be-hidden."

The social significance of this playing of "hide-seek" would be limited to the approximation of visual and social contours, if further forms of play were not immediately related to it. But the use of masks to cover one's face, the use of exotic costumes (Indian or cowboy) to cover one's body, and finally the make-believe notion of having a spiritual "totality" to cover one's whole being[64] are reifications immediately related to this form of play. Mask and dress serve as symbolic types which cast the perspectives of relevance into stereotyped patterns of "how-to-hide" and "how-to-seek."

An analysis of the triadic relevance structure in masked interaction may reveal the *social significance of the mask.* Take the following example: A few weeks before Christmas, Georg (5;11) asked for a Santa Claus mask. Upon my answer that there were still a few days left until Christmas, and he did not need it right away, he protested vehemently: "No! I need it now! Otherwise Santa Claus can see me. Otherwise he can stick me into his bag."[65] For the boy, the mask becomes the mutual object of his and Santa Claus' tendings. Georg's tending toward the mask implies Santa Claus' tending toward him and toward the mask. Georg needs to master this dif-

[64] See Berger-Luckmann's notion of "universe-maintenance": *Social Construction,* pp. 96–118.
[65] In Middle European Christmas tales Santa Claus comes to visit with a big bag, into which he packs all the naughty children.

fuse (and dangerous) situation. By covering himself with the mask, Santa Claus is confronted with his own mask, as if he were looking into a mirror. But this forces Santa Claus to turn away from Georg and to tend only toward the mask. Santa Claus, however, implies, in his own tending toward the mask, Georg's tending toward Santa Claus and toward the mask. This result leaves the person, who wears the mask, in control of the situation. He is "safe." There is no tending toward him any more. If Santa Claus takes the mask as a mere mirror of his features, very well, he has been fooled. If he does not and takes the mask as a social object, then in tending toward it he implies the double tending of the Other, of Georg, which is in any case controlled by the boy.

The high degree of reification in masked interaction is obvious. The two perspectives of relevance 1. of the masked person and 2. of the person impersonated under the mask become "meshed" into one. They are controllable by the masked person. This, of course, includes as yet only "interaction" between the masked person and the one impersonated. "Anyone" who is playing the rôle of the masked person, falls, of course, under the control of the mask. Only in this rather intricate sense is it correct to say that a mask (like a boy's dressing himself like an Indian) implies an identification with the impersonated being. Mutual masking and dressing within similar attire implies, therefore, mutual control and subsequently mutual subordination. Military uniforms have always served that purpose. More subtly, however, a playboy looking at the "bunny" in his club might, perhaps, reflect for a moment which creatures of the animal kingdom the *bunny* is to control.

This topic will be pursued further in discussing team-audience formations. But, some reflection seems to be called for in order to warn against any too hasty generalizations. All initial examples of masked interaction were related to children's play. In these cases, the mask refers always to some incipient event, while the notion of one's own body is still rather vague. Typification of context by the incipient event, i.e., by that "being" impersonated under the mask, takes place: The lawn indeed *is* the prairie hiding those Indians. And all typificatory schemes relating to one's body are still diffuse: The murderous Comanche, who nails me to the stake and cuts my throat, isn't doing anything to *my* body.

CHAPTER 7

TOWARD A UNIFIED THEORY OF GAME, PLAY, AND SOCIAL ACTION

THEME:

Sociological theory has to deal with processes of type formation within frames of social relevance. Modes of interaction like games, plays, and projected social actions have to be differentiated on the background of a theory of social types. Most discriminative for such an endeavor are differences in the temporal dimensions and in the relevance structures of interactional situations.

The paramount incipient event "body" becomes part of all relevance-maintaining typificatory schemes. But incomplete intersubjective "testing" of the social type of the "body" and especially of the later typical specifications into "my" and "your" body leaves those typificatory schemes precariously "open." Arising inconsistencies in such situations are numerous.[1]

The structure of these inconsistencies, the typical social conditions for their arisal and the interactional modes of their solution may be now examined to see whether they account for contextual differences between the modes of play, of game, and of social action.

The inconsistencies related to the mode of play can be grouped according to three major characteristics of play that were determined before: 1. *Reduction of types* is a prerequisite for all modes of interaction, especially between adult and child, because the child's stock of types is very limited. 2. In play, *symbolic types* are constituted. Their enactment posits *social* limits. Symbolic types arise initially as incipient events. They structure play and induce social temporality. 3. Paramount among all incipient events is the body. The *body as social type* becomes, in play, a composite part of all typificatory schemes and posits social limits itself.

ad 1: Inconsistencies related to the reduction of types in play were men-

---

[1] The question (see *sect.* 4.42) of what determines the chance for an arisal of social inconsistencies has thus been answered for an important instance. The prevalence of playing-at-a-theme, of play and also of game, especially in the "play-world of the child," is a consequence of the incipient state of the child's typificatory scheme of "body."

tioned in relation to what I have called the "protective cover" for the child's interacting with an adult. Take, for instance, the play of a child giving a toy and taking it back soon after. Which inconsistencies are to be seen? a) The child's giving is to assure relevance for the child. Its vague typificatory schemes concerning its own body are differentiated only diffusely: the body of a parent or a friend cannot yet be apprehended as a *social* object distinct from and interactive with its own body. My appearance as a "stranger" threatens the coherence of these typificatory schemes. By means of the "gift" as an incipient event, the child may bridge the inconsistency. The child's play reduces relevant types and attempts avoidance of further inconsistencies. b) But though the child's playing-at-the-gift (his taking it back, for instance) is to be expected in the child's process of type formation, this constitutes an inconsistency for the adult: Taking back a "gift" threatens its symbolic character. More precisely, the child's play creates an inconsistency within the temporal typifications of the adult's action patterns. In order to maintain social relevance from the adult's perspective he typifies the child's performance as "mere play."

ad 2: The enactment of symbolic types in play constitutes social limits and every such limit, if played at, leads into inconsistencies. For these limits, as I have pointed out, circumscribe the range of social relevance in those situations which cannot be united into a context by some typificatory scheme. Take again the symbolic type of a fool, and in order to contrast this problem still further, assume some rather frequent impersonation by the same individual. The fool's interacting with his partners or his audience soon institutes such reified patterns in the context that hardly allow him to leave these patterns "off stage," i.e., in "normal" daily life. Limits have been set so definitely that any playing-at-the-limits invokes inconsistencies.[2]

ad 3: The human body is paramount among all incipient events. Hence, it is also a paramount source of social inconsistencies. The most difficult and largely unsolved problems of the theory of intersubjectivity immediately relate to this fact. I cannot pursue this problem to any extent.[3] In principle, however, the significance of social inconsistencies constituted by bodily

---

[2] Marilyn Monroe's attempts to free herself from the limits set by the symbolic type of "sexbomb" show the tragic consequences and the personally uncontrollable inertia of these inconsistencies. – It need not be stressed again that these phenomena are entirely different from the well-known problem in role-theory that reciprocal role typifications also have a certain inertia.

[3] The studies of *Plessner* and of *Merleau-Ponty* are among the most important in this field. See: Helmuth Plessner, *Die Stufen des Organischen und der Mensch* (Berlin, DeGruyter, 1928), and Maurice Merleau-Ponty, *Phenomenology of Perception* (London, Routledge–Kegan Paul, 1962).

involvement in social interaction is to be clearly recognized. These social inconsistencies must be studied further, insofar as they lead to a distinction between play and the interactional mode called "game."

G. H. Mead saw the distinction between play and game as being based on interactional differences in both modes of interaction:

The play antedates the game. For in a game there is a regulated procedure, and rules. The child must not only take the rôle of the other, as he does in play, but he must assume the various rôles of all the participants in the game, and govern his action accordingly. If he plays first base, it is as the one to whom the ball will be thrown from the field or from the catcher. Their organized reactions to him he has imbedded in his own playing of the different positions, and this organized reaction becomes what I have called the "generalized other" that accompanies and controls his conduct.[4]

The concept of "generalized other" circumscribes a notion of intersubjective relations: it is a state, in which social control may be exerted on the basis of one's internalizing the attitudes of others toward each other, of others toward oneself, and of others toward some common activity. In other words, the mutual tendings of all individuals in a given situation toward each other *and* toward a common object can be apprehended *in toto* by each actor.

This complicated net of relations can be described in more detail: If my tending toward some social object implies the tending of the other, say of x_1, toward the object and toward myself, then x_1's tending toward the object implies the tending of x_2 toward the object and toward x_1, and in turn, x_2's tending implies . . . etc. The triadic intentionality of perceiving social objects leads to a complicated net of mutual tendings in social interaction between many actors. But if this net were merely composed of mutual tendings, it would be highly fragile. I showed earlier that the individual has an enormous destructive power to disrupt social relevance, because *he* can refuse to tend toward a common object and thus can make *my* perceiving the object – at least very difficult, if not impossible. The more individuals interact in a situation, the more potent grows this power of the individual. This may be observed often in children's play: the more children interact, the faster the topics of play change and the greater seems to be the "chaos" for some detached observing adult.

Mead's notion of "generalized other" relates to this problem. The net of individual tendings between "particular others" prevalent in play has to be "generalized" in order to lose its fragile and accidental character. Individual

4 G. H. Mead, *Present*, p. 186.

consent in mutual tending toward common social objects has to be subsumed under the generality of norms and rules typically prevalent in games. But how can this process be described?

I shall be guided here by Goffman's approach to this problem.[5] He described the interactional attempts to overcome social inconsistencies as "impression management" by competing teams trying to impress their definition on the situation. The formation of teams and audiences will reduce the destructive power of the individual to disrupt social relevance that is based on mutual tendings toward a common social object. Team-audience formation and the interactional mode of game are intrinsically related.

7.1 Common Symbolic Types in Play and Game

Symbolic types arise in play and counter the disruption of relevance. *In play interaction is structured by arising symbolic types* which set definite social limits. Their arisal brings about *social temporality.* But the reified character of the symbolic type, which structures play, removes to a certain extent ongoing interaction from individual control. A player may disrupt a play, but he cannot significantly influence the course of play. To use a metaphor: A play does not have an individual conductor, its "beat" is determined by the symbolic type. Or, as Buytendijk called it, play is always a play with something that also plays with the player.[6]

In *game,* the situation is quite different. In Mead's words, "in a game there is a regulated procedure, and rules." Relations unifying the situation into a context do not merely arise with the mutual tendings toward a symbolic type, but they are determined by a prevalent typificatory scheme. "Regulated procedures" and "rules" of a game are first of all typificatory schemes inducing "regulated" relations in the context. In other words, the passage of interaction is structured according to "rules," while in play it is structured by some symbolic type. In general, however, "rules" are not symbolic types but typificatory schemes. They determine the relations within the context. If "rules" indeed structure social interaction in games analogously to symbolic types in play, one must assume a close relationship between play and game. This relation can be readily explained, if one assumes that play and game have some *common symbolic type.*[7]

Such a common symbolic type may, for instance, structure the passage of interaction in a play of Give-and-Take. Enactment of this symbolic type sets, however, limits for all interaction in that situation. (I cannot "give" the

[5] Compare *sect.* 1.3.
[6] Quoted by Plessner in *Lachen und Weinen,* p. 102.
[7] This is a hypothesis. The subsequent analysis will explore and test ist implications.

toy with my nose; it is difficult to "give" it with my "feet"; the adult does not "take" the toy with his teeth; he will not "take" a "chair"; if I "take" the toy back, he protests; etc. etc.) A multiplicity of limits arises with the enactment of this symbolic type in play: these limits will be apprehended as social types. *As soon as a typical mode of interaction comes about that is patterned by those limits and which is restricted to such pattern, one may speak of a game.*[8] For this pattern is a typificatory scheme unifying the situation into a context of game. The common symbolic type is thus also a determinant of the typificatory scheme of a game. The limits which arose by enactment of the common symbolic type in play pattern the game's typificatory scheme. In short: *In games the common symbolic type is ordered into the passage of interaction.* Hence, no social temporality arises on the basis of the common symbolic type in games as it does in play.[9]

The typificatory scheme "baseball" in Mead's example refers to a common symbolic type "give-and-take," resp. "throw-and-catch." *The passage of interaction is structured by an elaborate network of rules:* "throw there," "catch here," etc. It is not structured, as in play, by the symbolic type itself. (Interaction would be simply interrupted if the pitcher, for instance, threw the baseball straight up into the air and tried to catch it himself.) In game the symbolic type is ordered according to specific limits. It is subordinated, so to speak, to the rules. It is "ordered into the passage of interaction."

Is therefore a game of baseball, for instance, no play? This is what Mead would say. The terms play and game are meant by him to label *distinct* phases in the genesis of a social self. However, within the present study of typificatory processes, the game of baseball has to be called a play, too, if in this game incipient events arise leading to new symbolic types, which structure the passage of interaction and come about through a significant rôle of the body. (These "new" symbolic types may, therefore, induce social temporality!) I have shown that in games "an elaborate network of rules" comes about which is built around a common symbolic type like "give-and-take." But enactment of the rules may lead to new symbolic types. Rules are apt to be reified in notions like "correct-false," like "good-poor," leading to

---

[8] Some excellent illustrations may be found, for instance, in Eric Berne's *Games People Play*. What he describes as "Sexual Games" (pp. 123–131) are "strategically" structured patterns of interaction: hence they are also "games" in the above sense. Their pattern is composed of limits set by enactment of the common symbolic type of "making love." These limits are *social* and can hardly be explained by "sexual instincts" as Berne suggests. The interactional mode of "making-love-to-each-other" is, of course, play.

[9] See *sect.* 5.23: The "more stringent definition of social temporality" stipulates that the passage of interaction has to be *structured by* the incipient event, resp. by the symbolic type.

typified notions of "cheating" and "false-play," to types like "amateur" and "professional." These are symbolic types arising in playing games. They are not applicable to plays which are not games.

If I visit, for instance, some friends and their little boy greets me by placing a toy in my hand, the child is playing. In this "give-and-take" social relevance is constituted for him. If he takes the toy back, he is "cheating" only from an adult perspective, in which the child's play is falsely taken for a game. This experience can be quite irritating for an adult. I observed, for instance, my own son, in what I assumed to be a game: he "learned" to build in "correct" order cubic blocks of various shapes upon each other, and after he "knew the game," he purposefully started making "mistakes" in changing the order at will. While he was delighted about it, I could not help feeling irritated. My tending toward the object in a mode of game conflicted with his tending toward it in play. This discrepancy between the two modes of interaction can neither be solved by the child's starting a game that he is not prepared for, nor by the adult's starting a play, which would always retain the character of a game. Typically, the adult takes refuge in an imposing "you-ought-to-do-it-that-way," he tries to impose rules of an adult game. However, this is not an imposition within the relevance structure of *mutual* play or game, but an imposing by means of the symbolic type "father-who-knows-everything." It is, in other words, an imposition of "rationality" encompassing (and often trespassing upon) the specific rules of the present game.[10]

7.2 Inconsistencies and Relevance in Play, in Game, and in Social Action

All social action is preceded by a project. This conception was already discussed in some detail.[11] The project is a typificatory scheme which unites an anticipated series of interactional situations into a projected state of affairs. A project of social action has to anticipate that arising inconsistencies can be dealt with in typical ways: either they can be anticipated as *typically* occurring in a specific course of action, or they can be anticipated as *potentially* occurring through intervention of antagonistic opponents. The first case can be dealt with explicitly in projecting an anticipated course of

---

[10] This "imposition of rationality" is a phenomenon not sufficiently clarified in sociological theory. It is related to the problem of intersubjectivity. I should like to state a conjecture: If Peirce' and Durkheim's claims that logic and rationality have a social basis are correct, then this basis could be clarified by studying further the intermediary phases between play and game. For *Peirce* see *Coll. Pap.*, 2.654ff, 5.311, 5.354–357, 5.378, 5.384. For *Durkheim* see especially his *The Elementary Forms of the Religious Life* (London, Allan, 1954) esp. p. 418.

[11] See *sect.* 5.11.

action that avoids inconsistencies. The latter has to anticipate relatively unprogrammed, intermittent phases of play, in which symbolic types may have to be constructed ad hoc to assure dominance of some thematic field throughout the situation. (The malicious trouble-maker, for instance, may fall into the "pit" of a fool's rôle.) But in both cases, the typificatory scheme of the project imposes the temporal dimension. In all its phases social action is maintained by typificatory schemes not induced by the project, but by reciprocal communicative face-to-face relations.[12]

An important source for inconsistencies arises, when play and social action are merged with one another. For, while a child plays, the adult often perceives the situation in terms of social action. In this case, both modes of interaction overlap. One has to see most clearly how difficult it is for an adult to give up his position and start playing himself. He cannot divest himself of the typificatory schemes which are an integral part of his stock of experiences and determine his perspectives of relevance. The adult typifies the child's behavior within a typical frame, and this is most often a frame of social action. The child's play is apprehended by the adult as a reified action pattern which he calls "mere play." As such, the child's play fits into the adult's typificatory schemes of social action. As such, it bridges most inconsistencies the child's play creates for the adult. Play as "mere play" becomes a symbolic type (for the adult) assuring the maintenance of relevance between adult and child. It is a symbolic type ordered by the adult into his frame of social interaction. Hence, according to the earlier definition, the child's play is taken by the adult as a game.[13] The adult apprehends the child's play as a set of reified (and for him irrelevant) rules posited ad hoc by the child. The adult plays along these rules in his stiff and wooden attempts to converse with the child.

In other words, interaction between adult and child is seldom mutual play. The performance of the adult leads to symbolic types like "gift" or "body" which the child brings about in his play. They assure social relevance for the child in a situation, where the stock of types of interacting partners differ considerably. This form of interaction is merely an unintentional, though unavoidable creation of inconsistencies by the adult which the child tries to bridge in typificatory attempts. But in order to assure that these typificatory attempts of the child and his creation of symbolic types in play are uninterrupted by the adult, the adult calls the child's play in toto "mere play." Thus he assures relevance in the situation from his perspective. The

---

[12] See sect. 5.13.
[13] Sect. 7.1.

adult brackets, so to speak, the otherwise unrestricted validity of his typifi-catory schemes of social action in the realm of play.

As soon as one studies the interactional modes of play, game, and social action from the perspective of social inconsistencies, it becomes evident that the transition between the different modes is fluid. *Mutual* play presupposes a vague situation in which both, resp. all, actors can maintain relevance only by playing at a symbolic type.[14] Interaction between child and adult seldom will be mutual play. The adult typifies the child's behavior as "mere play," but this typification – as I have shown above – apprehends the adult's interaction with the child as a game. Its "rules" are given ad hoc in the child's performance, which the adult can apprehend only in a regulated form: as a game. Mutual understanding arises only when the child himself advises the adult: "Now, listen, let's play it this way." As soon as this stage is reached by the child, he typifies the ongoing interaction himself as play. More precisely, his assigning explicit rules suggests that he is now taking his own playing for a game. More importantly, however, he is becoming aware of projected actions himself. The early phase of mere enactment of project-formations in playing at a symbolic type thus passed, and projected social actions can be pursued by the child.

The study of the transitional phases between social action and play again leads into problems of the theory of intersubjectivity. *Social action* is based upon types "for anyone," valid for typical actors pursuing typical goals in typical situations. It is a mode of interaction in which, at least in principle, everyone can act with anyone else, anywhere and at any time. In *play,* to the contrary, the situation is structured by the symbolic type and gains a unique temporal dimension. The incipient symbolic type is determined by the spe-cific perspectives of relevance of those present in the situation. Hence, the intersubjective validity of play does not exceed its present situation. In *games,* however, mutual rules have already been tested in similar situations. They form mediary modes of interaction spanning what otherwise appears to be a gap between play and social action.

This problem cannot be studied to any extent. But it may be clarified in respect to the characteristic inconsistencies and the structure of relevance prevailing in this transitional mode of game. A hint may be found in the

---

[14] Relevance maintained by symbolic types and relevance maintained by typificatory schemes in role interaction must be distinguished. If I talk about "degeneration of social roles into symbolic types" I do not connect any value judgement with the term "degen-eration." I suggest, however, that role interaction has been overestimated in recent sociological theory and that the consequences of the enactment of symbolic types for personal identity and for the perception of social values are considerable.

structure of projects of action. In a certain sense, projects and games are both "mediaries" between play and action. Enactment of interactional sequences constitutive for later formation of projects takes place in play.[15] On the other hand, projects are constitutive for all social action. Furthermore, games order the common symbolic type arising in play into the passage of social interaction.

Apparently, game and social action have not yet been clearly distinguished. Are, for instance, all games also preceded by projects? A game of bridge, for example, or a game of baseball requires a performance based on typificatory schemes projecting specific lines of interaction. All games are structured by rules. They lead to at least a rudimentary "strategy," to some choice between alternate lines of acting. But this describes also a project of action. Projects are antecedent to social action. Are they also in the same sense antecedent to games?

In the typificatory scheme of a project potential inconsistencies (that are to be avoided in later action) are anticipated. The scheme has, however, only limited influence on the arisal of these inconsistencies. That is to say, in a project potential situations may have to be considered (say of fool-creation), but a successful completion of action can never be guaranteed. The "horizon" of an actor in social action, to use a metaphor, is never closed in respect to the field of his possibilities.

In games, on the other hand, the inconsistencies serve a definite purpose. Take, for instance, the game of baseball. The common symbolic type of "give-and-take," which also structured multiple forms of play in various earlier situations of type-formation, is ordered here into a definite passage of interaction. From pitcher to catcher, from batter into the field, etc. etc.: the bodily enactment of this symbolic type is ordered along a definite course of interaction. The typificatory scheme, which regulates this line of interaction, is composed of limits which were set by certain bodily enactments of this common symbolic type in earlier plays. These limits assure 1. that inconsistencies arise only within these limits (I am not going to suddenly catch a ripe tomatoe), and 2. that all potential inconsistencies are only consequences of an enactment of this symbolic type (this ball has been pitched too high). Games, in short, are a mode of interaction, in which inconsistencies arise within specific limits and in line with specific rules. Fun in games results from the assured knowledge of the participants that the inconsistencies in their game are manageable. Any player can play at these inconsistencies with perfect ease. And this includes the so-called "spoil-sport," too.

[15] See *sect.* 6.24.

This reveals the principal difference between play and game. Playing at the limits set by the symbolic type in play invokes inconsistencies that threaten social relevance. For social relevance in play is maintained by the symbolic type. Quite differently, social relevance in game is maintained by the game's typificatory scheme: the situational relations are structured according to "rules." These inconsistencies arise, of course, also in game *only* on the background of intersubjective relevance. In other words, the game's system of relevance and typificatory scheme (rules) delimit also the arisal of possible inconsistencies. In contradistinction to social action, where the arisal of inconsistencies is always an open possibility, in games one finds them to be an inherent characteristic: *games are structured by a system of "pre-defined" inconsistencies.*

7.3 The Closure of a Game's Typificatory Scheme

Which interactional mode distinguishes a game like baseball from, for instance, the game of poker? The boy next door would probably answer that baseball has to be played outside on a field and that poker can be played even within a telephone booth. *Playing* these games implies different degrees of bodily involvement. Modern mathematical game analysis and the development of high-speed computers have even shown that games can be "played" by machines. Bodily involvement may be dispensed with altogether in games. But in this case, according to the previous definition of play, *no playing* of the game goes on. Playing a game, in addition to bodily involvement and reduction of social types, implies the positing of social limits by enacting some symbolic type.[16]

The point of interest: Playing of games has to be distinguished from the interactional mode of game, and the latter may be reduced even to the limit case of excluding all bodily involvement (for instance, in chess "played" between computers). These differences, which still allow one to speak of "game" in all three instances, may be clarified by studying more closely the notion of "purpose" or of "goal" in game. A comparison with the structure of social action and its project will again further this clarification.

A project of action implies a typificatory scheme outlining a purposive

---

[16] If *any* of these three characteristics is missing, no *playing of a game* takes place. In this case, the *interactional mode of game* prevails as such. A systematic study of games would have to introduce further distinctions here. For instance, Goffman distinguishes *game,* as a "body of rules," and *play* as a "particular instance of a given game played from beginning to end." *Playing* is the "process of move-taking," whereas the "varieties of interaction that occur among persons who are face to face" in order to play a game is called *gaming.* (E. Goffman, *Encounters,* pp. 35f.) – My terminology, obviously, is different from Goffman's.

course of action. This does not *necessarily* hold for a game. The convention-al *goal* of "loss" or "success" in a game is, I contend, an additional imposi-tion *not* resulting inherently from the rules or the typificatory scheme of the game.[17] Its imposition is an arbitrary or a traditional convention. Everyone knows that the boys in the neighborhood can "play some baseball" in the backyard without counting innings or runs scored. But "foul play" or "per-fect pitch," like all other symbolic types arising in playing a game, can occur without tending toward the game's "goal." In other words, while a project of action can never guarantee a later success of action and fails totally if the "final goal" is not being achieved, *playing* a game has no *inherent* goal and is in that sense always "successful" even in the most rudimentary phase of playing it. Thus, if the notion of "success" is to be discriminative at all for the interactional mode of game, it has to be assumed to be an *imposed* notion.

This "imposition" has to be made more precise. My contention that the "goal" is not inherent to the game's typificatory scheme follows from my earlier definition of this concept. Typificatory schemes, which unite the situ-ation of game into a context, are composed of all relevant situational rela-tions. Relevance, i.e., the interlocking of mutual perspectives of relevance is assured in game by the rules which tell where to tend to and how to tend toward the other partners. This mutual tending is not as precariously latent as in play, where any individual can easily disrupt relevance. Mutual tending, i.e., the set of relevant relations is "assured" within the formation of op-posing teams and audiences, a phenomenon which will be studied further in the next chapter. But this set of relations determining the typificatory scheme of a game can be described sufficiently without referring to a "goal" of who won or lost the game. If this "goal" is introduced by agreement be-tween the participants, I want to call this imposition a *closure of the game's typificatory scheme.*

Three characteristics of game were described. 1. In game, a symbolic type, which arose in play and determined the structure of play (it is thus common to play and game) is ordered into the passage of interaction. 2. En-actment of that symbolic type in play led to a multiplicity of social limits, certain of which are taken over as "rules" into the typificatory scheme of the game. 3. The "ends" of game (its "purpose") has two aspects. 3a) In *playing a game,* symbolic types arise which may be socially highly significant.[18] Playing at these symbolic types is playing with a purpose at purposefully

[17] Mathematical game analysis similarly speaks of goals as "imputations." Compare Neumann–Morgenstern, *Theory of Games,* pp. 34–37.
[18] See *sect.* 8.2 for the "tough guy" constituted in playing football.

constructed social inconsistencies. It is a source of "fun in games." [19] *These ends of game are intrinsic to the game's typificatory scheme.* They arise even in rudimentary phases of playing a game and do not imply or presuppose any "ultimate" or definite goal of game. 3b) Very different from intrinsic ends of a game is *its "goal"* which *imposes a purposive closure on the game's typificatory scheme.* Relations in the situation of game are united into a purposive goal. It determines how to start and when to end the game. It determines, in short, a *temporal span* of the game.

The notion of "closure" may be clarified further by studying the temporal differences between games and social action. Nearly all theories of game, as for example Huizinga's and Caillois', insist that games take place within assigned spatial and temporal boundaries. But how do these boundaries come about? A goal or a temporal limitation of a game apparently does not *have to* be assigned by those playing a game in order to make playing a game possible at all. However, the participants in a game *may consent* to an imposition of such boundaries.

Since in a game symbolic types are ordered into the passage of social interaction, this "ordering" or "structurization of passage" does not lead to social temporality. The imposition of a "span" on this structurization of passage is, however, a perfect example of "temporal typifications." [20] The "span" of a game may be defined in various ways. It may be a definite period of cosmic time (the game lasts 45 minutes). It may be defined by counting and/or measuring (the ball has to touch the opponent's half of the field 21 times without his being able to hit it back immediately to my half). It may be an exhausting of some resource (I am going to risk 20 dollars). In all of these instances, a game's span is defined by temporal typifications. Playing a game gains a temporal and spatial unity by means of a certain *goal* of the game. This goal is to be realized by performing a specific sequence of game interactions determined by the game's span. This unity results from typifying all ongoing interacting in game by the "span" of the game. [21] For example: "The game has just started"; "it is going as expected"; "they ought to throw now everything they have into the game". These are temporal typifications of the game determined by the game's span. Realizing a goal of a game within an imposed span implies a temporal typification of playing a game. The goal imposes a *closure* of the game's typificatory scheme.

The next question, most naturally, is to ask for a comparison between the

---

[19] Compare Goffman's essay "Fun in Games" in: *Encounters,* pp. 17–81.

[20] See *sect.* 5.11.

[21] Compare the similar formulation of Schütz for the span of the project. See *Social World,* p. 62.

closure of games and social action. Is the typificatory scheme of a project, being basic for all social action, also closed in a similar sense? The question was answered implicitly in the investigation of the inconsistencies occurring in both modes of interaction. A closure of the game's typificatory scheme would not be possible, if games were not structured by a "universe of inconsistencies." In social action the arisal of inconsistencies is always an open possibility: success of social action depends entirely on the successful realization of a preconceived project and can only be judged in retrospect, after the act has been performed. In games, on the other hand, the ease of one's playing at the game's inconsistencies is a central mode of interaction and constitutive for the "fun in games." Relevance is never threatened by these inconsistencies, as long as the typificatory scheme is "closed," i.e., as long as this closure directs all interactional relations toward a common goal. One could stress this important difference between game and social action also by a special term: *the system of inconsistencies in a game and the imposed closure of a game's typificatory scheme lead to "total relevance" within the situation.*

7.4 Conclusion: Game and Social Action

My presentation of games was based on the hypothesis that play and game have a common symbolic type. This symbolic type arises in play and constitutes its relevance structure. Playing at this symbolic type posits social limits which are "ordered" subsequently into the typificatory scheme of a game circumscribing its "rules." Empirical evidence, aside from generally known common-sense observations, could not be collected here to check this hypothesis. But I intend to apply these theses in a final chapter to some problems of social mobility and status maintenance in order to test their usefulness (although not their validity) in the context of empirical studies.

The temporal dimensions of game and social action are so closely related that an approach which does not consider carefully the different relevance structures of game and social action, leads easily to a confusion of both modes of social interaction. To be more specific: The "span of the project" in social action constitutes temporal typifications based on inner time. But the temporal typifications in games are of the same character. The close relationship between game and action rests on their having the same temporal structure as soon as closure of the game's typificatory scheme is somehow defined. It is possible to *perform* a game as if it were social action. (It is, of course, *not* possible to *play* a game as if it were some social action.)

In other words, games can be dealt with analytically in terms of a theory of social action without major distortion of their temporal structure. The mathematical theory of games takes advantage of this fact. Similarly, Berne has attempted to grasp all social action in terms of games.[22] In certain theories of social action, for instance in Parsons', it is nearly impossible to distinguish social action from game. In one way or another, the game's goal is taken in these theories as an *inherent* teleological principle, from where the game's "meaning" may be revealed. It makes only little difference, if such a principle is tied to the project of action or to the goal of games. The mathematical theory of games, for instance, achieves closure of the game's typificatory scheme by the notion of utility. Berne refers to so-called "ego states" of "Parent-Adult-Child." Parsons introduced the motivational goal of an "optimization of gratification."[23] In reference to games, any of these notions leads to a closure of the game's typificatory scheme: Temporal typification of *all* game interaction becomes possible and the boundaries between game and action start to fluctuate.

Disregard for the different relevance structures of game and social action is also typical for sociological attempts to deal with play and game as total phenomena. This approach was criticized frequently above. If game and play are taken as total phenomena with the intent to derive all social structures from them, usually a closure of the game's typificatory scheme in the form of some teleological principle slips in. For instance, Gehlen introduced the notion of "discipline" (Zucht) in order to explain the transition from the mode of play ("Spiel") to the realm of social action ("ernste Aufgaben") and work:

(Es) liegt dieser Übergang in der Einengung des Spielinteresses auf bestimmte Endziele, in der Festlegung des Verhaltens im Sinne der Regelmäßigkeit, und des Dabeibleibens und in dem Sachgehorsam, in dem Übergewicht, das die Gesetze der Sache selbst erhalten, so daß endlich sie es sind, die das regelmäßige Verhalten bestimmen.[24]

"Obedience to the inherent laws of things" (Sachgehorsam) has for Gehlen an entirely different conceptual value than the notion of "chosé-ité" for Durkheim or Husserl's insistence on "Sachgerechtigkeit." For Gehlen takes play from the outset as a total social phenomenon. The notions of "Zucht" and "Sachgehorsam" are inherent teleological prin-

---

[22] See *sect.* 1.3.
[23] See *sect.* 5.14.
[24] A. Gehlen, *Mensch*, p. 224. – Gehlen quotes immediately following George H. Mead's notion of "generalized other." It is hard to see how this Meadian notion can support a teleological concept like Gehlen's "Zucht." See *sect.* 6.12.

ciples (closures) necessarily implied in a total theory of play that attempts a transition from play and game to phenomena of social action.

Sartre has dealt with the problem of "closure" of game's typificatory schemes from another perspective. He has shown that an "alien temporality" may arise in men's economic transactions, if the notions of profit and compound interest become *the* ordering principles for all economic events and actions.[25] In this case, a "fetishizing" of economic events takes place.[26] The event becomes an "independent reality," determining rather than being determined by social interaction: it "imprisons men in its apparatus." The "fetishizing" of profit in economic interaction refers precisely to the same closing of the margin between game and social action described above. The total relevance system of games (economic transaction) is, in those cases, closed by the notion of "success," by measurable monetary rewards. The mathematical theory of game, the "fetish" of cybernetical models for economic behavior rests altogether on certain assumptions concerning the "utility" of games. By this notion of utility, the typificatory schemes of economic games may be "closed," temporal typifications and unity of game arise. If the notion of "utility" can be supported further by an *inherent* teleological principle, like an ideology of profit, then economic interactions – indistinguishable as to games or actions – will dominate the situation. Increasingly, they will be withdrawn from man's cooperative influence.[27]

Sartre's argument is rather convincing. But is it also conclusive? I contend it is circular in respect to the major point of my last presentation. The closure of typificatory schemes was assumed in advance in Sartre's attempt to include all significant social interaction in a frame of historical ends of action.[28] His narrow notion of social relevance leads to the assumption that all typificatory schemes are reified. Sartre does not need a teleological principle to bridge the gap between play and social action: all means-end schemata are already posited under such a closure. Subsequently, interaction occurs only between competing teams who "compose the event" by trying to impress their definition of historical reality on the situation. In other words: team-audience formation is *the* mode of social interaction within Sartre's narrow frame of social relevance, which the individual may cut across only in his Project. A wider notion of relevance, which I con-

---

[25] See *sect.* 5.4.
[26] Sartre, *Search*, pp. 128f.
[27] Durkheim described this state of affairs as "economic anomie." See esp. his foreword to the 2nd ed. of *Division of Labor*.
[28] Compare *sect.* 5.4.

sidered necessary for a study of the interactional modes of play and game, left – for the time being – the relationship between closure of typificatory schemes and formation of teams and audiences unclarified. But Sartre's argument concerning the "alien temporality" of economic transactions, which is related to the phenomenon of total relevance structures prevalent in certain games, is convincing. Interaction between teams and audiences shall be studied, therefore, in the chapter which follows.

CHAPTER 8

TEAM AND AUDIENCE

THEME:

The division of a social context into team and audience is a fundamental form of interactional organization. Team-audience-formation occurs in two structurally different ways: First, a symbolic type may impose a reified representational pattern on the context delimiting its relevance. Secondly, closure of a game's typificatory scheme may impose total relevance.

Two lines of argument lead to the problem of teams and audiences. Closure of typificatory schemes and interaction between competitive teams are (in Sartre's theory) intrinsically related. The second argument relates to Mead's notion of "generalized other." The constitution of intersubjectively valid consent within the mutual tending of interacting partners toward common social objects is to be regulated by social rules prevalent also in games. Questioned more closely, however, the constitution of the "generalized other" remains conceptually unsatisfactory.[1]

Goffman's suggestion may help to bridge that difficulty: social inconsistencies may be overcome by "impression management" of competing teams. This suggestion led to the notion of common symbolic types in play and game. The seemingly intrinsic relationship of symbolic types in play and games, the possible closure of their respective typificatory schemes, and the formation of teams and audiences remain to be clarified.

8.1 Team and Audience: Theory

A further examination of the fundamental triadic intentionality of perceiving social objects may offer a clue. My perception of a social object, constituted within a context of mutual interaction, implies both the tending of the Other toward the social object and toward me. This interlocking of mutual perspectives of relevance may find an interesting "amplification"

---

[1] This is not to degrade in the least Mead's ingenious intuition in proposing this conception. For if the constitution of the "generalized other" were satisfactorily solved, the problem of intersubjectivity would have found its solution.

ın certain social contexts. Emile Durkheim already noted this phenomenon in the "particular attitude of a man speaking to a crowd" who experiences an "exceptional increase of force":

It comes to him from the very group which he addresses. The sentiments provoked by his words come back to him, but enlarged and amplified, and to this degree they strengthen his own sentiment. The passionate energies he arouses re-echo within him and quicken his vital tone. It is no longer a simple individual who speaks; it is a group incarnate and personified.[2]

Obviously, the "sentiments" aroused and amplified in the group depend very much on what the speaker is talking about. If the thematic field were the Pythagorean theorem and its theme its application among the ancient Babyloneans, his audience, say at a camping site, would become less aroused than if he announced the introduction of free love for everyone. Thematic field and choice of appropriate themes, knowledge and careful references to common symbolic types, all determine the effect of his speech on the audience.

If the speaker, for instance, plays at some prevalent prejudice in his audience, he may be almost sure of an amplified response. That is to say: the speaker could not "create" such an amplifying effect if it were not based on a most careful choice of thematic field and relevant symbolic types pertaining to the specific prejudice cultivated by his audience. The structure of this "mechanism" was described by Alfred Schütz in a study of the prejudices an "in-group" may impose upon an "out-group" by simply relying on subsequent self-typifications of the "out-group" inherent in that "mechanism":

A vicious circle is thus set up because the outgroup, by the changed reaction of the in-group, is fortified in its interpretation of the traits of the in-group as highly detestable. In more general terms: to the natural aspect the world has for group A belongs not only a certain stereotyped idea of the natural aspect the world has for group B, but included in it also is a stereotype of the way in which group B supposedly looks at A. This is, on a major scale – i.e., in the relationship between groups – the same phenomenon which, in respect to relations between individuals, Cooley has called the "looking-glass effect".[3]

Schütz has outlined here the crucial "mechanism" for team-audience formations. The only remaining difficulty is to explain, how on a "major scale" the phenomenon of the looking-glass effect may work between

---

[2] E. Durkheim, *Elementary Forms,* p. 210.

[3] "Equality and the Meaning Structure of the Social World," *Coll. Pap.,* vol. 2, p. 247.

social groups; its working on the individual level is an immediate consequence of the triadic structure of social relevance.

First of all, symbolic types, which seem to play a significant rôle in instituting such "vicious circles," are social types. Hence, they indicate in their typicality already the typical triadic perspectives of their constitutive social context. In simpler words: A white teacher's referring to the symbolic type "Black Man" in front of a class of Negroe students implies for his audience two aspects: *first*, the teacher's tending toward the typified social object "Black Man," *secondly*, his tending toward his class.

But since I am not simply talking about social, but about *symbolic* social types, their specific characteristics have to be taken into account. Symbolic types exhibit a significant degree of reification and delimit the range of relevance; they are taken as representations, i.e., they may stand for a typificatory scheme which otherwise would assure the maintenance of relevance in the situation.[4] These characteristics have the "amplifying effect" to which Durkheim and Schütz referred in their studies. Take, for instance, the symbolic type of "fool" discussed earlier in detail.[5] Unlike the enactment of social roles, which takes place in reciprocal, continuously readjusted typifications, the symbolic type "splits" the context into "fool" and "non-fool". Situational relations in a fool-making context are reified to such a degree that reciprocal typifications and constitution of social objects do not take place. Relevance is maintained and determined exclusively by the symbolic type.

This phenomenon of exclusive determination of social relevance also occurred in an earlier case. The closure of the typificatory scheme of games led to "total" relevance. The "splitting" of a context into "team" and "audience" is, furthermore, *the* characteristic of such games. *Sartre* assumed such a closure from the outset by his insistence on the predominance of means-ends schemata in social interaction and described subsequently all interaction in terms of competing teams. *Goffman*, despite fundamentally divergent assumptions about social reality, also describes all individual performances as team-performances.

A notion of "total relevance" can be methodologically significant only, if a distinction between "relevant" and "other" social phenomena is implied. The latter ones are also observable and copresent, but they are "marginal" or "not determinant" for relevance. One may say: *Total relevance in a social situation splits the context into a team, which controls the situational relations constitutive for the relevance structure, and into*

---

[4] See *sect.* **6.21.**
[5] See *sect.* 6.22.

an audience, which is subject to and has at most marginal control over the relevance structure. Hence, team-audience formation may occur in two structurally entirely different manners: 1. a symbolic type imposes a reified, representative pattern on the context delimiting its relevance; 2. closure of the typificatory schemes of games imposes total relevance.

The notion of "control" in this definition requires further clarification. In the case of games proper the question is answered right away by the rules of the game. They determine who is to control the situation and how control may "legally" be seized by Others. Obviously, the notions of "team" and "audience" in the case of games proper refer first to the two competing groups of players: one is the team and is in control and the other is the audience and tries to seize control. The spectators form an "audience" only in a very different sense, namely in respect to the symbolic types those players are enacting on the field.[6] This distinction, often overlooked in sociological studies of games, becomes obvious by a look at the "mechanism" of control in games proper. For, the question of who is team and who is audience, according to my definition, is to be decided by the exercise of and competition for control in the situation.

But the notion of "control" is less precisely defined in those cases, where 1. either total relevance is imposed by some symbolic type or where 2. some "inherent" teleological principle leads to a merger between the interactional modes of game and social action.

ad 1: In a situation dominated by a symbolic type the context is "split" because of the reified action patterns pertaining to the symbolic type. To give an example: For those who "cared," Marilyn Monroe "froze" their total sexual relevance structure. However, this does not imply that they selected their bed-fellows according to their symbolic type. This, besides being a probably frustrating enterprise, would have led to immediate interaction with the symbolic type and hence to "realistic" reciprocal typifications allowing the male to seize control of the situation. Rather, the symbolic type is to assure certain self-typifications within the audience by partitioning the context. That is to say, Marilyn Monroe as a symbolic type re-enforces the precarious self-typification of the male in modern society. But precisely this "re-enforcement," this "amplification," as Durkheim has called it, must still be clarified.

---

[6] Common sense reacts quite distinctly to these differences: poor games (where no socially significant symbolic types are enacted) have few spectators. But nevertheless, groups of players are fighting for being "in" as team and sending the others "out" as audience. That this lack of spectators is not solely dependent on poor play is obvious: the World Series held in Frankfurt, Germany, or a soccer game in Chicago's Wrigley Field would prove this point.

Schütz proposed that the looking-glass effect occurs also on a "major scale" between social groups, i.e., between team and audience. Since the triadic structure of social types already implies a reference to the constitutive context of interlocking perspectives of relevance, one merely needs to add that the splitting of the context into team and audience enforces this triadic structure. Not only *my* tending toward the social object implies now the double tending of the Other, but *our* tending, the tending of everyone in the audience implies now the double tending of the impersonator of the symbolic type. I am looking at "making-love" (symbolic type) not merely by taking into my tending Marilyn Monroe's tending toward it and toward *me,* but her double tending toward "making-love" and toward *us.* Thus, *the symbolic type throws a "shadow" over the partitioned context, in which every one in the audience may feel alike.* In other words, the symbolic type induces total relevance in the situation by situational relations splitting the context and unifying team as well as audience.

To give one additional example: Goffman refers to the "shadow" in his notion of "impression management":

> We know that the formal code of British civil servants and of American baseball umpires obliges them not only to desist from making improper "deals" but also to desist from innocent action which might possibly give the (wrong) impression that they are making deals. Whether an honest performer wishes to convey the truth or whether a dishonest performer wishes to convey a falsehood, both must take care to enliven their performances with appropriate expressions, exclude from their performances expressions that might discredit the impression being fostered, and take care lest the audience impute unintended meanings.[7]

The American baseball umpire, who has to "desist from innocent actions" in order not to "foster a wrong impression" has simply to perform his actions in accord with his "shadow." If he were not, his audience could not feel at ease that "everything is under control." Every Western fan knows how deadly it is for a poker player to casually hide his cards in a game.

This notion of the "shadow" of symbolic social types can help to answer the earlier question, how the "spectators" in a game proper like football may become an audience and interaction on the field may be considered a unified performance of some team. For in a game proper, as I have shown earlier and am going to discuss in detail in the final section,[8] symbolic types like "foul play," "expert," or "tough guy" are enacted. And it is in respect to the enactment of these symbolic types that the spectators

---

[7] E. Goffman, *Presentation,* p. 66.
[8] See *sect.* 8.2. and also the earlier *sect.* 7.1.

form an audience. Into the "shadow" of these types they may retreat either in comfort or in rage.

ad 2: The final question is that of control in a situation where game and social action are merged with each other, since the game's closure is supposed to be an inherent teleological principle. Most prominently, such a merger occurs in contemporary conceptions concerning the "utility" of economic endeavors that can be grasped also analytically in the theory of economic games. One empirical aspect of this problem will be studied in the next section.

The closure of typificatory schemes by inherent teleological principles has been discussed before in detail at Sartre's notion of "objective ends of action" and at Gehlen's notion of "Zucht." [9] I suggest that Heidegger's notion of "anyone" (das Man) implies a similar closure. For it is nothing but a most careful explication of the phenomenon of the "shadow":

Das Man hat selbst eigene Weisen zu sein. Die genannte Tendenz des Mitseins, die wir die Abständigkeit nannten, gründet darin, daß das Miteinandersein als solches die *Durchschnittlichkeit* besorgt. Sie ist ein existenzialer Charakter des Man. Dem Man geht es in seinem Sein wesentlich um sie. Deshalb hält es sich faktisch in der Durchschnittlichkeit dessen, was sich gehört, was man gelten läßt und was nicht, dem man Erfolg zubilligt, dem man ihn versagt. Diese Durchschnittlichkeit in der Vorzeichnung dessen, was gewagt werden kann und darf, wacht über jede sich vordrängende Ausnahme. Jeder Vorrang wird geräuschlos niedergehalten. Alles Ursprüngliche ist über Nacht als längst bekannt geglättet. Alles Erkämpfte wird handlich. Jedes Geheimnis verliert seine Kraft. Die Sorge der Durchschnittlichkeit enthüllt wieder eine wesenhafte Tendenz des Daseins, die wir die *Einebnung* aller Seinsmöglichkeiten nennen.[10]

Being-with-another in the same "shadow" is based on an "average," on a "median" consent on what is considered to be appropriate and valid fur mutual success. Any individual ambition is limited by the fringes of the "shadow." All relevant aspects of the situation are open to anyone in the audience, which fights deliberately and with great success against secret deals within the range of its competence.

Heidegger's notion of "Man" is most interesting as a description of the existential modes and posibilities of human action within the "shadow" of a symbolic type. But it becomes entirely unacceptable where Heidegger identifies this mode of social existence with social life at large. This is the moment of closure in Heidegger's theory. For he summarizes the passage quoted above in the sentence:

[9] See *sect.* 7.4.
[10] Heidegger, *Sein und Zeit,* p. 127.

Abständigkeit, Durchschnittlichkeit, Einebnung konstituieren als Seinsweisen des Man das, was wir als "die Öffentlichkeit" kennen.

Public life (Öffentlichkeit) certainly has more dimensions than existence within the "shadow" of a symbolic type.[11] What Heidegger seems to want, and what he finds nowhere in social life, is a realm dominated totally by the decision of an autonomous individual. Heidegger, like Sartre,[12] insists that somewhere there ought to be a realm of life, where one is free from all intersubjective bonds, where one is free to determine one's fate oneself. The "repressive" influence of social life, of the "collective conscience" in Durkheim's terms, makes itself most obviously felt in the "shadow," in the "inauthentic state" of the "Man":

Das Man ist überall dabei, doch so, daß es sich auch schon immer davongeschlichen hat, wo das Dasein auf Entscheidung drängt.[13]

It is Heidegger's insistence on "the decision," on man's freedom "to play or not to play" (as Schiller has stated it most clearly in his attempt to achieve political renovation by avoiding the murderous turmoil of contemporary revolutions) that leads Heidegger to an a-social conception of human existence.[14]

8.2 Practice: The Relation between Career Patterns and the Structure of Games.

Are problems of social control also in larger social settings related to the structure of games played in that society? This question has found little attention in sociological literature.[15] Caillois' opinion that play and game are "in principle devoid of important repercussions upon the solidity and continuity of collective and institutional life"[16] seems to express a general consensus among sociologists.

But Caillois' statement does not find universal support. In their "Study

---

[11] A similar reduction of social life to a mere "ostensible, overt" level of human conduct was criticized earlier in respect to Berne's foundation of his *Games People Play*. See *sect.* 1.3.

[12] See *sect.* 5.4.

[13] *Sein und Zeit*, p. 127.

[14] For a most interesting study of the historical development of "decisionism," which is closely related to aesthetic and rationalistic conceptions especially of German political thought, see Christian Graf von Krockow, *Die Entscheidung. Eine Untersuchung über Ernst Jünger, Carl Schmitt, Martin Heidegger* (Stuttgart, Enke, 1958).

[15] There are some exceptions. For instance: David Riesman and R. Denney, *Football in America: A Study of Culture Diffusion*, American Quarterly, 3, 1951, pp. 309–325.

[16] Roger Caillois, *Unity of Play: Diversity of Games*, Diogenes, 19, 1957, p. 99.

of the Culture of Suburban Life" Seeley, Sim and Loosley have tried to make the career patterns in upper-middle class suburban Crestwood Heights transparent by comparing them with the competitive structures of "typically male, typically North American games" like hockey and football which "seem to represent symbolically the structure of competition." [17]

Since these authors refer to games (and especially Canadian football) only metaphorically, i.e., since they do not see an *immediate* interactional link between the competitive settings in playing a game and in pursueing some occupational career, I shall attempt to construct this link from the very material and description they present. For, unfortunately they insist, after some very enlightening passages about the structural competition in games:

Career considerations seem to "come from nowhere" in the environment of the young child. He senses them only at the deepest level and expresses them in those flashes of insight which surprise and amaze parents. Yet from the beginning these considerations shape his orientation towards adulthood.[18]

In fact, I contend, career considerations are closely intertwined with the competitive setting of games which are played resp. appreciated in the larger social setting.

1. Rules and symbolic types. As in baseball, soccer, basketball, or tennis, the common symbolic type of football [19] is constituted in mutual "give-and-take." But unlike these other games, in football bodily involvement in playing at this symbolic type is nearly unlimited and highly combative. Thus, bodily enactment of this symbolic type, i.e., the positing of social limits constituting the typificatory scheme of the game and circumscribing its "rules," requires an aggressive and often violent "typically male" performance. Rules restricting bodily contact with the ball or restricting the "give-and-take" of the ball within that team, which is in possession of the ball, are only few. Rules concerning the bodily involvement with the opponents' team, which tries to block by vigorous bodily opposition any advancement of the ball, are still less restrictive. The player in

---

[17] J. R. Seeley, R. A. Sim, E. W. Loosley, *Crestwood Heights* (New York, Basic Books, 1956), p. 121.

[18] *Crestwood*, p. 124.

[19] In Crestwood Heights one plays "Canadian Rugby football." The analogies seen by Seeley et al. between the competitive settings of the suburb and of the game refer to that game. However, the authors pointed out the close relationship between American and Canadian football (p. 450 n. 7). The differences in the rules of both games are not significant enough to influence their stock of similarities. Though I refer in the following always to American football, a more detailed study should, of course, take account of these differences.

possession of the ball has to be "tackled" by the opposing team and such a tackle with its pile of limbs, legs and other unsortable bodily accessories is one of the most scenic configurations of the game.

A symbolic type arising with such vigorous, often violent, but in any case courageous, bodily involvement is that of "tough guy."[20] If transformed into the combat image of the "leathernecks" or into more refined "Profiles in Courage," on a rather wide scale of personal identity formation the "tough guy" is a basic determinant. William James considered the dualism between the "tender-minded" and the "tough-minded" to be of such a profound social reality that he described "The Present Dilemma in Philosophy" in his popular lectures on pragmatism as a consequence of these personal symbolic types:

"Their antagonism, whenever as individuals their temperaments have been intense, has formed in all ages a part of the philosophic atmosphere of the time ... The tough think of the tender as sentimentalists and softheads. The tender feel the tough to be unrefined, callous or brutal.
Their mutual reaction is very much like that which takes place when Bostonian tourists mingle with a population like that of Cripple Creek. Each type believes the other to be inferior to itself; but disdain in the one case is mingled with amusement; in the other it has a dash of fear.[21]

Rather than having grasped here a typology of philosophical minds, I contend, William James has acutely sensed the social types of "tough guy" and "tenderfoot" which have become identity-determining symbolic types in a specific social setting. Whether one plays football in this social context *because* those types are prevalent there, or vice versa, would be an altogether pointless question. However, I suggest that the modes of bodily involvement in the game of football are conducive for the constitution of the symbolic type of the "tough guy."[22]

---

[20] Severe limitations arise for any mere description of a symbolic type. It could be attempted by a study of the semantic field out of which this profile is carved, for instance, in the annual "Pro Football Almanac." To give only one example here: "Y. A. Tittle, New York Giants. The Bald Eagle never was more gallant. With a hostile sell-out crowd at Chicago's Wrigley Field howling for blood, aging quarterback Y. A. Tittle continued to play despite his injured, painwracked leg; desperately trying to toss just one more touchdown pass that would give the New York Giants a victory and the 1963 NFL championship." Bill Wise, *1964 Official Pro Football Almanac* (Greenwich, Fawcett, 1964), p. 46.

[21] William James, *Pragmatism* (New York, Meridian, 1955) p. 22f.

[22] The consequences of the arising dualism between the "tenderfoot" and the "tough guy" cannot be studied in any detail here. But they are immediately apparent in other competitive settings, for instance, in American politics. The types of "dove" or "hawk," the "egghead" and "liberal" as opposed to a conservative Birchite: these types become politically potent on the background of typificatory schemes which relate to constitutive

A closer view at the constitutive processes of this type formation will further support this contention. One has to remember that a boy's tending toward the "tough guy" has to imply his peers' or his team's tending toward him and toward the "tough guy." Apparently, an individualistic "overdoing" in one's own tending to become a "tough guy" would jeopardize the constitutive triadic relations of the perspectives of relevance which are fundamental for every social context. In simpler words, an individual's ambitious temptation to become a "tough guy" *at the cost of others* forecloses their tending toward the tough guy and toward him. Hence, the constitution of the *social* symbolic type does not succeed and the caricature of the "meat-head," a conglomeration of some merely perceptually affirmable traits of physical fitness, arises as Seeley et. al. found out:

> There is an endless constraint, however, against "overdoing". The star in Crestwood Heights must constantly practise "modesty," and pass the honor of victory on to the coach, his team-mates, or even his mother who has fed him so well. He must strive to establish the record, but once it is established he can be confident it will not be forgotten provided he properly disclaims credit for the victory. He can quickly submerge himself in the group, the team, or the firm.[23]

However, the authors' reasoning "that a star who excels too well puts himself out of his own league" and hence, as a "deterrent to over-performance," is inclined "to relate himself more co-operatively to the team" grasps only peripheral traits of the phenomenon. To become a "star" implies nothing but a specific reification of one's "shadow." [24] In this case, there is not an ongoing constitution of the type "tough guy" from one game to the other, depending on the more-or-less incalculable imponderabilia of playing against various teams, but the "Bald Eagle" *is* a star.[25]

---

contexts of games which have been played by "everyone." William James' statement may be requoted again since it becomes especially transparent in the political context, say of "doves" and "hawks": "Each type believes the other to be inferior to itself; but disdain in the one case is mingled with amusement, in the other it has a dash of fear."

[23] *Crestwood,* p. 123. – Again, the already quoted *Pro Football Almanac* may be studied for further support of this thesis. On about 150 pages the "unsung heroes" and the great stars of the game are portrayed. But consistently, quotations praising their achievements refer to teammates' statements, while they speak out themselves in direct speech only to remark on some mishap, like some injury or suspension, or on their intent to "help the Giants win."

[24] See *sect.* 8.1.

[25] The typification of Y. A. Tittle from the New York Giants as *the* star of the game is so consistent that he is never referred to in the *Pro Football Almanac* by his first name: "Y. A. injured his leg" (p. 13) or "Y. A. Tittle was on the shelf" (p. 15) etc., etc. No other player seems to have reached the symbolic stage of being typified by his initials only. They are the "Jimmy Brown" from Cleveland or the "Mean John" of the Redskins.

He has to impersonate the "tough guy" and his only chance to remain in the game *and* to take part in a "free" (i.e. a non-reified) constitution of social relations is to "submerge himself in the group, the team, or the firm."

The symbolic type of "tough guy" arises from the specific style of bodily involvement in playing football. He is a "personal type," while a particular symbolic "action type" arises immediately from the rules of the game.[26] Typically for the game of football (as well as for baseball and golf) interaction between both teams is broken up into distinct phases of interaction. To score a touchdown, a touchback, or a fieldgoal is not to be achieved in a constant uninterrupted flow of interaction (like for instance in soccer). The rules of the game specifically assign for the beginning of each phase of interaction to one team the initiative to advance toward the goal and to the opponents a defensive rôle of blocking any advancement. Offensive and defensive rôles of the two teams may change, of course, immediately after a phase of interaction has begun, but its starting situation is clearly defined. Furthermore, offensive and defensive rôles for the starting position of each phase of interaction alternate between the teams only in case the offensive team is unable to advance at least 10 yards. Most important, however, for the structure of competition in football: The offensive team is given 4 chances to gain the required ground from the opponents.

Summary: Interaction in football is patterned into alternating sequences of "action" (offense, defense, tackle) and "planning" (huddle). Both phases are strict team performances, while only the "action"-phase counts toward the playing-time. Defensive and offensive rôles are precisely defined for each team in each phase. A team may reach its ultimate goal of scoring some goal in accumulating certain minimal gains (cumulative credit system). A team loses its right to an offensive initiative only after it has had at least a "second chance."

The description of this pattern of interaction could also come from the pen of some school or college administrator who attempts to characterize the two teams he is supposed to keep running: his students on the one side and his teaching staff on the other. A change of only a few descriptive labels leads to the following statement: Interaction in school (college)

---

[26] I cannot present a comprehensive study of the game of football at this time. Further symbolic types concerning, for example, typical team-audience formations, typical deviations like "foul play" etc. ought to be studied further in more detail. My present task is merely to demonstrate the applicability of the conceptual scheme of type formations to the problems studied by Seeley et. al. in Crestwood Heights. Hence, I point out only the constitution of *one* personal type and *one* action type.

is patterned into alternating sequences of "action" (teaching, writing, showing-off in class) and "planning" (reading, doing research, "study hall"). Both phases are strict team performances ("my" students are doing research, "my" teaching staff has published), while only the "action"-phase counts toward the total performance ("publish or perish"; report cards). Defensive and offensive rôles are precisely defined for each team in each phase. A team (i.e. each of its individual members) may reach its ultimate goal of scoring some goal (graduation, promotion) in accumulating certain minimal gains (credits, one publication a year). A team (i.e. each member of the team) loses its right for an offensive initiative (to advance to college or to be kept on the list for promotions) only after it had at least "a second chance."

This hypothetical transference of the action pattern of football into the action pattern of a school seems to be possible without major distortions of the different institutional orders,[27] because the action pattern had hardened into the reified status of a closed symbolic typificatory scheme. The imposed goals of ultimate success are closely related. Any interaction in either system, more specifically, any "playing" at some symbolic type of this scheme ("equal chance," "second chance," "doing research") posits social limits for all other interaction within the respective system. The legitimating devices, which the football coach or the school administrator may "invent" to "justify" those symbolic interactional patterns, can "work" and may save the inhabitants from "anomic terror" only, as long as those social limits may come about in mutual interaction.

2. *The social setting.* Seeley and his collaborators studied the game of football within the larger social setting of Crestwood Heights. However, as was noted earlier, they do not see an immediate *interactional* tie between the mode of playing this game and other modes of social interaction in Crestwood Heights. The larger social setting converges, in their opinion, only on a highly institutionalized level with the game of football, where, for instance, economic and financial interests may merge with those of playing the game.[28] In their own words:

The game is played by two competing teams. The teams are evenly matched in number, in ascribed roles, and, if possible, in strength – for the odds for winning should be as even as possible. Equal strength depends on player ability, coaching and management skill, and the eye appeal of the playing grounds, uniforms,

---

[27] It would be easy to collect empirical data to support this hypothetical opinion of a typical administrator concerning "his" school or "his" staff.

[28] Methodologically, this conception derives from their implicit presuppositions concerning the dualism between "fun" in "mere play" and "discipline" in the realm of "serious" endeavours.

equipment, and drum majorettes. The two teams are members of a league, and the league is tied in series of relationships to other leagues devoted to the promotion of the game. In a single game, therefore, the issue at stake is not simply the final score of the game but actually the interlocking interests of all the teams in the league, of all the leagues, officials, players, coaches, and subsidiary parties to the game – of distributors of sporting equipment, news and radio commentators, and so on.[29]

Those seemingly innocent final words "and so on" indicate the institutional convergence they assume to prevail between the social setting of Crestwood Heights and the game itself. It is based on one core argument: "The odds for winning should be as even as possible." And indeed the whole social lay-out, as far as it concerns the crucial question of status-maintenance and a constant fear about and fight against the danger of downward mobility for adolescents being raised in Crestwood Heights, is encompassed in that theme.[30] Two consequences may be drawn from their approach:

1. On the one hand, their limitation to a study of the competitive structure of the football game, as if "everyone" plays the game, leads necessarily to a polarization of the social setting in Crestwood Heights: a male realm of "sentimental toughness and realism" is clearly separated from the female world of "idealistic fadism" (terms used similarly by Riesman in criticizing this supposed polarization). The polarization into "typically male" and "typically female" attitudes, for instance, toward the child's potential failure,[31] is a consequence of their approach; it is not based on a deduction from empirical data presented in the study.

2. On the other hand, however, it is precisely their hypothesis of the convergence between the competitive setting of football and that of the male world in Crestwood Heights which allow Seeley and his colleagues to translate their observations into a remarkably vivid portrait of that suburb. There are, however, three major presuppositions on which this hypothesis is built, and they are all fulfilled for this specific study. They indicate the close relations between the interactional mode of playing

---

[29] *Crestwood*, p. 121.

[30] David Riesman in his very critical introduction to "Crestwood Heights" takes issue with the authors' attempts to grasp the social setting within the scheme of competitive efficiency: "I wonder whether it is I who bring to the material a sardonic reaction or whether I find it there, in the use of the term 'efficiency,' in the comparison with the club or office, and in the awkwardness – neither quite jargon nor quite literature – of such phrases as 'highly regarded token of love and esteem.'" (p. ix) – I intend to show that the authors' had good reason to choose that approach.

[31] "The father ... would be more inclined to elbow the child out of the driver's seat" while the mother tends "to drive, so to speak, from the back seat." *Crestwood*, p. 127.

football and the "serious" style of everyday social action in Crestwood Heights.

Presupposition 1: The closure of the typificatory scheme of football is compatible with the general career orientation. – This closure, i.e., the imposition of the non-immanent "goal" or "purpose" for playing the game concerns many more facets of the game than the authors recognize. They restrict their argument to one major competitive ideal: "The odds for winning should be as even as possible."

The game is won by that team accumulating the highest number of points within 60 minutes of playing-time. There are four major ways of scoring[32]: 1. a touchdown, i.e. propelling the ball beyond the opponents' goal line, counts 6 points; 2. a touchback, forcing the opponents to touch the ball to the ground behind their own goal line, counts 2 points; 3. a fieldgoal scores 3 points, if the ball can be kicked from the field over the crossbars of the opponents' goal post; 4. as a kind of "bonus" after a touchdown, the scoring team is allowed to attempt a kick of the ball over the opponents' goal post, collecting 1 point in case of success. Touchdown, touchback, and fieldgoal are, of course, immanent characteristics of the game; i.e. they are rules of football. However, altogether alien to the rules of bodily interaction are a) the weights for each particular scoring (6; 2; 3; 1),[33] b) the introduction of the "bonus" after having been successful in scoring a touchdown, and c) the decision to count the points made during exactly 60 minutes of strict playing-time. These three characteristics circumscribe the closure of the typificatory scheme of football. They are imposed on the interactional rules of the game and are major determinants of the adopted strategy of each team.

I have previously noted that the closure of a game's typificatory scheme allows for the transition between the mode of playing a game and the mode of social action within the larger social setting.[34] This thesis may be now explicated.

ad a: The assignment of specific weights (6; 2; 3; 1) for the different possibilities of scoring in the game is an attempt to even the odds for winning in those situations. Closer statistical analysis of the model of a football game would probably reveal the fact that the chances of scoring

[32] These rules of scoring are subject to frequent changes by agreement between the major leagues. Hence, it may be that other rules are valid today. This does not significantly influence the argument, but only supports it: these rules are imposed.

[33] Of course, the ongoing interaction is also determined by these weights in that they influence the "strategy" of the game. This, however, is a *consequence* of a *particular* closure of the game. Different weights lead to a change of strategies.

[34] See *sect.* 7.4.

in any of these 4 ways correlate with these weights. The situations are comparable to the rank assigned to different hands in a poker game. However close such a model would approximate the real game, the important point is the effort (or – if seen on the background of a once-adopted type of game like football – the necessity) to balance by calculated rational assignment of weights the chances of winning in the game. *Comparison:* The parental efforts to plan such balancing of the odds in their children's education toward a prospective career have been the major theme of Seeley's report on Crestwood Heights. These efforts aim at keeping the child within a favorable competitive position of its team and not, as may be considered appropriate in another social setting, at developing the child's individual capacities into a personal totality.

ad b: The chance to collect a "bonus" after having been successful *already once* is reminiscent of the proverbial attitude that "one is to help those who help themselves." This rule or attitude definitely favors those who are winning. It does not support the competitive ideal that "the odds for winning should be as even as possible," though the imbalance is somehow corrected by assigning to it merely the minimal possible score. – *Comparison:* In the larger social setting of Seeley's study this attitude becomes compatible with their competitive ideal of "even odds," since first of all nobody seems to be a loser in Crestwood Heights, and secondly, even the smallest competitive achievement of the child is systematically and generously rewarded by the parents.

ad c: The time limit of 60 minutes of "playing-time" induces a typical attitude toward the manageability of time. Only the phases of "action" count against the total playing time, while the intermittent phases of "planning" (huddle) do not. Each phase of action is so short, lasting often only a few seconds, that – in comparison to the long span of total playing time – the phases of "action" may seem to be nearly independent of the major time limits of the game. This holds true for at least the first three quarters of the game, while only toward the end in the final phases of action awareness of the "last minute left" of playing-time will determine strongly the pattern of interaction. In other words, in a typical mid-game situation of high tension, say in a tackle on the opponents' one-yard line, where the phase of action may last perhaps 10 seconds, the interaction is *not structured by outer playing-time.* Both teams attempt to structure the anticipated phase of action by adopting some strategy, though in this situation nearly all success depends on the force and vivacity of bodily charge of the attacking team. I have already shown that the symbolic type of "tough guy" is related to this style of interaction. The incipient event constitutive for this symbolic type comes about through combative interaction between the opposing teams in this situation. And it is the incipient event of mutual combative interaction which structures this situation. Since, on the other hand, the symbolic type of "tough guy" may penetrate the whole typificatory scheme of football which unifies the situation of action into a context, one may conclude, that in this typical situation of interaction *social temporality arises.* The typical mid-game situation of high combat tension is not structured by outer "playing time" but by an incipient event constituted in team interaction, which unites the situation into a context and leads to the arisal of social temporality. However, social temporality may structure more-or-less intensively only certain phases of action, which are always broken off shortly by the imposed phases of "planning," and which are judicially called by a whole team of umpires.[35] – *Comparison:* Arising incipient events structuring the passage of social interaction and inducing social temporality are being kept under the tight rule of imposed strategic planning. It is the individual in his capacity for *temporal typifications,* who is to project and pursue his *own* path of action. There has to be sound rational management and action in order that *social temporality,* which is itself not subject to individual control, may not arise to structure long and perhaps socially decisive passages of interaction. This characteristic of strategic and purposeful parental attitudes, again, has been reported extensively by Seeley et. al. in their report:

The parental role has to be one of careful management, in which protection of the child is delicately balanced against exposure to difficulty.[36]

Summary: The first presupposition concerning Seeley's hypothesis of a convergence between the competitive setting of football and that of the male world of Crestwood Heights is built on the compatibility between the closure of the typificatory scheme of football and the general career orientation in that suburb. The three characteristics of that closure have been shown to relate immediately to specific aspects of that career orientation: a) The assignment of specific weights to the different possibilities

---

[35] The high bodily involvement in football, nearly unlimited as compared to games like soccer or baseball, reduces the main task of the umpires to judge if the ball has been touched to the ground, that is, it is their main task to decide if an action phase has to be terminated. – In which ways the symbolic type of "judge" arising in these games penetrates into the judicial system in the larger social setting is open for further analysis. In any case, the football leagues have developed their own "judicial system." In the NFL, James Kane was the "field judge" in 1963 and it seems worthwhile reporting in the annals, for instance, that "his honor was knocked down" by a "pair of frisky Colts." See: *Pro Football Almanac,* p. 71.

[36] *Crestwood,* p. 128.

of scoring in the game correlate with the general competitive ideal of "even odds" for every member of his team. b) The granting of an additional "bonus" for those who have proved to be successful corresponds to a widely practiced system of incentives as a stimulus for competitive achievement. c) Careful strategic management tries to delimit the range of possibly arising social temporality: incipient events have to be kept under social control.

Presupposition 2: Crestwood Heights and its games are set within an "open society." – Several references have already been made to the notion of "strategy" in games. Though a comprehensive study of that notion cannot be undertaken in this context, since it would imply an analysis of the rôle of rationality within different social settings and would rely ultimately on some theory of intersubjectivity, two points were clarified to some degree:

1. The "strategy" of interaction in a football game is a consequence of the particular closure of the game's typificatory scheme.[37] Only an ultimate strategy of "how to win the game" forces all interactional relations into a closed means-end schema. *Comparison:*

The money which the father earns in a schedule-dominated life is used to purchase whatever is considered necessary – including leisure.[38]

The phases of "action" and the phases of "leisure" (or "rest" or "planning how to spend the earnings") are cast in Crestwood Heights into an all encompassing competitive scheme directed to and by the father's unquestioned capacity to earn.

2. "Strategic games" are also studied in the mathematical theory of games. The notion of rational behavior basic for the concept of "strategy" presupposes, at least hypothetically, the role of an "umpire" who may know "everything that happened in a particular play." This presupposition may be characterized by the term "open society."[39] If individual access to the labor market and to economic positions of strategic influence were restricted, if access to the various institutions of learning and "equality under law" were limited to certain sectors of Crestwood Heights' population, then the total social setting would lack its typical permeability. In other words, the competitive structure of a strategic game like football may penetrate the social setting and especially its dominant economic

---

[37] This notion of strategy, by the way, is equivalent to the one prevalent in the mathematical theory of games.
[38] *Crestwood,* p. 64.
[39] Neumann-Morgenstern, *Theory of Games,* pp. 68–72.

styles of cooperation, competition, and career orientation (and vice versa) only in a sufficiently homogenious setting.

As a simple *correlate* to this second presupposition, Seeley's and his collaborators' conception of "social time" can further support the argument. They state:

Social time, then, is derived from physical and biological time, in the sense that the logic and symbolism of these two are the foundations upon which a system of social time is built.[40]

The "logic and symbolism" of "nature time" is, however, isomorphic to the "time of Cartesian rationality" which Sartre has shown to be at the basis of the economic conceptions and transactions in a "capitalistic economy."[41] Consistency and transferability between the temporal dimensions structuring both the specific realm of play and game as well as a specific social setting are presuppositions for the "permeability" noted above as prevailing in an "open society." As if to support this argument, the authors of "Crestwood Heights" continue:

In the measure of time in Crestwood Heights, a pendulum-like swing occurs and recurs – between tension and relaxation, preparation and realization, work and leisure, application and dalliance.

Without any difficulties, these characteristics could be translated into Parsons' notion of pattern variables, which are thematic temporal typifications based on "nature time."[42] Incipient events are for Parsons not subject to study in an "analytical science of social action"; in Crestwood Heights they seem to vanish altogether. Social temporality, as an intersubjectively constituted phenomenon of context, does not arise within the competitive setting, at least as far as it is projected by their men's unbroken confidence in their career orientations.

Presupposition 3: The social setting of Crestwood Heights is characterized by the relative irrelevance of any occupational mobility ethos for the career orientations of the adolescents. The mobility ethos, which becomes problematic for the formation of personal identity for any adolescent with lower parental occupational status,[43] has in Crestwood Heights no significant impact. An all-out attempt to assure status-maintenance for the child is the major problem:

[40] *Crestwood,* p. 63.
[41] See *sect.* 5.4. and 7.4.
[42] See *sects.* 5.21.
[43] See: Peter Berger and Thomas Luckmann, *Social Mobility and Personal Identity,* European Journal of Sociology, 5, 1964, pp. 331ff.

The parents face a solid dilemma. Their resolve not to intervene (with the career plans of their children) may be a common-sense recognition that in a changing world one cannot make specific plans, that arranged marriages and careers belong to other and bygone time. On the other hand, no one knows better than the parents in Crestwood Heights that there is "nothing left" for the child if his career goes awry.[44]

David Riesman indicated in his introduction that Seeley and his other field workers occasionally seem to be "taken in" by the "very niceness of the Crestwood Heights people" which made them in a certain sense "defenseless" in the face of their informants.[45] This criticism definitely applies to their judgement quoted above. The dilemma of a mother, who puts a plate of food in front of her child hoping the unwilling brat will start eating sometime, while knowing that the kid may starve otherwise, is a universal human problem. But this dilemma is clearly defined and constituted within the immediate social context, especially of the family. Its possible solutions are, however, also based within this same interactional context.

However, in a very different sense, one can argue indeed that the parents in Crestwood Heights face a "solid dilemma" in respect to the careers of their children. The three presuppositions listed above all support the major contention of Seeley, Sim, and Loosley that the competitive setting in football converges with major characteristics of the general career orientation in Crestwood Heights. It is the very limitation of these presuppositions to the specific social setting of Crestwood Heights which leads to the notion that there is "nothing left" outside its highly protective social context.

Is it perhaps possible to "teach" a mobility ethos and its implicit protective and identity-producing mechanisms to overcome the mobility dilemma? Or are there any games or forms of play which can perform this important social function? Very probably, the question cannot be raised in this explicit form. The "troubled" parents of Crestwood Heights will not be relieved from their "solid dilemma" so simply. But sociological research in this direction would not be totally undirected. And the thesis of Caillois that games are "in principle devoid of important repercussions upon the solidity and continuity of collective and institutional life" can hardly be maintained.

---

[44] *Crestwood,* p. 127.
[45] *op. cit.,* p. ixf. – The study of Crestwood Heights does not penetrate what Vidich and Bensman have called the "separate and hidden layer of community life," i.e., the realm of community gossip. This realm seems to be largely structured by symbolic types, which are related to the more intimate games the people play in Crestwood Heights. See for instance, Arthur J. Vidich and Joseph Bensman, *Small Town in Mass Society* (Garden City, Doubleday Anchor Books, 1960), pp. 30–46.

CHAPTER 9

CONCLUSION: THE CONSTRUCTION AND SOLUTION OF SOCIAL INCONSISTENCIES

Within the larger framework of sociological theory, this study dealt with preliminaries to the theory of social roles. Typical lines of action can be reciprocally pursued only within typificatory frames of social relevance. Innovation and variation of such frames occur as a process of intersubjective constructing and solving of social inconsistencies.

The major positions of what one could call "relevance theory" have been developed by Alfred Schütz and Aron Gurwitsch from a phenomenological perspective and by Charles S. Peirce and George H. Mead as correlates to their pragmatistic conception of social reality. Relevance theory deals with a peculiar problem: If social reality is conceived as a construction of and by social types, social inconsistencies have to be studied as inconsistencies between social types, as inconsistencies arising within typificatory schemes that pattern social interaction. The conceptual danger of reifying social inconsistencies is apparent. Inconsistencies between social types are likely to be taken as typical social phenomena, as types themselves.

The circularity of such an approach has been recognized. Mead studied social inconsistencies as eruptive "natural" phenomena which lead to emergent events within the temporal phenomenon of the present. Schütz described social inconsistencies as "explosions" of the individual actor's anticipatory action patterns. Both studies of social inconsistencies focus on different but correlated aspects of one and the same social phenomenon. Both deal with the emergence of incipient events in face of social inconsistencies. But Schütz had considerable difficulty grasping the situational constitution and relevance of social inconsistencies, since he derived his notion of social relevance from the individual's structure of interactional motives. Mead's difficulties were to delineate the social from the situational aspects of emergent events.

Social relevance as the phenomenal structure of context was described by Aron Gurwitsch in his studies of "The Field of Consciousness." Applying his notion of relevance to a study of social objects required few conceptual changes. A situation of social interaction gains *relevance* by a specific relational structure unifying the *social situation* into a *context*. Social objects are constituted by mutual interacting of partners, and their intersubjective tending toward the arising social object has some import for this constitutive process. The relational structure (and this is the major alteration I proposed) is triadic: my tending toward a social object has to imply the tending of Others toward the object and toward me. In other words: the *intentionality of perceiving social objects* has a triadic structure, which becomes an inherent characteristic of social types and determines the relational structure constitutive for a relevant social context. Two different, though related ways of maintaining social relevance in a situation have been described:

1. Most generally, relevance as a unification of situational relations into a context is maintained by some *typificatory scheme*. Every member of a social group has always at his disposal some stock of social types. This is his only means of coming to terms with his social environment. These types may be very rudimentary, as in the case of very young children, they may be precariously fragile, as in the case of psychiatric patients: as long as one talks of "social beings" with whom one is involved in some "social intercourse," intersubjective social types lead to a mutual constitution of social objects. The situational relations between those social types, which make such intercourse possible (i.e., which maintain relevance) are called a typificatory scheme. All social action, as well as certain forms of game, maintain relevance by means of typificatory schemes.

2. In certain social situations, relevance may be maintained by *symbolic social types:* they are constituted in the interactional mode of play. The symbolic type of a "fool," for instance, may be created by a team which is in danger of losing its control over a specific situation. This symbolic type, which may be impersonated by anyone, reifies all situational relations and patterns all mutual interaction; it represents the order of situational control; it legitimates all intersubjective conduct in the situation. Relevance is induced by the symbolic type.

The creation of symbolic types is a major means of constructing social inconsistencies. For maintenance of social relevance, say, by invoking a fool-making situation, can prolong the situational dominance of a certain team, but it brings about "frictions," "ambivalence" and "uncertainty" by its reification of all situational relations. These terms indicate the vagueness of a social situation in which social inconsistencies arise. They may arise either by purposive construction or by an insufficient stock of social types: the process of type formation is the same in both cases. The notion of "purpose" becomes significant only on the interactional levels of game and social action. Individual interactional goals and their subjectivistic implications arise in specific modes of transition between game and social action.

Social inconsistencies indicate a gap in the context, i.e., a situation which can be unified into context only on its fringes. It is a situation where the mediate presentation of context (the tending of the Other toward common social objects and toward me) cannot be "tied" with the immediate presentation of context (the context as it presents itself to me). There is no social type available which "ties" the two modes of presentation together. In other words: The mediate presentation of context by other participants in a social situation constitutes a *thematic field*. This thematic field is diffuse if a social inconsistency occurs: attempts to clarify the thematic field by turning thematic interest toward specific constituents of the situation does not lead to a satisfactory typification of the context. *Theme* after theme, (they stand in an intrinsic relationship to the thematic field) comes up in typificatory efforts to come to terms with the situation.

These incipient typificatory processes are to be understood as specific modes of interaction, if the claim of interactional construction of social reality is to be taken seriously. *In playing-at-a-theme* an interactional solution to the social inconsistency is constituted: some theme leads to a satisfactory clarification of the diffuse thematic field; an *incipient event* as a rudimentary social type (still indistinguishable from the social object) comes about. In typifying first the whole context by that incipient event and then also other situations with the rudimentary social type, an iterative constitution and separation of social type and social object takes place. This innovatory process has an abductive structure, as first described by Charles S. Peirce in his epistemological analyses. Applied to the present social context: though the constitutive processes start from some appropriate theme, social object and social type arise as "antecedent" to the "consequent," the theme. "Understanding" social phenomena in intersubjective typificatory processes of an abductive structure avoids some of the subjectivistic and solipsistic fallacies known from the theory of intersubjectivity.

The interactional modes of playing-at-a-theme, of play, of game and finally of social action proper (which is preceded by a project) have been distinguished by contextual differences, especially by its temporal dimensions. *Social temporality* has been described as a phenomenon of context:

if the arisal of an incipient event leads to a structurization of the passage of social interaction, thus bringing about a typificatory scheme unifying the situation into a context, then this process is structured by "social temporality." However, the typificatory scheme of a project, which is constitutive for social action, does not constitute social relevance. It does not lead to social temporality, but to *temporal typifications* based on "inner time."

The relationship between the contextual phenomenon of "social temporality" and "inner time" (i.e., the temporal dimension of the stream of consciousness) has not been studied at all. A second problem has been left out. Though it is of equal importance (and probably closely related to those temporal phenomena) the triadic intentionality of perceiving social objects has not been linked to the perception of visual objects "in the modus of naive certainty." The unsolved problems of the theory of intersubjectivity, which Edmund Husserl outlined in his great "Cartesian Meditations," have appeared only at the horizon of my study. They circumscribe the particular unsolved questions mentioned here.

These problems may be approached, perhaps, by further analysing the *rôle of the body* in play. I have shown that the human body is paramount among all incipient events and becomes a constitutive part of all typificatory schemes. The emergence of symbolic types in play has been closely linked to this constitutive rôle of the body. Bodily enactment of the symbolic type constitutes limits for all social interaction: these limits delineate the range of social relevance and save the situation from the ever imminent danger of anomie. To look at the "nomic" side of this phenomenon: the boundaries of socially relevant reality do not have to coincide with the delimitations set by the human body.

Anomie occurs as a "destruction" of the abductive level of type formation, as a situation in which incipient events cannot arise and the typical contours of social objects become blurred and unapprehendable. The phenomenon of *reification,* on the other hand, describes a total separation of the abductive level from the realm of social types. Those situational relations between social types, which maintain relevance, are taken in this case as types themselves. For instance, enactment of symbolic types in play implies a considerable reification of the context.

Symbolic types "split" the context into *team and audience.* They impose a total relevance structure on the situation since they reify all situational relations in respect to the one symbolic type. Either one belongs to the impersonating team or one is part of the observing audience. Situational control over the social setting is delineated along the team-audience division. The control is amplified by the *"shadow"* of the symbolic type: the triadic intentionality of perceiving social objects, which remains a constitutive characteristic also of the arising symbolic social types, becomes "enforced" or "amplified" by the possibility of an individual's submerging into the anonymity of "his" team or audience.

Total relevance may also be imposed on a situation by *closure of a game's typificatory scheme*. Play and game are related modes of interaction, since they have a common symbolic type. Enactment of this symbolic type in play posits social limits, certain of which constitute the typificatory scheme describing the rules of the game. Closure of this scheme is achieved by imposing a "goal" or "purpose" on the game, which is arbitrarily agreed upon, or traditionally derived. The important point: closure of the typificatory scheme is not inherent to the rules of the game. But as soon as some closure has been adopted by consent, total relevance structures enactment of the game. A division of context into team and audience occurs.

Finally, some methodological questions related to the construction and solution of social inconsistencies should be mentioned. Concerning sociological studies of game and play, two often stated premisses have become questionable. 1. Studying the interactional modes of playing-at-a-theme, of play and game, and of social action proper, from the perspective of contextual differences in the immediate situation of interaction does neither rely on nor lead to a dualism between "mere play" and "serious action." 2. Play and game have considerable repercussions on the solidity of collective and institutional life.

The modes of play, game, and social action merge into one another under precisely determinable contextual conditions. One such condition, team-audience formation, is of special methodological interest. For it questions the widely held opinion that the social sciences can be based on and developed from a notion of social action, say, for instance, in the Parsonean adaptation of Max Weber's theory. Social action is *not* an irreducible social phenomenon. It is just one mode of interaction among others. It is not even the most important one, if one stresses those interactional processes, in which social types are constituted.

These methodological questions go beyond the intended scope and practicable range of this study. They were bracketed earlier in favor of contextual analyses of the structure of social inconsistencies. But they have to be taken up in order to establish or dismiss a final conjecture, with which I would like to conclude this study. The notion of rationality, which by ways of largely reified conceptions like "rational" or "logical" action, like "objective" as opposed to "subjective" reality, has permeated many concept formations of the social sciences, may reveal itself as a derivative of transitional phases between plays, games, and projected social actions. This conjecture may direct further sociological research in a realm already staked out both by Charles S. Peirce' dictum that "logic is rooted in the social principle" and by Edmund Husserl's analyses of the "life-world."

BIBLIOGRAPHY

BENSMAN, JOSEPH and Vidich, Arthur. Small Town in Mass Society (Garden City, Doubleday Anchor Books, 1960)

BERGER, PETER L. and Kellner, Hansfried. Marriage and the Construction of Social Reality, Diogenes, 46, 1964, pp. 1ff.

– and Luckmann, Thomas. Social Mobility and Personal Identity, European Journal of Sociology, 5, 1964, pp. 331ff.

– and Luckmann, Thomas. The Social Construction of Reality (Garden City, Doubleday, 1966)

– and Pullberg, Stanley. Reification and the Sociological Critique of Consciousness, New Left Review, 35, 1966, pp. 56–77.

BERGSON, HENRI. The Creative Mind (New York, Wisdom Library, 1946)

BERNE, ERIC. Games People Play (New York, Grove, 1964)

BERNSTEIN, RICHARD J. Perspectives on Peirce (New Haven, Yale Univ. Press, 1965)

BRIGGS, RAYMOND. The Mother Goose Treasury (New York, Coward-McCann, 1966) – A first collection of these rhymes attributed to "Mother Goose" appeared between 1765 and 1781.

BUSCH, WILHELM. Max and Moritz (München, Braun-Schneider, 1965) – First published in 1865.

BUYTENDIJK, F. J. J. Het spel van mensch en dier als openbaring van levensdriften (Amsterdam, 1932) – German translation: Wesen und Sinn des Spiels (Berlin, Wolff, 1934)

CAILLOIS, ROGER. Unity of Play: Diversity of Games, Diogenes, 19, 1957.

– Les jeux et les hommes (Paris, Gallimard, 1958) – English translation: Man, Play, and Games (New York, Free Press of Glencoe, 1961) – German edition: Die Spiele und die Menschen (München-Wien, Langen-Müller, no date)

CAMUS, ALBERT. The Rebel (New York, Vintage Books, 1961) – First French edition "L'Homme Révolté" in 1951.

COOLEY, CHARLES H. Human Nature and the Social Order (New York, Scribner, 1902)

DENNEY, R. and Riesman, D. Football in America: A Study in Culture Diffusion, American Quarterly, 3, 1951, pp. 309-325.

DURKHEIM, EMILE. The Division of Labor in Society (New York, Macmillan, 1933) – First published in French in 1893, second edition in 1902.

– The Rules of Sociological Methods (Chicago, Univ. of Chicago Press, 1938) – First French publication in 1895.

– Le Suicide (Paris, Presses Univ. de France, 1960). – First published in 1897.

– The Elementary Forms of the Religious Life (London, Allan, 1954). – First French edition from 1912.

– Sociology and Philosophy (Glencoe, Free Press, 1953) – First published posthumously in French in 1924.

FESTINGER, LEON. A Theory of Cognitive Dissonance (Stanford, Stanford Univ. Press, 1957)

GEHLEN, ARNOLD. Der Mensch (Bonn, Athenäum, 6. Aufl., 1958). – First edition published in 1940.

– Die Seele im technischen Zeitalter (Hamburg, Rowohlt, 1957)

GLASER, B. G. and Strauss, A. L., Awareness of Dying (Chicago, Aldine, 1965)

GOFFMAN, ERVING. The Presentation of Self in Everyday Life (New York, Doubleday Anchor Books, 1959)

– Asylums (New York, Doubleday Anchor Books, 1961)

– Encounters (Indianapolis, Bobbs-Merrill, 1961)

GROOS, KARL. Die Spiele der Thiere (Jena, Fischer, 1896)

– Die Spiele der Menschen (Jena, Fischer, 1899)

GURWITSCH, ARON. The Field of Consciousness (Pittsburgh, Dusquesne Univ. Press, 1964) – The original French edition "Théorie du champ de la conscience" was published in 1957.

HABERMAS, JÜRGEN. Erkenntnis und Interesse (Frankfurt, Suhrkamp, 1968)

HEIDEGGER, MARTIN. Sein und Zeit (Tübingen, Niemeyer, 10. Aufl., 1963) – First edition in 1927.

HERMES, H. Enumerability, Decidability, Computability (Berlin–Heidelberg–New York, Springer, 1965)

HOFFMANN, HEINRICH. Der Struwelpeter (Stuttgart, Loewe, no date) – The physician author lived from 1809–1894.

HUIZINGA, JOHAN. Homo Ludens (Leiden, 1938) – English translation under the same title published by Beacon Press, Boston, 1955.

HUSSERL, EDMUND. Ideen zu einer reinen Phänomenologie und phänomenologischen Philosophie (Den Haag, Nijhoff, 1950). 1. Buch. – English translation by W. R. Boyce Gibson, Ideas (New York, Macmillan, 1931). First German edition in 1913.

– Cartesianische Meditationen (Den Haag, Nijhoff, 1950) – First published in French in 1931. – English translation by D. Cairns, Cartesian Meditations (The Hague, Nijhoff, 1960).

– Die Krisis der europäischen Wissenschaften und die transzendentale Phänomenologie (Haag, Nijhoff, 1962) – Some parts were already published in 1936.

– Erfahrung und Urteil (Hamburg, Claassen, 3d ed., 1964)

JAMES WILLIAM. The Principles of Psychology (Dover Publications, 1950), vol. 1. – First edition published in 1890.

– The Will to Believe (Dover Edition, 1956) – Originally published in 1897.

– Pragmatism (New York, Meridian, 1955) – First publication in 1907.

KELLNER, HANSFRIED and Berger, Peter. Marriage and the Construction of Social Reality, Diogenes 46, 1964, pp. 1ff.

KANT, IMMANUEL. Kritik der Urteilskraft, in: Kants Werke, 6. Buch (Berlin, Weichert, no date) – First published in 1790.

KEMENY, JOHN G., Snell, J. Laurie and Thompson, Gerald L. Introduction to Finite Mathematics (Englewood Cliffs, Prentice-Hall, 1956)

KETCHAM, HANK. Dennis the Menace (New York, Fawcett, 1966)

KLAPP, ORRIN E. The Fool as a Social Type, Am. Journ. of Soc., 55, 1949, pp. 157–162.

– Symbolic Leaders, Public Dramas and Public Men (Chicago, 1964)

KROCKOW, CHRISTIAN GRAF VON. Die Entscheidung, Eine Untersuchung über Ernst Jünger, Carl Schmitt, Martin Heidegger (Stuttgart, Enke, 1958)

LINDGREN, ASTRID. Pippi Langstrumpf (Hamburg, Oetinger, 1968)

LOOSLEY, E. W.; Seeley, J. R.; Sim, R. A.; Crestwood Heights (New York, Basic Books, 1956)

LUCKMANN, THOMAS and Berger, Peter L. Social Mobility and Personal Identity. European Journal of Sociology, 5, 1964, pp331ff.

– and Berger, Peter L. The Social Construction of Reality (Garden City, Doubleday, 1966)

– On the Boundaries of the Social World, in: Phenomenology and Social Reality. Essays in Memory of Alfred Schutz, (ed.) Maurice Natanson (The Hague, Nijhoff, 1970).

MAUSS, MARCEL. The Gift (London, Cohen 1966) – First French edition in 1925.

McGILVARY, E. B. The "fringe" of William James' psychology, the basis of logic. Philosophical Review, 20, 1911, pp.138ff.

MEAD, GEORGE HERBERT. The Philosophy of the Present (LaSalle, Open Court, 1959) – First published in 1932.

– Mind, Self and Society (Chicago, Univ. of Chicago Press, 1934)

MERLEAU-PONTY, MAURICE. Phenomenology of Perception (London, Routledge-Kegan Paul, 1962) – First French edition published in 1945.

MILLS, C. WRIGHT. The Sociological Imagination (New York, Grove Press, 1961)

– Sociology and Pragmatism (New York, Oxford Univ. Press, 1966)

MORGENSTERN, OSKAR. Spieltheorie, in: Handwörterbuch der Sozialwissenschaften (Göttingen, Vandenhoek, 1956)

– and Neumann, John von. Theory of Games and Economic Behavior (New York, Wiley, 1964) – First edition 1944.

NATANSON, MAURICE. A Critique of Jean-Paul Sartre's Ontology (Lincoln, Univ. of Nebr. Studies, 1951)

NEUMANN, JOHN VON. Zur Theorie der Gesellschaftsspiele, Mathematische Annalen, 100, 1928, pp.295-320.

– and Morgenstern, Oskar. Theory of Games and Economic Behavior (New York, Wiley, 1964) – First Edition 1944.

OETINGER, FRIEDRICH. Partnerschaft (Stuttgart, Metzler, 1953) "Friedrich Oetinger" is a pseudonym of Prof. Dr. Theodor Wilhelm used only in this first book.

PARETO, VILFREDO. The Mind and Society (New York, Harcourt and Brace, 1935) – First Italian edition in 1916.

PARSONS, TALCOTT. The Structure of Social Action (New York-London, McGraw-Hill, 1937)

– Essays in Sociological Theory Pure and Applied (Glencoe, Free Press, 1949)

– The Social System (Glencoe, Free Press, 1951)

- and Shils, Edward A. (eds.). Toward a General Theory of Action (New York-Evanston, Harper and Row, 1962) – First published in 1951.
- The Social System: A General Theory of Action, in: R. R. Grinker (ed.), Toward a Unified Theory of Human Behavior (Basic Books, 1956)
PEIRCE, CHARLES SANDERS. Collected Papers of Charles Sanders Peirce, vols. 1–6 edited by Ch. Hartshorne and P. Weiss, vols. 7–8 edited by A. W. Burks (Cambridge, Mass., Harvard Univ. Press, 2d and 3d printing, 1965–1966).
PIAGET, JEAN. Die Bildung des Zeitbegriffs beim Kinde (Zürich, Rascher, 1955)
PLESSNER, HELMUTH. Die Stufen des Organischen und der Mensch (Berlin, De Gruyter, 1928)
- Die verspätete Nation (Stuttgart, Kohlhammer, 1959) – First published in 1935 under the title "Das Schicksal des deutschen Geistes im Ausgang seiner bürgerlichen Epoche".
- Lachen und Weinen (Bern-München, Francke, 3d. ed., 1961) – The first edition appeared in 1941.
- Diesseits der Utopie (Düsseldorf-Köln, Diederichs, 1966)
PREYER, W. Die Seele des Kindes (Leipzig, Grieben, 4. Aufl., 1895)
PULLBERG, STANLEY and Berger, Peter L. Reification and the Sociological Critique of Consciousness, New Left Review, 35, 1966, pp. 56–77.
RIESMANN, D. and Denney, R. Football in America: A Study in Culture Diffusion, American Quarterly, 3, 1951, pp. 309–325.
RUSSELL, BERTRAND. A History of Western Philosophy (New York, Simon and Schuster, 1945)
SARTRE, JEAN-PAUL. Critique de la Raison Dialectique (Paris, Gallimard, 1960)
- Search for a Method (New York, Knopf, 1963)
- The Words (Greenwich, Fawcett, 1966)
SCHILLER, FRIEDRICH. Über die ästhetische Erziehung des Menschen, in einer Reihe von Briefen, in: Schillers sämtlichen Werken (Stuttgart, Cotta, 1889), Vol. 12. – First published in 1795.
SCHÖNBACH, PETER. Dissonanz und Interaktionssequenzen, Kölner Zeitschrift für Soziologie und Sozialpsychologie, 18, 1966, pp.253-270.
SCHÜTZ, ALFRED. The Phenomenology of the Social World (Northwestern Univ. Press, 1967) – Translation by G. Walsh and F. Lehnert of the original German edition: Der sinnhafte Aufbau der sozialen Welt (Wien, Springer, 1932)
- Collected Papers; vol. I: ed. by M. Natanson, vol. II: ed. by A. Broderson; vol. III: ed. by I. Schütz (The Hague, Nijhoff, 1962; 1964; 1966)
- Reflections on the Problems of Relevance, ed. by Richard Zaner (New Haven, Yale Univ. Press, 1970).
SEELEY, J. R.; Sim, R. A.; Loosley, E. W. Crestwood Heights (New York, Basic Books, 1956)
SHILS, EDWARD A. and Parsons, Talcott (eds.). Toward a General Theory of Action (New York-Evanston, Harper and Row, 1962) – First published in 1951.
SIM, R. A.; Loosley, E. W.; Seeley, J. R.; Crestwood Heights (New York, Basic Books, 1956)
SNELL, J. LAURIE; Thompson, Gerald L.; Kemeny, John G. Introduction to Finite Mathematics (Englewood Cliffs, Prentice-Hall, 1956)
SPENCER, HERBERT. The Principles of Psychology (London, Williams and Nor-

gate, 3rd ed., 1890), vol. 2. – The theory of play (part. IX, chap. 9) was first published in 1872.

STRAUSS, ANSELM. Mirrors and Masks (Glencoe, Free Press, 1959)

– and Glaser, B. C. Awareness of Dying (Chicago, Aldine, 1965)

SZASZ, THOMAS S. The Ethics of Psychoanalysis (New York, Basic Books, 1965)

THOMPSON, GERALD L.; Kemeny, John G.; Snell, J. Laurie. Introduction to Finite Mathematics (Englewood Cliffs, Prentice-Hall, 1956)

VIDICH, ARTHUR J. and Bensman, Joseph. Small Town in Mass Society (Garden City, Doubleday Anchor Books, 1960)

WEBER, MAX. Gesammelte Aufsätze zur Religionssoziologie (Tübingen, Mohr, 1934), vol. 1.

– Gesammelte Aufsätze zur Wissenschaftslehre (Tübingen, Mohr, 2d. ed. 1951)

WISE, BILL. 1964 Official Pro Football Almanac (Greenwich, Fawcett, 1964)

INDEX

I. NAME INDEX FOR REFERENCES TO THEORIES OF PLAY AND GAME

Berne, Eric, 8–10, 112n2, 143n8, 152, 161n11.
Buytendijk, F. J. J., 2–4, 6, 142.
Caillois, Roger, 4n10, 111, 113n4, 114, 150, 161, 173.
Gehlen, Arnold, 116–117, 119, 152.
Goffman, Erving, 10–12, 148n16, 150n19.
Groos, Karl, 2, 128n43, 136n60.
Hall, Stanley, 2.
Huizinga, Johan, 3–4, 6, 111, 113–114, 116, 128, 150.
Kant, Immanuel, 5.
Leibniz, Gottfried Wilhelm, 2n2.
Mead, George Herbert, 3–4, 6, 52–53, 127–128, 130, 135, 136n60, 141–143, 155.
Morgenstern, Oskar, 2n2, 11–12, 149n17, 171n39.
Neumann, John von, 2–4, 6, 11–12, 149n17, 171n39.
Pareto, Vilfredo, 42–43, 52.
Peirce, Charles S., 51–52.
Plessner, Helmuth, 2–3, 6.
Preyer, W., 128n45.
Sartre, Jean-Paul, 103, 107–108, 136n60.
Schiller, Friedrich, 3, 111, 114, 116–119, 161.
Schütz, Alfred, 17.
Spencer, Herbert, 2, 136n60.
Szasz, Thomas, 10, 130n49.

II. SUBJECT INDEX FOR REFERENCES TO MAJOR CONCEPTS

abduction, 40–42, 47, 74, 182.
alienation, 103, 125–126.
ambivalence, 54–55, 64.
anomie, 73, 119–121, 125–126.
audience, 157–158.
body, 131–133, 135–136.
closure, 149–150, 158.
common symbolic type, 142.
compatibility, 55.
context, 48–49, 131–132.
control, 158.
diffuseness, 54.
dramatic situation, 54, 56–57.
game, 143, 146, 149–150.
gap, 56–57.
goal, 148–150.
hide-seek, 136–138.
immediate presentation, 48–51, 55.
imputations, 16.
incipient event, 62–63, 100–101.
incipient typification, 66–67.
inconsistency, 50–60.
inner time, 25–26, 77–79.
intentionality, 20–21, 33.
intersubjectivity, 15, 131–132, 146.
looking-glass self, 17, 156.
mask, 137–138.
mediate presentation, 48–51, 55, 112.
perceiving, 14–15, 42, 46–47, 134.
permanent gap, 56–58.
perspectives of relevance, 20, 51, 74.
play, 130, 146.
playing-at-a-theme, 53, 101.
playing games, 148–149.
project formation, 129.
protective cover, 135, 145.
reduction of types, 112–117.
reification, 73, 103–104.

relevance, 48, 50–51, 125.
roles, 122, 129n47, 146n14.
rules of games, 142–143.
shadow, 159.
social limits, 112, 123, 125.
social object, 14–15, 28, 47–48, 62, 72–74.
social situation, 46.
social temporality, 77–79, 96–97, 109–110, 133.
social types, 55–56, 61–62, 74.
social typification, 56, 61.
split of context, 157.

strategy, 72, 147, 171.
subjectivism, 47, 49, 73, 119–120.
symbolic types, 122, 125, 130.
team, 157–158.
temporal typification, 78–79, 109, 150.
thematic field, 46, 48–50, 73–74.
theme, 46, 48–50, 73–74.
total relevance, 151, 157–158.
triadic structure, 17, 20–21, 32, 50.
typificatory scheme, 55, 77, 120, 131–133.
vagueness, 34–35, 44, 54.